*To Ric,*

*Best Regards*

# THE FAMILY BUSINESS

*Memoirs of a Boston Private Eye*

By
John DiNatale

with
Roland Merullo

The Family Business
*Memoirs of a Boston Private Eye*

PFP, INC
publisher@pfppublishing.com
144 Tenney Street
Georgetown, MA 01833

October 2013
Printed in the United States of America

ISBN-10: 0989237257
ISBN-13: 978-0-9892372-5-3
(also available in eBook format)

Cover Painting:
Paul Shea
*used with the kind permission of Mike Shea & the Shea Family*

*For my mother, Big Evie.*
*She knew, and she always did.*

# Author's Note

Nothing in these pages is made up. Because of the nature of our business, and because of the necessary respect for our clients' privacy, I have changed names and identifying details in almost all the cases described here. If those names and details resemble real people and events, that is purely coincidental. Some of the conversations took place more than forty years ago. While not claiming to recall them verbatim, I have done my best to be true to the spirit of them. Information from the Boston Strangler case, in Chapter Three and elsewhere, comes mainly from conversations with my father, and from his thousands of pages of files, photos, police records, letters and drawings. In some instances, facts were checked against Gerold Frank's *The Boston Strangler*, as well as against various newspaper and magazine articles from that time.

*To read more about Phil DiNatale's investigation of the Boston Strangler case and view the web series and documentary showcasing Phil's files and research, please visit:* http://www.strangleholdthemovie.com

# Foreword

According to my grandfather's records, he left Messina Italy as a young boy of nine on August 19, 1897. He arrived in Boston on September 13, 1897 and there, Salvatore DiNatale began his pursuit of the great American Dream.

Appointed to the Boston Police Department on December 26, 1919, he served with distinction until his retirement in 1953. Along the way, he was promoted to "special officer", later achieving the rank of detective and on February 1, 1950 was assigned to investigate the "Great Brinks Robbery" in the North End of Boston. It was the greatest crime of his generation and Detective DiNatale worked on the case until his retirement, chronicling his daily investigations in very neat typed and handwritten notes.

Four of Salvatore's sons followed his footsteps into the police department: my father Phil, and my uncles Joe, Frank, and Tom.

My father learned his dad's lessons well and, beginning in 1948, he too started to chronicle his own career — keeping a daily diary of his professional life as a Boston Police Officer. If Phil DiNatale arrested you in 1949 for theft, his files today contain a sealed envelope with your name, a copy of the arrest report, a mug shot, and whatever else he had thought important to the case. Phil was also promoted through the ranks and became a station house detective. He was awarded numerous citations including the Department Medal of Honor for Bravery. And, like his father, he worked on the greatest crime of his generation: the Boston Strangler case. Just as my grandfather did with the Brinks robbery investigation, my dad recorded his day-to-day investigations of the case from the first murder in June 1962 to his retirement from the department at the case's conclusion in 1968.

To anyone who would listen and despite numerous claims to the contrary, Phil DiNatale insisted that Albert DeSalvo was the Boston Strangler. He knew it, could prove it, and tried until his death in 1987 to tell the real story of the investigation. On July 18, 2013 the Boston Police Department, with the aid of some of the most recent advances in DNA testing, revealed that there was a 100 per cent match with DeSalvo to the last murder victim. The BPD had finally solved the case that one of their own had initiated. At last, Phil and his partners who worked so diligently, had been proven to be right. Albert DeSalvo *was* the Boston Strangler.

My father started the DiNatale Detective Agency on Beacon Hill in October of 1968, and as a sixteen-year-old, he taught me how to drive and follow people at the same time. Some teenagers work their first jobs bagging groceries at the local market, I bagged cheating spouses working at my dad's agency.

I grew up in the private detective business, as did my brother Richard, and today we operate one of the oldest agencies in Massachusetts. The business shaped our lives and after a while it was not what we did for a living anymore, it was who we were. It had taken us over, lock, stock and barrel.

Working as private investigators with my dad, (who we affectionately called "Phil"), in the 1970s and early 1980s was entirely different than it is today. Our storefront walk-in office, located in the shadow of the Boston Statehouse, attracted more characters from every walk of life than one could possibly imagine. Back then, surveillance was an art. Now, with the advent of GPS and other technologies it has become a science. In those days, clients came to you for information because you were skilled enough to know where it was and how to extract it from people and not simply because you knew how to perform a search on Google. Developing personal contacts with thousands of people from every walk of life enables one to hone communication skills and to be comfortable enough to interview anyone.

This is a story of growing up in the family business, a look inside the private investigation field as it once was and how those activities shaped my life and the lives of my family members.

A toast we make as our extended family gets together for dinner on Thanksgiving and Christmas includes the Italian phrase: *La Famiglia e Tutto* — *"Family is Everything"*. While I may be the one writing about our business, I cannot take sole credit because my younger brother Richard has been an equal and integral component in its success. I do not think I could have lasted as long in this field without his love and immeasurable contributions because he is one of the best private investigators in the business. I could not imagine doing what we do without him.

My sister Jean typed the first reports from my father, and has been such an important supporter to me during this book's journey. Her encouragement over the years helped me to finally see the project through to its completion.

I was introduced to author Roland Merullo by a former client, Bob Jasse. Bob was a very successful businessman who came from a rough background in the city of Revere. He loved listening to the stories of my father's investigations and of the strangler case and for years insisted that I meet Roland, (another Revere kid), who was an immensely talented and accomplished writer.

Roland and I finally met several years ago over a round of golf. We walked for 18 holes and shared one of those conversations where we discovered how uncanny it was that our lives were so similar. I was quite fortunate that Roland agreed to write this memoir with me. I remember reading the first chapter and thinking how he had captured my voice, and then crying when I felt he had portrayed the essence of the relationship with my father. That was special, and we have become not only business partners in this project but golfing buddies — which to the two of us, is much more important.

Baseball Hall of Famer, Reggie Jackson, was once asked after he had become a member of the New York Yankees, how he fit in with all of the great players on that team.

"I'm the straw that stirs the drink in the dugout," he replied.

In our dugout, my wife Dorothy is the straw that stirs the drink. She was hired by Phil in 1976 — shortly after I started, and she is the love of my life. Along with my two daughters Lindsay and Jackie, she has encouraged me to tell this story. Without her, I would be a wandering gypsy. Dorothy runs our office today, allowing Richard and me to do what we do best. She is "office mom" to some of the younger staff and while Richard and I, might be able to run the business without each other, neither one of us could do it without Dorothy.

To the rest of my family, my twin sister Evelyn, who prays for me daily, my nieces and nephews — especially Myles David Jewell, thank you for your love and support. Myles spent most of the winter of 2010 filming me discussing the private investigation business and visiting some of the actual locations where our cases occurred. We would film six to eight hours of material and then send Roland the video every week. This I think really contributed to Roland hearing my voice. Myles is the best.

Thank you to Peter Sarno, my publisher, for taking a chance in a publishing world that does not seem to know what it is anymore.

"Family is Everything"

*John DiNatale*
October 2013

*"Try to be one of the people on whom nothing is lost."*
                                    - Henry James

# BOOK ONE
## The Agency's Roots

# ONE
First Surveillance

*"The atrocious crime of being a young man, which the honorable gentleman has with such spirit and decency charged upon me, I shall neither attempt to palliate nor deny; but content myself with wishing that I may be one of those whose follies may cease with their youth, and not of that number who are ignorant in spite of experience."*
- William Pitt

In the same way other people might recall their first date, I remember my first surveillance case. I was sixteen years old. Six months earlier, my father had left the Boston Police Department to start his own private investigation agency, and, before that cold winter night in 1969 — though my mother kept the books and one of my sisters typed up reports, he had never asked me to do anything to help out.

But on that Saturday in January, for reasons known only to him, my dad decided it was time for my introduction to the family business. We climbed into his 1964 Chevy Impala and made the twenty-minute trip from our home in West Roxbury to a section of Boston called the Back Bay. In those days, Boston's Back Bay was not exactly the mix of elegant red-brick townhouses and trendy shops that it is today. The neighborhood — land that had been reclaimed from salt marsh and tid-

1

al flats in the early 1800s, and the only part of the city with streets in an even grid — runs along the western edge of downtown, from the Public Gardens west to Fenway Park, a distance of about two miles; and from the Charles River south to Huntington Avenue, about a mile. There were some expensive townhouses then, of course, as well as insurance company headquarters, lawyers' offices, and clothing stores; but there was also a collection of seedy bars, a pair of strip clubs called The Mouse Trap Cabaret and The Teddy Bear Lounge, a maze of dark alleys that ran between the main streets, and a combination Greyhound/Hudson/Michaud/Bonanza bus station that was home to an eclectic crowd of travelers, pick-pockets, streetwalkers, drunks, and cruising gay men. If you wandered a little farther west, to Massachusetts Avenue, or too far south, across Huntington, you could find yourself in even more lively neighborhoods, places where cab drivers did not like to wait around after dropping off a fare, and where the crack of gunshots was not a rare occurrence. Parts of those neighborhoods and most of the Back Bay have since been "gentrified" to use a word I dislike (The old Boston Police Headquarters on Berkeley Street is now the $300 a night Back Bay Hotel; The Mouse Trap is now a Four Seasons Luxury Hotel). But in the 1960s, along Boylston and Stuart Streets and the alphabetical side streets running perpendicular to them, you had a spicy stew of city life — rich and poor, hardworking and lazy, honest and corrupt, decent and indecent — the whole spectrum of humanity on full display.

From his twenty-four years as both patrolman and detective on those streets, my father knew the territory the way a chemist knows the table of elements. It was his stomping grounds, his native soil, the place he felt at home in the way only a beat policeman can. Even before he became a local celebrity, a man on a first-name basis with Hollywood stars, my dad could hardly walk three Back Bay blocks, have his hair cut, buy a shirt, or stop for a drink there without seeing a friend, a colleague, somebody he'd pressed for information, or a guy he'd chased down a dark alley and sent away on a minor rap a few years earlier.

On that afternoon, my father was behind the wheel. There was a learner's permit in my wallet, but my only driving experience consisted of a handful of Driver's Ed classes, and those few times my mother let me drive when she helped me out with my 6:00 a.m. paper route. As we made our way into the city, turned right on Clarendon Street and parked, my dad gave me the rough outlines of the case: A woman in a North Shore suburb suspected her husband was cheating on her, telling her he needed to work overtime on Saturdays, then leaving early and picking up women in bars. Her lawyer had "retained us", as my dad liked to put it, to try to get some proof of the man's infidelity. Up to that point, my sexual experience consisted of sitting with a girl I liked, watching TV in her parents' house (usually with the parents close by). I knew nothing of the physical joys and emotional stresses of marriage, and even less about the divorce laws of the Commonwealth of Massachusetts. But, even to me, the assignment seemed straightforward enough: we had to catch this husband doing something he should not have been doing with a woman who was not his wife. Compared to some of the cases my dad had worked on in his detective days — the Boston Strangler investigation especially — it was not the most glamorous of assignments, but in those early years on his own he was happy to accept any legitimate job that came his way.

My father had already been on the case a week or so and had done some preliminary surveillance. He had a description, knew where the man lived and where he worked — in the old John Hancock Life Insurance Building directly across Clarendon Street from where we were now parked. (Though much of the Back Bay has changed, you can still find that building — eight floors, tan-colored stone, four wide columns out front and a dozen-step stairway.) We sat there with the motor running, watching the winter darkness settle across the city, streetlights fluttering to life, students and musicians and workers hurrying along in the cold air. My father, as was his habit, said little. His powerful upper body hidden beneath a short, wool-lined jacket, his close-cropped hair covered by a gray fedora, a .38 pistol strapped against his ribs, he watched the street the way a hunter watches for a deer to step out of a stand of trees.

I thought it was strange for the husband to be working so late on a Saturday afternoon — to be working at all on the weekend, for that matter, but I did not risk saying so. My father was treating me as a grown man, an apprentice, part of the business; the last thing I wanted was to say or do anything that would make him see me as a boy.

When we had been there an hour and a half, he said, without turning to look at me, "You get out and watch for him, Johnny. I gotta go find a place to take a leak. He's gonna have to come out that door, right there. Don't take your eyes off it for one second."

I got out. He drove away. I was on my own.

As architects and engineers would learn two years later when the new sixty-five-story John Hancock Tower was being erected almost on that exact spot, and dozens of the four-foot-by-eight-foot glass panes that formed its exterior walls would be sucked out and sent smashing to the pavement ten, twenty, or fifty floors below, the winter wind whips through that part of Boston as if it is in training for a next life in the ice fields of Mount Everest. Maybe it has something to do with the straightforward alignment of the streets, or maybe it is the proximity to the river — which is deep and cold and half a mile wide at that point, a few blocks north — I do not know; but especially in winter and especially after dark, there is a particular species of chill that slices through that neighborhood. Unfortunately, though I was dressed in the high school fashion of the day — beige Barracuda jacket, black chinos, penny loafers, no gloves — I was not dressed for the Back Bay on a winter night.

At first, I waited where my father had left me, in the mouth of an alley at the back side of Trinity Church. But the alley smelled so strongly of urine and stale beer, and the wind had such a cold bite, that I soon took refuge beside the columns of a nearby building. According to my watch, it was just after 6:00 p.m. I was sure my dad knew a bar close by where he could find relief, and that he would return in a few minutes to bring me back into the warmth of the Impala's front seat. But half an hour passed and he did not show. I assumed then that he must have gone to one of his favorite watering holes, maybe Gino Capelletti's The Point After, or swung down to see friends at Jimmy's Harborside, or was picking up sandwiches for us at Ken's, the two-story deli on Boylston Street with its high-calorie lineup of cheesecakes and pies in the window. Whatever bar or restaurant he'd gone into to use the bathroom, he had probably caught sight of a friend, stayed for a Seagram's and ginger or a cup of coffee. Or maybe he was at the deli, waiting for someone to throw our sandwiches together, looking at his watch, worrying about me out there alone in the frigid air.

But then, when an hour had passed without any sign of him, I started to wonder if I had been abandoned, if this was his idea of a joke, some kind of initiation into the exotic life of the private detective.

At which point our client's husband stepped out of the building opposite me.

The man hurried off along the sidewalk. I gave him a little

space, and then followed. As my dad no doubt understood, the advantage of using a sixteen-year-old on a surveillance case — the only advantage — was that no cheating husband expects to be followed by a teenager. As I tailed him along the dark, cold street, the husband never made so much as a second backward glance. He walked to the first corner, turned left on Stuart Street, went another block or so and stepped into a bar called My Brother's Place.

The front of My Brother's Place (308 Stuart Street, now the food prep room for a trendy Italian restaurant) does not take up much space in the line of buildings and storefronts along that block. There is a narrow door inset between two small plate-glass windows. Then, as now, the windows were covered with metal grating, the sidewalk out front was cracked; overhead hung a three-story fire escape, looking like it would break loose in the first strong gust of wind and crash to the ground. I put my hands to the glass and peered in, made sure the man had not slipped out through a back door, then crossed the street to the bus station. The air had not gotten any warmer. There was no sign of my father, and not much chance, if he came driving back to the first stakeout spot, that he would be able to guess which way I had gone. In the winter of 1969, the cell phone existed only in the fantastical imagination of a few science-fiction writers, and our agency was not yet equipped with the high-tech, forty-mile-range Motorola walkie-talkies we would later use. My only option was to find a pay phone, call in my location to our answering service, and hope my father thought to check in with them when — and if — he came back to Clarendon Street. The answering service people were used to this kind of thing. Later, I would even get the feeling they enjoyed it: relaying messages among private eyes sneaking around the city must have been a kind of spice in the bland diet of their usual duties.

At that moment, though, the thrill of our profession was lost on me. I went into the bus station and placed the call, but it took me almost half an hour to build up enough courage to cross the street and step through the door of My Brother's Place. It was a shadowy, unpretentious bar, sawdust on the floor and ten-cent drafts, the kind of place where you ask for vodka or gin without mentioning a brand name. I know this because, years later, my friends and I would meet there for a drink after work. But I was too young to buy alcohol then and had no notion that a martini made with Popov might taste any different from one made with Grey Goose. I asked the bartender if I could use the bathroom ("Yeah, yeah, but hurry."), and on my way to the back of the room I surreptitiously took a closer look at the man I had been following. He was sitting with a woman, all right, chatting her up at a table near the wall. But, to my adolescent eyes at least, she was so singularly unattractive it seemed almost impossible that he would be risking his marriage to spend time with her. Passing them, in one direction then the other, I made a mental note of what she looked like. Then, in what I hoped was a mature way, I nodded my thanks to the bartender, went out and across the street and took up a position in the glass-fronted lobby of the bus station.

While I stood there, hoping for the best, I was approached by a succession of friendly men I had never met before. I was not a completely naive kid; I had some vague idea what was going on. But I had been raised to be polite to my elders, and it was a struggle to carry on a conversation with these affable strangers and keep an eye on the door of My Brother's Place.

"What are you doing here?"

"Just waiting around."

"Waiting for somebody in particular, or just waiting?"

"Waiting for somebody."

"Not taking a bus and going away someplace, are you?"

"Nope."

One of the men must have still been hitting on me when the blue Impala came screeching to the curb, because my father charged up to us — chest forward, big arms swinging — and told the guy to get the hell away from me or he was going to kick his ass all the way into the river.

"He was just being friendly," I told my dad when we were out on the sidewalk, teasing him a bit, maybe as payback for the long, cold wait.

"Friendly, your ass," my father said out of the side of his mouth.

By then, he had flipped some kind of internal switch, shifted into a more intense version of his ordinary personality. I had seen that side of him before: a concentrated attention that made it seem like the cells in his eyes and neck were bouncing, energy swirling in his arms and shoulders. "You got the guy in there, huh?" he said, sounding surprised and a bit eager. Before I could ask where he had been for the last hour and a half, he told me to get behind the wheel of the Impala and watch the door again; he was going in for a drink and a closer look. I sat behind the wheel, turning it lazily this way and that, pretending I was driving in the city at night, half-watching for my dad. I had been there only a few minutes when he came hustling back out, jumped into the passenger seat, and told me to drive around the block. The guy was ready to leave, he knew where his car was parked, we would swing around and wait outside the garage entrance. In the excitement of the moment my father did not seem to consider the fact that a few snowflakes had started to fall, making the roads slick, and that I had logged a lifetime total of about twelve hours behind the wheel, none of them at night, and none in the famously chaotic traffic of downtown Boston. "Go! Go!"

So we went. I looped carefully around the block. We waited

until the car came out of the underground garage, and began following it. As I gripped the wheel with both hands and pressed on the accelerator, my dad kept up a running commentary, a professor's first lecture in Surveillance 101. "Okay, don't get too close, Johnny. Okay, he's got his turn signal on, see it? All right, make sure you don't get caught in the light. Okay, good. Move up now. Don't let this jerk in the van get between us. Up a little more. That's good. Right there." I turned where my dad said to turn, following the sedan — left on Charles, right on Beacon, across in front of the State House, left on Bowdoin and downhill there, past my father's storefront office, through the Haymarket and into the Callahan Tunnel that runs under Boston Harbor and links the city with its northern suburbs.

In those days a double line of grimy white tiles separated the tunnel's two lanes; crossing them was illegal. I tried to stay close to the sedan, while steering the Impala — which seemed about twice as wide as it had a few minutes earlier — between the tunnel wall on one side and the line of tiles on the other. My father yelled at me to keep up, keep up Johnny. And I pushed down on the gas and then somehow momentarily lost control so that the left-side tires crossed onto the tiles. I jerked the wheel hard, too hard: the car veered across the lane and the right front fender grazed the concrete wall. The impact knocked us left again. My father screamed: "What the fuck are you doing!" And I screamed back at him, and then the sedan got a ways ahead of us so that I had to pick up speed instead of slowing down as we approached the tolls.

My dad's explosions — my brother and sisters and I were intimately familiar with them — usually lasted less than half a minute. By the time we came out into the open air again, he had already calmed down. A light snow had started to fall, the roadway was wet and slippery. We paid the toll and soon caught up to the sedan, and my father moved into a slightly more advanced level of what would be a fifteen-year tutorial in the fine points of tailing someone. Surveillance 102. Most cars did not have passenger-side mirrors in those days, so he told me to stay in the guy's blind spot — right hand side, a couple lengths back. Through East Boston and Revere we went, and then west on two-lane roads into Malden and Medford. My dad made sure I did not fall far enough behind to get caught by a turning traffic light, and did not stay close enough to arouse the straying husband's suspicions.

Somehow, in spite of the snow and the dark roads and my father giving me blunt instructions, I was able to keep the sedan in sight until it turned onto the quiet suburban street where the man lived. We made a last loop around the block, went past his house one time and saw the sedan in the driveway, made sure we had "put him to bed," in the parlance of the profession. No cheating on that day, nothing much to report beyond a drink with a woman in a seedy bar. But the whole thing was, for me, a major accomplishment. I had driven the car in the city, through the tunnel, in light snow; I had followed somebody.

My dad let me stay behind the wheel and told me to head back into "town", as we called Boston then. Like so many parents of his generation, he had a strong dislike of rock and roll music, preferring Connie Francis and Tony Bennett to the Beatles and Stones. But on that return drive he said, "Go 'head and listen to the zoot-suiter music if you want to," and I could tell from that small indulgence, and from his tone of voice, how proud he was of me. I tuned the radio to AM 1510, WMEX. Feeling that I had passed my first test, I took the liberty of asking my dad where he had been all that time.

He kept his eyes straight ahead, pushed the fedora back off his forehead, and said, "None of your fucking business."

And that was my father, Phil DiNatale, who loved me, and came to trust me, and, after that night, welcomed me into the family business.

# TWO
The Promotion

*"A 27 year old Back Bay woman and her sister from Charlestown were fined $100 each in Roxbury District Court today for assault and battery upon a policemen. He said the women kicked and scratched him and tore his uniform."* Each had to pay $5 to the policeman for damages to his clothing and $12.50 to city of Boston for damage to his uniform. *"Victim of the assault was Patrolman Philip J. DiNatale, who said the women lit into him when he stopped to question them on Peterboro Street at 3 a.m. on March 25. He said they also spat in his face."*
-Boston Herald American

I t is tempting to think of it as just a career, but the business my dad introduced me to on that night has turned out to be much more than that. It is the way I met my wife, the place I formed a bond with my brother, made lifelong friends, helped thousands of people solve personal and legal problems, and learned — through the approximately ten thousand cases we have been a part of over the past forty years — about a layer of human life that, most of the time, lies hidden from public view.

And it is tempting to look at my father as just a tough-guy cop, his dad a cop, three brothers and a cousin on the force, his working life immersed in the world of murderers and rapists, thieves and con-artists. But there was much more to him than the badge and gruff exterior, and if I am going to tell the full story of our family business, I have to try to paint a picture of him first.

He was, in fact, a tough guy, a kid who grew up in the inner city, enlisted in the U.S. Navy as a twenty-three-year-old, and spent part of World War Two in New Guinea. From what little I know of his early life, it was not a study in tenderness. To protect himself from the hard body-blows of lower-class Boston society, he built a full suit of armor — a no-nonsense way of talking and thinking about things, a way of carrying himself that was formidable, sometimes volatile. That armor served him well in his beat cop and detective days, but it stayed with him, even years later, when he moved to a suburban house with a swimming pool and counted lawyers and judges, movie stars and senators among his friends. In my high school and college years, his advice about being a good citizen went something like this: "If you ever get arrested, Johnny, you're going to see me at the door of the jail cell, and I'm going to hit you so hard that when you wake up your clothes will be out of style."

In his era, cops were not given workshops in cultural sensitivity. Like many of his colleagues in those days, and a few of them even now, he was not averse to administering a hard smack on the side of the head if the perpetrator resisted arrest too strenuously, or had committed some particularly unsavory transgression. I have newspaper clippings that show him arresting bloodied suspects, and it is a fair guess that the blood was not there before my father and his partner arrived on the scene. Twice, I saw him push grown men up against a wall with one of his huge forearms and lift them up onto their toes. And I am sure, in dark Back Bay alleys, there were plenty of similar encounters I never saw, ones that were not captured by *Herald American* photographers. Eddie Corsetti, the *Herald* reporter he later befriended, told me my father was famous for volunteering for assignments no one else wanted, and equally well known for getting people — suspects, included — to trust him.

I know that he carried a sawed-off baseball bat in the trunk of his car, and that along with two other officers, he won the Department Medal of Honor for subduing five muggers in the Boston Public Gardens at night. The muggers were armed with chains and screwdrivers; my dad did not pull his gun. I know that he received a series of commendations for "meritorious service and devotion to duty", that he worked his way steadily up the ladder from patrolman to detective second class, earning three nominations for officer of the month along the way. He chased down and tackled thieves and muggers, "pinched", as he liked to say, plenty of B&E men and gang members, broke down an armed murderer's door seconds before the man shot himself, collared more than one killer who had shot or beaten someone to death on the streets of the city.

But he was not an arresting machine, or, later, an investigating machine. He was a flawed, good man, expert at the work he did but not always at ease in the police bureaucracy, fond of his family but not always comfortable with displays of affection, more at home checking doorways in dark alleys and, later, in the rough and tumble world of business dealings, than with the tenderest aspects of domestic life. Still, even there, it is difficult to put one label on him. My friend Charlie Bell says that, when he first met my father as a teenager he felt he was being interrogated, about to have a flashlight shone in his eyes, but then goes on to describe him as "a personable and gentle soul."

We have old eight-millimeter footage that shows him hurrying out from behind the camera to sit close to my mother on a beach wall. He snuggles up and kisses her neck, happy as a schoolboy. My brother and sisters and I have memories of him splashing around with us in the surf at Miami Beach, big smile on his face. Jean remembers him hiding candies in the pockets of his blue uniform and letting her jump into his arms when he came home from work and search until she found them. Mule-stubborn, sentimental, generous at times, stingy at others, street-wise, protective, proud, irascible, funny — all true of Phil DiNatale, depending on the occasion.

He prayed and offered novenas in a downtown chapel — always alone, and carried a laminated picture of Our Lady of Perpetual Help in his pocket. He hated the smell of cigarette smoke, and never drank beer because he had been a mounted cop early in his career and said beer reminded him too much of a horse pissing. My father used so much aftershave that we sometimes joked with him that he never needed to take a shower, just douse himself with more Old Spice. Having eaten nothing but mutton during his service years in New Guinea (and contracted malaria there, besides), he refused to eat lamb.

He would have a glass of Blue Nun with my mother now and again — often while listening to Connie Francis — and became a fan of martinis only in the last years of his life. But, I never saw him drunk. He was partial to gray fedoras on the job, and socks with sandals and shorts when he was relaxing. Since he could not remember how to make a Windsor knot, he had me tie his neckties. When he was finished wearing them for the day, he took them off in such a way that he preserved the knot for the next time, and hung it in his closet in a loop. My dad could barely hear out of his left ear (from someone firing a rifle too close during the war, he said). And, Phil DiNatale liked to swear and tell stories; although open-minded in surprising ways, he was not even close to politically correct.

With us, though, the gruffness was in part an act, a habit, the way he had learned you were supposed to raise children in this world. If one of us did something to exasperate our ex-traordinarily patient mother, she would resort to the famous

15

phrase, "wait till your father gets home," and, in time, my brother and Jean and I learned to stuff books and magazines inside the back of our clothes as protection against a slap or spanking. The other sister, my twin, Evelyn, was constitutionally incapable of that kind of cringing, however. She faced my father's anger head-on, squinting her eyes up at him and telling him it was wrong to spank little kids, and she was not afraid of him anyway, that he could not hurt her no matter what he did. My dad had trouble keeping his gruff act in place against a force like that, could barely hide a smile, turned away from her with some vague threat about things going bad for her in the future if she did not straighten out. Sitting at the dinner table before heading off to the night shift, he would ask, "Did you do your homework?" and if I told him I had, he would say, "Good, go upstairs and do it again," rather than looking it over with me, answer by answer, the way a modern father might, the way I did with my own daughters.

In truth, though, my siblings and I have only a handful of memories of spending time with him when we were young. I remember, as a five-year-old, during the brief period when he performed his patrols on horseback, being taken down to the stables below District Sixteen on Boylston Street and having him hoist me up onto the back of Smokey, one of the Department's thoroughbreds. Every year in late June, when the rates were low, we would drive to Miami Beach for a ten-day family vacation.

My father would find a piece of foam rubber and cut it to fit the back of our station wagon, and that would be our bed because he got off work at two in the morning and wanted to head right out. For that three-day drive south — past cotton fields and sharecroppers' shacks, through territory that might have been another planet for northern city kids like us — and for the week or so we would spend at the Thunderbird Motel, we would have my father's undivided attention. He loved the ocean — if the water was warm enough. He would toss us around in the surf as if we weighed a few pounds; he would race with us along the sand. At times, he would loosen up and let his sense of humor show. We always made the trip with my uncle, and once, when they went in to check out the availability of rooms, the owner of the place told them no kids were allowed. "No kids, huh?" my dad said.

"Not under any circumstances."

"Okay." My dad let his jacket flap open, revealing his service pistol, turned to my uncle and said, "You wait here, Joe. I'll be right back. Goin' out to shoot the kids."

I think back on those vacation trips with a vivid fondness, but I also remember him missing every Little League game I ever played in, and not being present at most of our family meals. When we would go to my uncle and aunt's house for Sunday dinner, my dad would shake hands and kiss everybody, then disappear into one of the bedrooms for a two-hour nap.

It was hardly a matter of being anti-social. I saw his weekly paycheck once, in the early Sixties. Seventy-seven dollars. Barely enough to support a wife and four kids and keep up the payments on our very modest cape on Sherbrook Streeet in West Roxbury. There was some supplemental income: in those days it was customary for local merchants to give beat cops ("route cops" my dad called them, pronouncing the word "rout", unlike most Bostonians, who say "root") an envelope with cash or a bottle of Chivas at Christmastime. As is the case to this day, cops could make a little extra by volunteering for traffic or security details. My father worked the 4:00 p.m. to midnight shift at first, and after being promoted to detective, he started at 6:00 p.m. and got off at 2:00 a.m. He would come home and sleep for a few hours, then head off to his second job — making kitchen cabinets, repairing floors, trimming windows, painting houses. Before serving in the Pacific, he had graduated from the mechanical arts high school and spent time at the Charlestown Naval shipyard, and was, in fact, a skilled draftsman, mason, and finish carpenter. Thanks to his collection of hand tools and electric saws, our basement looked more like it belonged to a member of the carpenters' union than a member of the force.

Even when I was very young, he would sometimes take me with him on those jobs, and he would let me — or *make* me — help out with projects. He turned our second-floor attic into two finished bedrooms and surrounded the whole property with a neat stone wall. (When Route 128 was being built through the western suburbs — I must have been seven or eight — he would take me with him out to the construction site on a weekend afternoon and we would load so much scrap stone into the back of the car that the rear bumper was nearly touching the ground.) Later, if he had a house painting job, he would bring me along to do window trim. He was typical of a certain type of lower-middle-class father in those days: piecing together a living, doing whatever he could to hoist his family up onto the next rung on the ladder.

For a long time, it looked like he would keep to that pattern all the way to retirement, building bookcases for wealthy Needham homeowners, or remodeling a cellar for West Roxbury neighbors during the day, then chasing muggers across the Boston Common or investigating a Back Bay robbery at night. The fact was that he loved his job, loved the masculine camaraderie, the constant variety of life on the streets, the sense of doing something valuable in the world. "I knew the alleys," he said in a TV interview long after he retired. He had a wistful expression on his face, and said "alleys" the way someone else might have said "gardens" or "theater district". "I knew the alleys, and outa there I used to come up with some terrific pinches."

While the salary was not impressive in those years, there were plenty of side-benefits: free meals in the restaurant kitchens on his beat, parking spaces that would earn anyone else a ticket, respect for the power of the badge. You knew you would always have work, and that you could retire at a reasonable age and have a comfortable enough old age on your civil service pension.

But in 1962, when I was ten and my father had been a member of the Boston Police Department for fourteen years, something happened that would change his life — and our lives, and the life of pretty much everyone in Greater Boston — forever.

Though my father used to say District Sixteen in the Back Bay was the "Bon-Ton Division" (a phrase he had coined, I think), the place where "we had nice criminals, guys who robbed fur stores or didn't put money in the meters", and though he and his partner, Jimmy Mellon, had had some fun dressing up as women to catch purse-snatchers, there were always enough assaults and murders and rapes and muggings to keep him alert. It was the heart of a big city, after all, and he worked at night, and, especially after he was promoted to detective in 1960, he knew the job would not consist merely of talking to the occasional drunk in front of the public library, being spat on and scratched by streetwalkers, or keeping the fans in order outside Fenway Park.

In those days newspapers assigned a "photog" to the police beat, and I have a box full of newspaper clippings my father saved from almost every time his name or picture made the papers. Detective DiNatale arrested someone who was accused of beating an old man to death, someone else who had been conning hotel owners, stealing from parking meters, smashing plate glass windows, engaging in prostitution, committing armed rape. Detective DiNatale shot at a man who tried to run him and fellow officers over in a speeding car. He kept a gun in the house and wore it everywhere but in the shower, and my sister has vivid memories of him leaving his billy club on a table near the front door when he got home. In the 1960s, there was an outbreak of what everyone called "gangland killings". At one point, the feud between the McLaughlins and McLeans, two Greater Boston gangs, led to twenty-eight murders in a span of twenty months, and all the cops in homicide and most of the detectives, too, were under pressure from the press to solve this rash of brazen hits that seemed never to have any witnesses.

But on June 14, 1962, all that sordid business took a turn into a realm of human viciousness I think even my father never expected to encounter. On that day, a fifty-six-year-old Latvian immigrant named Anna Slesers was found dead in her Gainsborough Street apartment. She had been strangled with the cord of her bathrobe and sexually molested. Between that day and the 4th of January, 1964, twelve more women, aged nineteen to seventy-five years, were killed in similarly gruesome ways. Around their necks the killer tied lingerie or nylon stockings in a double-half-hitch, finished with a large decorative bow. Five of these murders occurred in my father's territory, and he was assigned to investigate them. But by the time the psychopath had been given the name Boston Strangler, and by the time Attorney General Edward Brooke had decided to form a task force people referred to as The Strangler Bureau, the city and surrounding suburbs were transfixed with a kind of terror no Bostonian has known before or since. Anyone who was alive then — but especially women who lived alone and children old enough to listen to the news — will remember the fear that buzzed in the air every time a new victim was discovered. Though the murders were eerily similar — the victims

20

often left in provocative poses, partly or fully naked, the younger ones killed on weekends and holidays, older ones during the week — the killer never seemed to have entered the apartments by force, and never left a shred of physical evidence — not a single fingerprint, not a mark from the sole of a shoe. Neighbors never heard the sound of a struggle, and could never seem to give a good description of the strange man who had slipped into and out of their apartment building like a shadow.

Brooke was contemplating a run for the U.S. Senate (in 1966 he would defeat Endicott Peabody in a landslide and become the first African American elected to the United States Senate by popular vote). Since the State and local cops — Boston, Cambridge, Lynn, Lawrence and Salem — seemed unable to catch the killer or killers and were overwhelmed by the gangland murders, the Attorney General came up with the Strangler Bureau idea and picked four men who were considered the finest investigators in the city: Andrew Tuney from the State Police, Steve Delaney from the Metropolitan District Commission Police (who had jurisdiction over certain beaches and recreation areas in Greater Boston), and two detectives from the Boston Police Department, Jim Mellon and Phil DiNatale.

# THREE

The Hunt, the Break, the Confession

*"The victims were, so far as could be determined, modest, inconspicuous, almost anonymous women, leading blameless lives. Beyond the mystery of their deaths, there was something terribly sad and pathetic about these victims who apparently either knew or were unafraid of their murderer, and let him into their apartments and did not even put up a struggle before they were finished off."*
-*The Boston Strangler,* Gerold Frank

No one involved in the investigation, and none of the city's terrified inhabitants knew that nineteen-year-old Mary Sullivan, killed on January 4, 1964, would be the last of the Strangler's victims. Two weeks later, when Attorney General Brooke announced the formation of his task force, no one knew that the man responsible for those thirteen horrific murders had recently been taken into custody on other charges. It was assumed the Strangler was still out on the streets, and that he would kill again. In part because of relentless criticism by the city's newspapers — at least two of which were carrying out their own investigations — the pressure on Brooke and his team to find the Strangler was immense.

After he was selected for what everyone called "The Strangler Bureau" — actual name "The Special Division of Crime

Research and Detection" — my father's hours changed: he started working days *and* nights, instead of just nights; and he started working Saturdays. (Even the occasional Sunday and holiday. The entry in his daybook for September 6, 1965 reads: *"Went to work half day with Lieutenant Tuney. Labor Day should be off — ")* My sister Evelyn says, "My father lived it, he drank it, he ate it. Our whole lives revolved around the Boston Strangler."

The office he reported to moved four miles due east, from Division Sixteen on Boylston Street to the State House on Beacon Hill. He was placed under the direction of a man named John Bottomly, a tall, bespectacled legal scholar with superb organizational skills but not much in the way of a personality. A friend of Attorney General Brooke from their Boston University Law School Days, Bottomly oversaw the Eminent Domain section of the A.G.'s office, but, as my dad put it, "wouldn't know a murder investigation if it came up and bit him in the face." Along with many of his colleagues, my father suspected that Bottomly had been chosen for the job of coordinating the Bureau largely on the basis of his friendship with Brooke . . . which was not a particularly unusual arrangement in Boston politics.

Whatever doubts he might have harbored about the political motives behind it, though, my father approached the investigation with a meticulous attention to detail. Throughout their careers, both he and his own father kept daily handwritten notes of every case they worked on, and it is interesting to consider that each of them was involved in the city's most notorious criminal case of his generation. I have inherited these notes, along with other files, boxes and boxes of them. They contain everything from the trivial to the remarkable, from an invitation "with one lady" to the Boston Police Relief Association annual Concert and Ball at Boston Garden in December, 1961, to thirty-three handwritten letters, sent to my dad from a prison cell by the Boston Strangler himself. Kept in red-jacketed hardcover notebooks with "Standard Daily Journal" on the front, my father's journals show, in shorthand, a daily record of interviews, conversations, leads, phone numbers, license plate numbers, street addresses, times he finished work and miles he drove that day. In the files there are photographs and diagrams of the murder scenes; verbatim accounts of interviews with DeSalvo under hypnosis; and hundreds of newspaper clippings. (My grandfather's notes from interviews he did during the investigation of the 1950 Brinks robbery are fascinating, and eerily similar to my dad's. In fact, my father used to talk about how "Pa" would tell them stories about his work as they sat around the dinner table: the Brinks robbery, at that time the largest robbery in U.S. history — $1.2 million in cash, another $1.5 million in securities — occurred in Boston's North End, and was eventually solved). The daybooks document an unforgettable chapter in the city's criminal history: extensive police work, on the one hand; and, on the other, the behavior of one of the most disturbed minds in the annals of American crime.

It seemed to me and my brother and sisters, that our father worked on the Strangler investigation every minute he was awake. I watched him with drafting ruler and pencil at the dining room table on Sundays, making scale drawings of each of the murder sites, where and in what position the victims had been found, the location of framed family photographs, bedclothes, plates, cups, silverware, and shoes in the apartments; the way the doors opened, the view from the windows. I have inherited these drawings, too. At first glance, they look like the work of an architect who is laying out a living space, suggesting where a table might be fit into a small kitchen, or in which corner of the apartment an armchair should be situated. Once they were drawn up, my dad studied them with a detective's eye, noticing things other people would have missed, and they yielded or reinforced key clues. For instance, from the way a spoon and coffee cup stood on the table at one of the murder scenes — where the Strangler had apparently had a chat with his victim before taking her life — and the way the contents of bureau drawers had been tossed to one side, my father surmised — correctly, as it turned out — that the Strangler was left handed.

He and his colleagues on the Bureau went through more than 30,000 documents relating to the murders. They interviewed or looked into 2,300 suspects, many of them with a history of sexual crimes — from peeping Toms to rapists. From profiles drawn up by the Bureau's medical experts, it was believed in some circles that the killer was likely homosexual, so certain bars and meeting places were raided and hundreds of known homosexuals questioned. The investigators put suspects under sodium pentothal and gave them lie detector tests — there were fewer legal obstacles to such practices in those days. My father tracked down and then worked with a man named Paul Gordon, who claimed to have ESP. Gordon knew so much about the crimes that, for a time, he was also considered a suspect. At one point, Bottomly called in a famous Dutch psychic named Peter Hurkos, who described photos of the murder scenes without having seen them, who "felt something" when he was driving by a building where — unbeknownst to him — a strangling had taken place, who somehow was able to tell stunned officers about their wife's childhood accidents, back problems, and their own recent sexual encounters, and who ultimately led them to a strange man he was sure had done the killings. The man had not.

There were telephone hot-line reports to track down, by the hundreds. There was no shortage of sex criminals who might have been capable of the stranglings. But neither was there so much as a shred of useful physical evidence. The Strangler, it seemed, did not make mistakes.

Like his fellow detectives on the case, my father called in all the old favors that were owed him, searching arrest records in the nearby cities, talking to parole and probation officers, inmates, psychologists, ex-cons, wise guys, and the people who lived or worked in or near the apartment buildings where the women had been killed. He made trips out of state — New York, Rhode Island, New Hampshire, Vermont, Pennsylvania, Maryland — to interview people who might have some connection with the crimes or the victims. He fielded calls from women claiming their boyfriend or husband was the Strangler, or that they had seen a suspicious man in the neighborhood, or that they had been receiving lewd notes or phone calls, and he and his co-workers in the Bureau looked into every one of these leads.

Bostonians were so terrified in those years, in what my father called "the Strangler season", that they often would not let police into their homes or apartments to conduct the investigation. Sometimes my father and his partner would stand out on the street, talking to witnesses or neighbors from sidewalk to second-floor window. This was ironic, because even after the Strangler had become front page news, and even after headlines like this one, "KEEP CHAIN LOCKS BOLTED", in the *Boston Record American*, whoever was committing the crimes seemed to be talking, not forcing, his way into the apartments. My father would later give a reason for this: "All the killings occurred in big apartment buildings," he said in an interview. "All those buildings were rundown. If somebody came to your door dressed like a maintenance man and said he was there to fix your running toilet, people would let him in. Everybody in those places had a running toilet, everybody had been trying to get their landlord to send somebody to fix it, or to do some other repair job. Sometimes they'd been waiting for years."

In TV cop shows, months of tedious research get compressed into a few minutes of script, and cases, no matter how complicated, fall into place neatly before the commercials at the turn of the hour. In reality, police work is always a combination of methodical, often monotonous investigation, the ability to talk to people and get them to talk, and good luck. You can see all that in my father's files, even the luck part: at one point in the investigation he had the first in what would be a series of heart attacks that would eventually lead to his death. Lying in his hospital bed, he was pleased to discover that two of the nurses he had been unsuccessfully tracking down, women who had been at a party with one of the victims the night before she had been killed, were employed at the hospital. He interviewed them from his bed.

After twelve frustrating months of crisscrossing Greater Boston following one piece of information after the next and enduring endless meetings with the Bureau's team, my dad was rewarded, finally, with his first real break in the case. The page marked Friday, January 8, in his 1965 daybook makes reference to it:

> The Chief of Security of the Mass General hospital called me. To Mass General and talked to Andy J. Palermo and while there made a few more checks.
>
> He told me about a good suspect and gave me some information on one Albert H. DeSalvo of Malden. An unknown nurse called — phone — Andy and gave him the information. Will check up on her. Andy will turn over more information later to me.

Palermo told my dad that the female hospital worker — who would ultimately be responsible for breaking the case, who would not give her name, and who, despite months of

effort by Palermo, my father, and others, would never be identified — claimed that a man she knew slightly had tied her up
in her apartment and assaulted her. From what she had been
reading about the Boston Strangler's peculiar method of gaining entry to his victims' apartments, and his way of molesting
and killing them, she thought she had been relatively fortunate.

This man, she wrote, should be looked at as a suspect. She
had his name, Albert DeSalvo, and provided a detailed description.

After two and a half years of frenzied investigation by legions of detectives and scores of reporters, in the thousands
upon thousands of man-hours that had gone into the hunt for
the Boston Strangler to that point, this was the first time the
name Albert DeSalvo appeared as a serious suspect on any police report or in any article.

Albert H. DeSalvo was thirty-one years old at the time,
and, as my father soon learned, was being held at The Center
for the Treatment of Sexually Dangerous Persons, a.k.a.
Bridgewater State Hospital, in connection with a recent arrest
in Cambridge. His early life reads like a Satanic prescription for
mayhem. His father was a violent drunk and sex fiend who
would bring home prostitutes and have intercourse with them
in front of his wife. In a drunken rage he broke his wife's fingers one by one — with young Albert and his five siblings
watching. He taught Albert, age six, how to shoplift. At one
point he sold Albert and one of his sisters to a farmer in Maine;
after several months they managed to run away. Albert himself
was introduced to sex by an older female neighbor; he was ten
at the time. He had already been arrested by then, and would
soon be caught burglarizing a store and sent to serve time in
the Lyman School for Boys.

When he surfaced again it was in the U.S. Army in Germany where he was the Army's middleweight boxing champion

and where he met his future wife, Irngard. He would later confess to assaulting hundreds of women while stationed in Europe, but there is no record of him ever being caught. Back in New Jersey, before being discharged (honorably, it would turn out, against all odds) he was accused of fondling a nine-year-old girl but the girl's mother did not press charges. By the late 1950s, after being arrested for breaking into apartments and houses, and after fathering two children with Irngard, he was living in Malden, Massachusetts, just north of Boston, and working at various jobs — housepainter, carpenter/handyman, furnace maintenance man. He had encounters with hundreds of women by that point, seducing some and assaulting or raping others, but had miraculously avoided arrest on sex charges. That bit of his good fortune was one reason the massive manhunt that began in the early 1960s had never turned its searchlight in DeSalvo's direction. Everyone was looking for a sex criminal; his court records showed him as a B&E (breaking and entering) man.

But in 1961, DeSalvo's incredible string of luck ran out — partially. Caught trying to break into the apartment of two young women in Harvard Square, he was tried for breaking and entering and assault, found guilty, and sentenced to two years in Billerica House of Correction. In another fateful twist, charges of lewd behavior were inexplicably dropped. It was shortly after serving that sentence that his killing spree began.

From January 8, 1965, when my father was first contacted by the head of security at Massachusetts General Hospital, his daybook shows DeSalvo's name dozens of times. He tried to find the anonymous woman at the hospital, checked out DeSalvo's rap sheet at Boston Police Headquarters, went to DeSalvo's hometown to see if he could speak to a family member, and then, later, to former employers. He learned almost immediately that DeSalvo was in Bridgewater on the Cambridge arrest. That piqued his interest even more, because that arrest, finally, *had* been for sexual assault. Once DeSalvo's photograph had gone out on the police wire — standard procedure — dozens of women in Connecticut came forward and fingered him as having assaulted them. He was known there as "The Green Man", because he posed as a maintenance man and often wore green pants. In Cambridge, his M. O. was different. There he was "The Measuring Man" because, hard as it may seem to believe now, he gained entrance to the women's apartments by telling them he was from a modeling agency and had been sent to measure them.

Having held his horrible secrets this long, upon being arrested in Cambridge on the sex charges, DeSalvo seemed almost eager to confess (in fact, Gerold Frank — who, my father said, was given unprecedented access to the case materials — notes that he did make a sort of confession to his then attorney, Jon Asgiersson, but Asgiersson, perhaps not believing the story, did not pass the information on). His wife and sister visited him at the station. In the presence of detectives, DeSalvo asked his wife's permission to tell them what he had done.

"Yes," said Irngard, "tell them everything" . . . and then she walked out.

DeSalvo confessed to a number of rapes, but when asked if he was the Boston Strangler, flat out denied it. He did not fit the profile, in any case. He was not homosexual, did not seem to have a problem relating to women, came across as meek and polite rather than enraged and vicious.

But the "Green man" connection had struck a chord with my dad. Looking through an old police file on the murder of the seventh victim, Patricia Bissette, killed on New Year's Eve, 1962, he had noticed that a neighbor had said she had seen a strange man in the building and that the man was wearing green pants.

*"Some checking on Albert DeSalvo,"* the daybook shows on February 16th.

My father put these two puzzle pieces together — the nurse's assault and the Green Man comment — and went to the Cambridge police. There, he was told that they had ruled out DeSalvo as a suspect in the stranglings because A) he had confessed openly to everything else but had denied killing anyone, and B) most importantly, in May, 1961, DeSalvo had been sentenced to two years in the Billerica House of Correction on the B&E charge.

That was the second reason why DeSalvo had never been considered a suspect during the Strangler season: some records showed him serving his full two-year sentence at Billerica. Since the first killing occurred in June of 1962, any investigator looking into Albert DeSalvo as a suspect would immediately rule him out because he had still been behind bars then.

Except, as my father figured out, he had not.

My father relied heavily on his intuition, and he had a sense that the Cambridge detectives were missing something. It was typical of him not to take someone else's word for anything connected to an investigation he was part of. Later, if we inherited a case from another agency, or files from a local police department, he would insist on gathering all the information again, on his own, making sure it was accurate, checking for missed opportunity or flimsy explanation. He liked to say, "We need to be standin' on firm ground before we can start makin' assumptions." This meant going over details as small as the correct spelling of witnesses names, one S or two, "William" or "Willard."

So, haunted by a whisper of doubt, on February 24th, he went to see his cousin, Tony DiNatale, who worked at the

31

Cambridge Probation Office. Tony gave him access to DeSalvo's probation records. Looking through them, my dad noticed what others had missed: DeSalvo had been granted an early parole, eleven months before his scheduled release date. The early release would have put him out on the streets in April, 1962. The Strangler's first victim had been killed that June.

At that point, along with his partners, my father still had scores of other leads to track down. Many of them had also seemed promising at first, then turned out to be dead ends. But, after the visit to the Cambridge probation office, the day-book reads: *"Albert case is getting interesting. Will have to talk to him soon."*

After a week of checking DeSalvo's work records, on March 5th, 1965, my father drove to Bridgewater to interview his newest suspect face to face. There, he was told — prematurely as it turned out — that DeSalvo had retained the flamboyant, newly famous, F. Lee Bailey as his attorney. In fact, Bailey was representing a man named George Nassar, accused of the fatal stabbing and shooting of a gas station attendant in the northern suburb of Andover. Nassar had been in a cell with DeSalvo and had listened to him brag about thirteen "big jobs" he had committed. Suspecting that his cellmate was actually referring to something other than robberies, Nassar advised Bailey to have a talk with him.

On that March 5th visit, my father tried to call Bailey to see if he would come to Bridgewater so the questioning could be done in the presence of an attorney, but Bailey was not available. In my dad's words, "I know that if I had talked to Albert he would have told me everything that very moment. He wanted to talk to somebody."

The next day Bailey came to Bridgewater, agreed to represent DeSalvo, and the Boston Strangler told him everything he had done — the break-ins, the rapes, and the murders. From that moment, though plenty of other men were still considered likely suspects, the Bureau's center of attention shifted to Bridgewater and the man who would become its most famous inmate.

You can see evidence of this shift of focus in the March 7th entry in my dad's daybook: *"Bottomly calls at home on Sunday. Report to Police Headquarters. Lieutenant Donovan and turn over all reports and work on Albert DeSalvo."*

Still, despite the fact that the confession was becoming known in police circles, the case was far from over. Not many serial murderers implicate themselves, and DeSalvo had always had a reputation for braggadocio. Several fellow inmates who were interviewed noted that tendency of his, and were either tired of his boasting about sexual conquests and break-ins, or did not believe them, or both. Other complications would arise, too.

Over the next week, looking for hard evidence to corroborate the confession, my father made a trip to Baltimore to interview a man who might have seen something at one of the murder sites. He went back to the Mass. General to try to track down the anonymous nurse or medical worker. He showed pictures of DeSalvo to neighbors of another victim, Sophie Clark, went back to the DeSalvo family home in Malden — no one there; he handed the Cambridge probation records over to Bottomly. My dad then checked the intake records at Bridgewater and noticed that DeSalvo had at first claimed to be unable to remember anything during an eighteen-month period: June, 1962 until January, 1964, the exact span of time during which the women had been killed. He painstakingly added factual details to what he called his "diagrams of death", creating something like a modern-day Excel spread sheet. These were 5' x 5' sheets of drafting paper, blocked out in even squares, with categories such as *"how killer got in"*, *"personal habits"*, *"type of the building"*, all of them filled in with a draftsman's neat printing. In addition to the scale drawings of each victim's apartment, my father and one of his colleagues on the Bureau, Lieutenant Andrew Tuney, made a more thorough check of work records, noted down the date, time, and place where DeSalvo had been on those days at those times. In every instance, DeSalvo's schedule and the victim's overlapped: there had been the opportunity for him to be away from his work at the hour of the killings, and he had also been working in or near the neighborhoods where they occurred.

At this point, in police parlance, my dad and the others on the Bureau "liked him". Nothing they learned after that point ever shook their conviction.

In my dad's laconic shorthand, all this seems routine enough. There are no exclamation points in the day book, no sense of excitement that they had finally caught the man they had been searching for, night and day, for three years. But on March 15th, after he records another visit to Cambridge and a talk with Captain Granger and Lieutenant Leo Davenport there, and writes about going over DeSalvo's background cases yet again, there is one telling clue in the handwritten entries. On that Monday, in red pen, my father made one small, precise check mark near DeSalvo's name. In that year's 365 pages, all of them marked with lines scrawled in various color ink, this is the only time the check mark appears. It is the same mark he used to make on his death diagrams, and his carpentry work — something to indicate he had gotten it right, that the measurements were precise, to scale, accurate as drawn, or that the cut should be made just to this side of the pencil line.

At that point, he knew.

# FOUR
## After the Confession

*"Reports have been received by Lieutenant Tuney that Bailey has said, "I will get that Brooke,".* McNamara's attitude toward you and your department is too well known to repeat. The connection between Collins' political ambitions and McNamara's attitude is subject to considerable speculation."* From a March 11, 1965 memo: from John Bottomly to Edward Brooke.

And then, in my father's words, "the political iron curtain came down."

When Ed Brooke found out about DeSalvo's confession and Bailey's visits, he took the unusual step of issuing an order denying anyone — even, for a time, the alleged strangler's own legal counsel — the right to talk to Albert DeSalvo. F. Lee Bailey tried to circumvent the order by sending telegrams to Nassar and by writing to DeSalvo's wife — even having someone make a phone call to her in her native German. Meanwhile, according to complaints my father shared with me on several occasions, the Boston Police Department was doing its best to secretly obstruct the investigation. The commissioner, he said in that same television interview, "was blind with hatred because a little guy like me come up with the answers."

All five city police departments where stranglings had occurred had been asked to send any information they had to the Strangler Bureau, but when my dad saw what the BPD had sent along, he knew it was only a portion of the evidence they had. In his opinion, it was clear what was going on: Ed Brooke wanted credit, via his Bureau, for catching the Strangler. But so did Edmund McNamara, commissioner of police, whose boss, John Collins, then mayor of Boston, was also contemplating a run for the senate seat.

Whatever the actual behind-the-scenes machinations, at this point John Bottomly began to make regular visits to Bridgewater to question DeSalvo in detail. My father often drove him there, and waited around while the interviews were being conducted. The situation did not please him. In fact, my dad and the others who had extensive experience as interrogators were extremely uncomfortable watching Bottomly assume that role. While they respected his grasp of the law and his organizational skills, they knew very well that interrogation techniques are not something you learn in law school, and they cringed at the way he conducted the interviews. Before every session, they would prep him in the hallway outside the interrogation room. In the film, *The Boston Strangler*, Bottomly moves DeSalvo from denial to confession like a master, but my father's remarks paint a very different picture.

The Bureau's secretary made transcripts of these sessions, and then the tapes and transcripts were handed over to my father and Lieutenant Tuney. The two of them often stayed up past midnight, in our basement, studying these pages and making notes. They spent most of the rest of 1965 checking DeSalvo's uncannily detailed memory against the facts of each case, trying to ascertain if he had faked the confession, if he had used details gleaned from newspaper reports or jailhouse conversations with George Nassar. Every statement DeSalvo made — what he had said to gain entry; exactly how he had killed each victim; what he had done to the body and in what position he had left it; what he saw in each apartment; what, if anything, he stole — everything had to be cross-checked against all the publicly available information on each murder. DeSalvo, it turned out again and again, knew facts known only to the police and never publicized: how much money he had taken from each apartment, and how much he had left behind; the exact position in which he had left the women; the fact that he had turned down a phonograph but not turned it off; that the paint in the hallway was chipped.

Working to undermine the credibility of DeSalvo's confession were two factors: the testimony of several neighbors and one assault victim who, when brought to Bridgewater, failed to make a positive identification; and the reports of Dr. Ames Robey, head of the psychiatric evaluation unit at Bridgewater, who had studied DeSalvo's records, had numerous conversations with the man, and had decided that he was a person incapable of serial murders. As most people in law enforcement know, however, eyewitness accounts and identifications are the least reliable evidence one is likely to encounter. And, as my father's letters from DeSalvo show, the Strangler would later brag about the games he played with Dr. Robey, putting on a false personality, telling lies, feigning mental breakdowns and memory lapses.

A whole book could be written just about the intricacies of this investigation (several have been), but the ultimate result of this huge tangle of competing agencies, less-than-ethical behavior, jealousy, confusion, criminal genius and political ambition was the deal F. Lee Bailey and Ed Brooke made in August, 1965: DeSalvo would confess privately to being the Boston Strangler, (which would help Brooke in his upcoming senate campaign) with the understanding that the confession could never be used against him in a court of law (which would help

F. Lee Bailey, who was going to enter an insanity plea on the hope of sparing DeSalvo's life and having him committed to a psychiatric facility instead of doing hard time.)

This arrangement infuriated my father, who felt it was good for the politicians and lawyers, but horribly unfair to the victims' families, and to a skeptical, still-terrified public that wanted to see a conviction in court. He saw it, too, as a larger opportunity lost: here was a serial killer asking to be committed to a mental hospital, begging to offer himself up for study; and here were the politicians, playing the case for their own advancement.

But, once the deal was cut, things dragged slowly and inevitably forward. It was not until January, 1967, that DeSalvo went on trial in Middlesex Superior Court in Cambridge for sexual assault, rape, and armed rape — many of these crimes had been committed before the stranglings began. Attorney General Brooke was gambling that he would be convicted on these charges, and — since a rape conviction in Massachusetts carried a life sentence — be kept off the streets for good. No one involved with the Strangler Bureau harbored any doubt that they had the right man in custody, but, as a legal matter, convicting DeSalvo of the stranglings would have been difficult. The physical evidence against him was non-existent. The case would rest on his confession, and on circumstantial evidence alone. You would have the bizarre spectacle of a serial murderer having to prove his own guilt.

Because the Strangler case formed the foundation of our detective agency, and changed my father's life, and my life forever, I have gone into some detail here. I will, however, skip over the complicated judicial proceedings that followed DeSalvo's confession. The political intrigue, the backstabbing, the legal maneuverings, the egotism and deceit — it would fill an entire and separate book. I will say only that I have been over my father's files many times, and, like him, have never possessed a second's doubt about who committed the murders. There were hearings to determine DeSalvo's competence to stand trial, there were measures taken by Bailey that stopped half an inch short of introducing the strangler confessions. There were more political machinations behind the scene, and hundreds more hours of police work: finding women who had known DeSalvo, and men who had been in prison with him, and checking out every last statement the man himself had made.

Ultimately, in a January 1967 trial covered by news outlets from around the world, a jury found DeSalvo guilty of multiple rapes and assaults, and he was sentenced to life in prison. In that sense, the deal brokered by Attorney General Ed Brooke and Attorney F. Lee Bailey accomplished its goal — the Strangler was kept off the streets forever. But neither DeSalvo nor anyone else has ever been tried, let alone convicted, for the thirteen murders, a fact that bothered my father until the day he died. (What bothered him even more was the legion of people who had never met DeSalvo and never worked on the case, but who stated with great confidence that he had not been the killer. "Strange, isn't it," he used to say, "the guy goes to jail and women stop dying.")

The epilogue to the story, and to this chapter in my father's life, is that, on February, 23, 1967, along with a burglar and a convicted murderer, Albert DeSalvo escaped from Bridgewater State Hospital. Just before he opened his cell door with a homemade key, slipped down an elevator shaft with the two other inmates and used planks to go over a twenty-foot wall, DeSalvo wrote the following letter to Charles W. Gaughan, the Bridgewater Superintendent. I found the letter — one page of looping handwriting — in my father's files, and include it here with all its punctuation and spelling errors:

*Thursday*
*Feb 23*

*Dear Mr Gaughan,*
*Sorry but I feel I've had it, I just don't understand the law or people. I truly thought I was doing the right thing, By telling the truth each day that goes by it seems to me a waste of time to be living. Everything I have inside me I felt could maybe clear up a few important matters, I had hope of trying to help others with problems such as mine, I'm not going out to hurt anyone, I just wish to die outside the wall. I know they will have orders to shoot me on sight. I am only sorry the people in our world don't even want to try and understand what makes a person what he "was," but not "now." I don't feel I could hurt a fly. I can't understand myself, so how can I expect you or anyone to understand what made me be. Everything I hate, and almost can't believe it was me.*
*Albert H. DeSalvo*
*It's dark in my room!*

My father was notified of the escape immediately, and he called my mother and had her take my brother, sister and me to my aunt's house in Somerville. This did not sit very well with my twin sister, Evelyn, who was planning to go to a school dance that night. He then hurried over to the Stop and Shop in West Roxbury, where my older sister Jean was working as a cashier. Jean also remembers that moment with acute pain. She was traumatized, at first because she had planned a night out with friends at the local bowling alley, and the sound of her name being called over the market's loudspeaker and then the sight of my dad driving up and bursting into the store was not exactly consistent with her hopes for a fun evening. But then, later and more seriously, the trauma came from the fact that, before joining us at my aunt's, she spent that first night alone in our house with my father. The lights were left on, she was unable to sleep, sure that DeSalvo was going to pay them a visit, kill him, and strangle her. At one point on that night the phone rang and she answered it. "This is Albert," said a man on the other end of the line. "Is Phil there?" Jean dropped the phone and ran to my father, screaming. After he hung up, my father told her it was just a friend playing a bad joke. But, forty-three years later, Jean still will not stay in a hotel room alone, or get into a taxi alone, or spend the night in her suburban home unless her husband or one of her sons is there with her. "I envy people when I hear them say, "I had the house all to myself," she says now. And in a memoir about that period, she wrote,

> "I can't be alone in a house like that . . . I believe that fear, no matter how hard one tries to ignore, disguise, or confront it, will color your thoughts and actions into adulthood. Imbedded fear will pop up like a fresh green weed in a heavily mulched garden. You think you've got it buried under layers of bark and pine, flowers bloom, life is good, but the weeds continue to sow their seeds and return."

It did not make it any easier for her when she saw a P.S. in one of DeSalvo's later letters to my dad: *"See if you can get me over your house. I've got a green thumb handy man's my trade."*

The morning after DeSalvo's escape, she joined us at my aunt and uncle's. Going their own way after a night together, DeSalvo's fellow escapees had a day of drinking in Charlestown and then turned themselves in. But the Boston Strangler was not with them, and the region simmered in fear for another 48 hours. While every cop in Greater Boston was looking for him, DeSalvo spent his last day of freedom riding buses back and forth across the city of Lynn — where the third strangling had occurred some five years earlier. He slipped into the basement of a triple-decker and spent the night there, dressed in a sailor suit he had found in a box. On the next afternoon, tired and hungry, with half the world, it seemed, looking for him and both the Attorney General and Bailey's office broadcasting an appeal that he surrender, he walked into a clothing store and asked to use the phone. Before he could make the call, a clerk recognized him. Moments later, without a struggle, he was arrested.

As he was being arraigned for the escape charges, DeSalvo and my father came face to face and talked. They had seen each other at the various court appearances, but this was their first conversation. Maybe, despite the fact that my father had testified against him, they sensed some kind of odd connection — father to father, hunter to hunted, Italian American handyman to Italian American handyman. Maybe DeSalvo was just working his notorious charm, trying to get whatever he could in the way of attention or favors. Maybe, after all those months of tracking him down, my father was fascinated with the man. According to my dad, after they had talked for a while, DeSalvo said, "Phil, would you mind going to the cellar in Lynn where I was hiding and getting my stuff and bringing it to me? I have a notebook there with names and addresses of people I want to be able to write to."

My father obliged. A few days later, on March 1, 1967, an entry in my dad's journal says, *"Received letter from Albert DeSalvo from Walpole."* DeSalvo had thanked him for the favor, and asked him to pick up his glasses and a few scraps of paper that were being held at the State Police crime lab on Commonwealth Avenue (walking distance from the home of his second victim). My father brought DeSalvo his personal items at 4 p.m. on Saturday the 4th, and stayed at the Walpole prison for six hours, talking to him.

For the next ten months, until the fall of 1968, they carried on a regular correspondence. As he did with everything else related to the case, my father saved these letters, thirty-three in all. The handwriting is fairly neat, the grammar fairly good, the lines — sometimes whiney, sometimes sentimental, sometimes showing the manipulative nature of a true sociopath, sometimes expressing a gratitude for *"someone who understands me"* — revealing a man who clearly knew what he had done, but not why he had done it. DeSalvo was in 10 Block at the notorious prison then, solitary confinement. The other escapees had tried to pin all the blame on him for planning their trip over the wall — which had resulted in DeSalvo attacking them physically in the courtroom. Bailey was no longer in contact with him. His wife had changed her name and moved away, taking the children with her after threatening to kill them and herself if he did not stop telling the world he was the Strangler. All he wanted, DeSalvo wrote to my dad, repeatedly, besides the chance to see his children, was for the state to decide to study him so that someone would understand the urge that came over him before he committed the murders, and possibly prevent such killings in the future. "I feel like a man without anything in this world," he wrote in his August 21, 1967 letter. "I sure miss my children very much, I'd like to have pictures seeing how they look now and would like to be kept informed that they are well."

His motives may have been altruistic, as he claimed, or they may have been a way of trying to trade time in the notorious maximum security prison in Walpole for time in a psychiatric hospital. Later newspaper reports suggest that he even clung to the frail hope that he had see the light of day again. My father visited with him often, bringing him books and going over the killings. Donald Conn, chief prosecutor in the case, knew about and obviously approved of these meetings, so, in certain circles, there was still the hope of finding a way to bring him to trial. "It would be a shame to leave this story as it is, undone," DeSalvo wrote in one of his last letters. Everybody but F. Lee Bailey and Edward Brooke seemed to agree.

Besides signing the letters ("yours truly, Albert"), DeSalvo had also signed an agreement with Bailey and 20th Century Fox, to allow a movie to be made from his story. The lawyer and Bottomly would both profit handsomely from the film, and my dad would end up making some money, too. On one of my father's visits to Walpole, he and DeSalvo heard a jet plane overhead. "Maybe that's the jet I bought my lawyer", DeSalvo said bitterly.

At some point in 1968, DeSalvo claimed he had not been of sound mind when he signed the agreement, and tried to stop the distribution of the film. This is from the October 1, 1968 issue of the *Boston Record American*:

> *Albert DeSalvo filed suit in Suffolk Superior Court seeking to prevent showing of the new movie The Boston Strangler because, he said, "it portrays him as 'a vicious and depraved individual' and constitutes an invasion of personal and private rights."*

The problem with this argument was that my father had letters in his possession in which DeSalvo talked about how great the movie was going to be. He produced these letters for the court, and that was pretty much the end of the not-of-sound-mind idea, and the end of DeSalvo's friendship, such as it was, with my dad.

It was not, however, the end of my father's connection to the Strangler story. In fact, long after the other major players in the saga had resigned, my father remained at the Bureau, working to bring the case to trial. Eventually, the Bureau was closed down and he was sent back to the Boston Police Department. Despite recommendations from both Attorneys General, Ed Brooke and Elliot Richardson, and apparently as punishment for his role in the case — which his superiors at the Boston Police Department saw as a disloyal cooperation with Commissioner McNamara's arch enemy, Brooke — my dad was reassigned. McNamara took him away from the street action he loved and made him do what he called "scut work", shuffling papers, even being asked to take the captain's car out to get it washed. In early 1968, 20th Century Fox was looking for a technical consultant to the film. My father and Bottomly were both approached by Hollywood, and were hired. Along with my father's position as technical advisor went a salary of $1,000 a week for twenty-four weeks — roughly eight times what he was earning then. He applied to the Department for a leave of absence. The request was denied. So he resigned, took my mother to Hollywood for a few months, had his own chair on the set, appeared on the *Joey Bishop Show* promoting the film, rubbed shoulders with Tony Curtis (who played DeSalvo, and bore some resemblance to him) and George Kennedy (who played Phil DiNatale, and did not look like him at all), enjoyed the high life for a while, collected his paycheck, and came home.

The story that director Richard Fleischman and screenwriter Edward Anhalt put together was gripping. And the performances — Curtis' especially, but Henry Fonda's as well, were widely praised, though the film bears only a passing resemblance to the actual facts of the case.

Albert DeSalvo passed the time at Walpole State Prison on

work details and making necklaces — of all things, in the prison workshop. On November 26, 1973, he was stabbed to death in the hospital ward. Despite two trials, no one was ever convicted of his murder. The Boston Strangler case remains officially unsolved.

A number of books have been written about the case. Two of the better known, Gerold Frank's, *The Boston Strangler*, and Susan Kelly's, *The Boston Stranglers,* take opposite points of view. Kelly, as her title suggests, argued that DeSalvo had either not been the killer, or had not been the only killer. Like the two other detectives who were closest to the actual investigation, John Donovan and Edward Sherry, my father was upset by Kelly's book. During the period when he was visiting DeSalvo at Walpole, Albert — as my father came to call him — talked to him in great detail about the killings. "He had a mind like a computer," my dad would later say. The oldest victim, Mary Mullen, had not actually been strangled. When DeSalvo took hold of her she had a heart attack and died instantly (my father and Lieutenant Tuney checked a nearby pharmacy and found that, yes, Mary Mullen had been taking medicine for her heart.) DeSalvo had laid her down on a sofa in her apartment, and he remembered the painting above that sofa — a deer running across a field. He also recalled, and related to my father, that the steps squeaked in one apartment building; he knew the color of the paint in another; the fact that, against the Boston building code, the apartment door opened outward not inward in the apartment of one of his victims. He revealed some of his techniques, saying that sometimes he would break in, using a piece of stiff cellophane to jimmy the lock, and sometimes he would talk his way in. If he stood in the lobby of an apartment building and saw BROWN or M. BROWN next to the bell, he would not ring it. If he saw a printed first name of MADELEINE or MARY, he would.

F. Lee Bailey, no stranger to con-artists, was certain DeSalvo had done the killings. Although there was never any physical evidence linking DeSalvo — or anyone else — to the murders, the circumstantial evidence was so consistent and so overwhelming, that, along with the detailed information contained in DeSalvo's confession and his jailhouse conversations, my father — who came to know DeSalvo better than anyone else involved in the case — was convinced beyond the smallest doubt that the Boston Strangler had been caught.

"They can say in one sentence that he wasn't the Strangler," he was fond of saying, "I could show you evidence for three days that says he was."

The Hollywood money was good, but not nearly good enough to retire on. My dad had burned bridges with his superiors at the Boston Police Department. He could, I suppose, have found work as a carpenter or handyman, but, after the intensity of the Strangler case, and after twenty four years of police work, there was a more appealing choice. For a brief time he sent out feelers and resumes for corporate security work. And then, in July of 1968, at the age of forty-nine, he decided to start a new career as a private detective. My mother agreed to this mid-life move on the condition that they use the Hollywood money to pay off the mortgage on their home. "This way," she told him, "if things don't go the way you want them to go, we'll at least still have the house."

And so, in one of life's strange twists, Albert DeSalvo's perverted viciousness led to the end of my father's police career, and the beginning of our family business.

# BOOK TWO
## The Early Days

# FIVE
The First Days

*"Look with favor upon a bold beginning."*
Virgil

Trading the bureaucratic confines of the Boston Police Department for the freedom of self-employment sounds like a step up the satisfaction ladder. But in the first months, my father's transition to the private sector must have been humbling for him. A year before, he had been part of a select group of investigators hand-picked to find the most notorious criminal in Boston's history. A few months earlier, he had been making a thousand dollars a week and keeping company with Hollywood stars. Now, in the fall of 1968, he found himself working out of a corner in the office of a lawyer he knew, Ed Swartz, "sitting on an empty orange crate" as he described it, with a telephone in his hand, trying to get his own business off the ground.

While he had little experience as an entrepreneur, he did have a long list of friends and contacts in the Greater Boston law enforcement community, and he had a way of making people feel comfortable around him, and of inspiring confidence. He was a simple, straightforward man, not particularly well educated, but street smart and with an excellent sense of people. My father misspelled and mispronounced words ("Leevites" instead of Levis, "birfday" instead of birthday, "goolie's stick" instead of goalie's stick, "Vouchwagon" instead of Volkswagen. Although we used to tease him about it mercilessly — "Dad, for your next birfday we're going to get you a goolie's stick to keep in your Vouchwagon" — he never changed), but he was adept at convincing people to reveal things they would not tell anyone else. He could not find the correct place to put a comma in a sentence, but he could ferret out the truth of a given situation with the instinct of a hunting dog. What he tried to do, in those first months on his own, was convince prospective clients that his particular skills were valuable to them. Years later, as he described this part of his life, my dad made the start of the business into a simple matter: "I had cards made up and I went all around the city, shaking hands, buying cocktails at a bar, telling them if you need me, call me." But he had bills to pay and three kids still to raise, and, on some days it must have felt like he was a middle-aged runner who had fallen a full lap behind the young guys and was pushing to catch up.

Contact by contact, case by case, conversation and free drink by conversation and free drink, he painstakingly took his reputation as a good cop and built it into a reputation as a good private investigator. In the library of documents he left behind, I found papers showing that his first P.I. license was issued on October 2, 1968. But the same neatly labeled folder shows that it was not for another year — October of 1969 — that he was really his own boss. At that point, for a hundred and eighty dollars a month, he rented one of two small back rooms of a storefront at 45 Bowdoin Street, in the shadow of the Massachusetts State House. He put in a phone line, a desk, two chairs, set out an inspiring, if unoriginal, framed inscription ("Though I walk through the valley of death, I shall fear no evil, because I am the meanest sonofabitch in the valley.") a sign over the front door (DiNatale Detective Agency and Security Patrol. All Types of Investigations. 227-4115.") And he was in business.

I was in high school then, at Catholic Memorial in West Roxbury, and, though my older sister, Jean, a recent graduate of what was then called The Chandler School for Women, was often pressed into service typing up reports for my dad, I was not called upon to do very much. There was that initial surveillance in the Back Bay. And, when Jean was not available — she had two young sons at that point and a husband in medical school — I sometimes edited the reports my father put together for lawyers, inserting or deleting commas, fixing spelling mistakes, trying to make his sentences sound more like what I thought a professional investigator should sound like, and less like the terse bulletins of a street cop. He admired my vocabulary and loved learning new words. "Reticent", I remember him saying, when I suggested that term to describe a less-than-forthcoming witness. "That's a good one. *Reticent*. Put that in."

A year after the Bowdoin Street office opened, I graduated from high school and started college at Boston State, but there still was not enough work for my father to hire me as full-time summer help. Often, on Friday and Saturday nights, I would do a bit of domestic or bar surveillance for him — sitting in Sammy White's lounge/bowling alley to make sure the bartender was not pouring too many free drinks for his friends; visiting what seemed like every Pewter Pot Muffin House and Signor Pizza in Greater Boston to assess the service and food quality; checking out the scene in Lombardo's, an East Boston function hall and bar where I was half the age of most of the other patrons. If my dad needed me, he would let me know. I would work, my mother would cut me a check — ten or twenty dollars, usually — but it was not by any stretch of the imagination a regular job. And it was not as if my father was pushing me to add criminal justice courses to my college load, grooming his older son to inherit the business. At that point, we did not really know if there would be a business to inherit.

From the reports I helped him with and from reading his case records, I know that my father's work in those days was often considerably less exciting that what he had done on the streets of the Back Bay. Sometimes he would investigate the crash of a private plane, trying to determine if the pilot had been drinking or if the equipment had malfunctioned. But a lot of his work had to do with personal injury cases, as well as criminal defense work, much of it for court appointed lawyers. He would stop in at police departments to get reports of an auto accident, speak with the investigating officer, identify and then interview witnesses, write out statements and have them sign it, then go to the scene and take careful photographs and measurements. Often, the police photographs would be close-ups of a skid mark, but my father thought the whole accident should be put into perspective, and so he would take a series of photographs that gave a fuller sense of the scene.

It does not sound like the type of work a P.I. would be involved in — surely it is nothing like what they do on TV — and, in fact, these days much of that work is handled by paralegals. But it helped pay the bills in those early months, and helped him establish a name among the city's legal community. Mixed in with those types of cases were a few missing persons jobs, and those had a bit more drama to them. One of these early cases hit close to home. Back from a day at college, I saw that my father had laid out some photographs on his bed. The photos were all of the same young man.

"Looks like a kid I went to high school with," I told him.

54

"Stevie O'Malley."

"That's exactly who it is."

"What are you doing with his picture?"

"Kid disappeared. His father wants me to find him."

In the late Sixties and early Seventies there was something like a communal encampment on the southern half of Boston Common. It was the time when the word "hippie" first entered the American vocabulary, when young people were pushing against the rigid social mores of the '50s and early '60s. Maybe because it was a place they could find the drugs and camaraderie they were looking for, or maybe because it was the heart of the city and they wanted the excitement of that, the visibility, a lot of suburban hippie kids about my age had gravitated to the Common. They would sit around there during the day, strumming a guitar, making out, furtively smoking a joint. In warmer seasons, some of them would spend the night there. It was a mostly harmless situation, and the police mostly left them alone.

From things Mr. O'Malley had told him, my father thought there was a good chance his son might be found among this crowd. My dad Shanghaied me to help with the search. We went down there together to have a look, did not see Stevie, but returned several times over the next few days to take an innocent-looking, father-and-son stroll back and forth across the Common. On the third or fourth visit, we caught sight of my former classmate. He had grown his hair to his shoulders, was sporting a scraggly beard, and he did not recognize me as we walked past. Instead of going into the group and talking to Stevie right then, which is what I expected him to do and hoped he would not, my father arranged for Stevie's dad to come down and talk to his son. The dad was not insistent on getting him back home, just wanted to know that Stevie was among the living and let him know he had a guaranteed bed if he ever wanted it. They got together, it worked out well. Years later at a high school reunion, I heard that Stevie's hippie stage had passed; he was doing fine, married, had a family and a good job.

At the time, those were the types of minor contributions I made to the DiNatale Detective Agency. Though, along with the police pension and whatever might have been left over from the Hollywood money, it was the way my parents put food on the table, and though my father was certainly experienced and professional in everything he did (he made a point of wearing a suit and tie every day, as we also do now), the whole enterprise had a catch-as-catch-can feeling about it: the one-room office, the single phone line, the sign over the door that suggested we did a couple of different things. My mother was good with money and kept the books. Squeezing time out of her household duties, Jean typed up reports. I was occasionally drafted to lend a hand in some other way, but it was mainly a one-man show (which is true of most P.I. agencies; we are a rare exception) and I think my dad would be shocked if he saw what the agency looks like now: six computers, four phones, file cabinets and meeting rooms, electronic counter surveillance equipment, all kinds of insurance. Serious as he was about his work in those early days, it felt more like the carpentry jobs he used to do to bring in a little extra cash. Maybe it would grow into something, maybe it would not. My dad worked hard — that was the way he did everything — but in the late 1960's and early 1970's, my father was still talking and thinking about his work on the Strangler investigation, and just measuring pieces of wood to see what kind of life he could build on top of that foundation.

# SIX
Managing the Theater

*"You had no taste when you married me."*
- Richard Sheriden

L ittle by little, as the months passed, my father's work grew more varied and interesting. He helped win some large awards in personal injury trials — fatal auto accidents and one tragic case that grew out of the death of a child. My mother helped him by finding — coincidentally, in a store where she had worked as a girl — a blanket that was identical to the one the child had been using on the night it caught fire. The blanket was set alight in court to show that the manufacturers had not, as they claimed, flame-proofed the material.

I found myself doing a bit more work for the family business at this point, mostly involving surveillances. A good friend named Mark Rose — also a twin and someone I had known since first grade — liked and admired my dad and was always interested in working for him. Whenever he could, my father would send us out on surveillances together. Mark stood six feet tall, 165 pounds of muscle, bright red hair and a face full of freckles. He had been something of a street brawler as a kid, and, like a lot of tough kids, had dreams of becoming a cop — which was part of the mutual affection between him and my dad. Mark was studying criminal justice at Northeastern University. Probably because he was an Irish kid — ours was a predominantly Irish neighborhood — and wanted me to be his Irish friend, Mark called me "Jack", as in, "Jack, what's Phil got us doing today?" He remains the only person in my life who has ever called me by that name.

One gorgeous fall Sunday my father assigned the two of us to follow a man who managed a movie theater not far from where we lived. As had been the case with the fellow who worked in the Back Bay, this man's wife suspected he was involved in an extracurricular romance, and wanted proof. On Sunday, an hour before the matinee was to begin, my father led Mark and me (driving a new beige Chevy Nova of which I was most proud) past the man's home so we could see what kind of car he owned. From there, we went to the rear entrance of the theater and my dad set us up with a description of the manager and a general outline of what we were supposed to do.

My father's intuition — and the wife's suspicions — proved accurate. A few minutes after the movie started, out the back door came the object of our attention: a bald man, about five-foot-four with drooping shoulders and a Casper Milquetoast expression. Such a fine specimen of masculinity, I thought, it was no wonder he felt he deserved to be sleeping with more than one woman at a time.

He climbed into his car and, for a little while, zigged and zagged through the back streets of West Roxbury and Dedham, making a couple of U-turns and acting just the way someone who expected to be followed would act. By this point in our young careers, Mark and I had done probably a dozen surveillance cases together. We liked the work and were fairly skilled at it. We gave the theater manager a little leeway, waited for him to straighten out his route and meet his friend — he picked her up outside a Dunkin Donuts in Dedham — and then we followed them according to the lessons my dad had given me years before — kept our distance, stayed in the blind spot when we could, did not get stuck at the lights. Steering my Nova through the busy streets, I could almost hear his voice in my ear, "Anticipate."

It was a fine day for a ride, the leaves turning, the October sun shining, foliage enthusiasts out crowding the roads. The theater manager and his friend must have been admirers of Thoreau, because they headed out to Walden Pond in Concord, parked there, and strolled around the pond, holding hands. Mark and I kept them in sight, sometimes slipping into the woods with our telephoto lenses and documenting any public displays of affection we saw.

Their loop around the lake complete, their foreplay finished, the couple returned to the man's car. He moved it to the far corner of the parking area. Eighty yards away, with a direct line of sight and a good camera, Mark and I sat in the Nova's front seat, listening to the Patriots' football game and watching the parked car. Usually on these surveillances, it would be difficult to actually catch a moment of physical affection. Sometimes there would be a bit of handholding, or a quick kiss, but this particular couple was quite active there in the front seat.

After a few snaps of the shutter, I must have taken my eyes off them, because the next time I looked the car appeared to be empty. In his typical tongue-in-cheek manner, Mark said, "Jack, what do you think they're doing?" Another minute and he had his answer: we saw the woman's bare feet come into view, pressed up against the windshield.

It is important for me to say here that we are not and never have been in the voyeur business. This is something we have to remind clients about again and again when they come to us with a potential domestic surveillance case. In fact, because of the loosening of divorce laws over the past couple of decades, domestic surveillance has become a much smaller part of our business: a divorce-minded husband or wife does not need proof of adultery anymore; he or she simply has to go into court and cite "irreconcilable differences" and no judge is going to force them to stay married. Occasionally now it is a question of money: if a breakup is going to mean some complications about parceling out great wealth, then clients might want concrete evidence to show their partner was cheating. Even in those cases, however, it is not like we perch on windowsills outside the adulterer's bedroom and take photos of the couple *in flagrante delicto* ("in the blazing offense"). The legal standard asks only for evidence that shows they had the *opportunity* to cheat. A couple in an apartment they do not share, especially at night or at an odd hour, a photo of them holding hands — that is almost always enough to convince a judge that something of a sexual nature was likely occurring.

It is a sordid business, and one I have not been sorry to see diminish as time has passed. On many, many occasions I have sat opposite a betrayed spouse and listened to her talk about the unraveling of the marriage, the loss of her husband's affection, the accusations, the fights, the feelings of confusion she saw in her children's faces. At such times, the private investigator has to have a bit of the counselor in him. Married more than thirty years myself, I have never been thrilled to hear about someone else poisoning his or her relationship in this way, but it is part of life, it has been part of married life for millennia, and it is part of the work we do. There were a few times — like that bright October afternoon at Walden Pond — when the event had a comical twist to it; and other times, when there were children and real heartbreak involved, that you wanted to be surprised, wanted to find out that the supposedly straying husband or wife was merely a passionate stamp collector consulting with a friend, or a secret beer-tester trying out a new recipe in a small club, or was sneaking out of the office thanks only to a penchant for solitary prayer.

Something like that happened only once, though, when a stocky, purse-wielding, very tough woman came into our office and retained us. This was shortly after my dad died. The woman suspected her husband of keeping secrets, perhaps cheating on her. Since he worked only a block from our office, she wanted us to follow him at lunch hour. She gave me a photo, wrote a check for $260, the four-hour minimum in those days, and said she would call to tell me what he was wearing when he left the house. On the following morning, dressed like a downtown businessman and armed with the description of the man's clothing choice for that day, I trailed the husband as he made a leisurely loop of downtown, along Cambridge to Tremont, left on School Street and then right on Washington Street, right again on Winter, to Tremont, and then back to his office. After two days of this, I called his wife and said, "Nothing. He walks around, has a smoke, goes into — "

"He WHAT!" she screamed into the phone.

"Nothing. He walks around, goes into a store, has a bite to eat someplace and goes back to the office."

"You said he smoked."

"Yes, he — "

"You're sure?"

"Cigarettes, we're talking, right?"

"That little sneak! He told me he quit! When he gets home to me he isn't going to believe the trouble he's in. He's not supposed to be smoking. I *despise* people who smoke!"

And so on. It was the only time in my career that I have ever been tempted to find the object of our surveillance and warn him about the consequences that awaited him.

On that October afternoon, however, I am fairly certain the theater manager and his friend were not just sharing a cigarette or comparing stamp collections there in the front seat of his car. After fifteen minutes or so the doors opened and out they came, pulling up pants, rearranging bra straps, tucking in shirts. More clicks of the telephoto shutter.

As is typically the rule, Mark and I never found out if the married couple got past their trouble or split up. We handed over the film to my dad and hoped it would not be too long before our next assignment. Though we laughed about the experience, I am sure it left a mark on our young minds. It is one thing, during the age when you are meeting young women and dating, to have an intellectual understanding of the ways relationships turn sour, to know the divorce statistics and hear the stories. It is something else to see it through the lens of your camera.

# SEVEN

A Close Shave

*"I seek a father who most need a son."*

- John Brinnin

C ases like the cheating theater manager were part and parcel of my maturing process — and of the agency's — another way in which my father's work reached its fingers into our family life and formed and molded us all.

By the time my younger brother Richard graduated from college, the business had evolved into something that offered a stable income, and it would make perfect sense for him to choose it as a career. For me, though, the situation was no so cut-and-dried. At Boston State College, I did take a few criminal justice courses (For my senior project in high school I had written a paper on the Strangler case, used my father notes, contacts, and diagrams, even interviewed the chief prosecutor, Donald Conn, and still got only a 'B'. "You haven't convinced me DeSalvo was the Strangler," the teacher said.), but I had studied Russian language in high school, and liked the challenge of it, and my real college interest was 20th Century Russian History. These were the Cold War years; people with degrees in Russian-related subjects were in high demand. After I earned my Bachelor's Degree, it seemed a sensible idea to pursue that study a little farther, move away from home for a while to attend graduate school, get to know another part of the country, and then see what options were open to me.

So from 1974-76, I spent two enjoyable years at Saint Louis University, earning a Master's in 20th Century Russian History, (and working on Cape Cod during the summers, tending bar in a wild place where female impersonators performed). For a Boston kid, someone who had spent all of his twenty-one years living with his parents in a tight-knit, ethnic neighborhood, life west of the Mississippi provided another kind of education. I called home during the first few weeks and told my dad I wanted to quit. I missed my friends and family, missed the neighborhood I had thought I wanted to get away from; I was not sure a Master's degree was the right career move. He convinced me to stick it out. At Thanksgiving, after I had made some friends and been invited to the home of one of them for the holiday meal, I called back with a slightly different report: "The people here are so friendly, I'm still trying to figure out what they want from me."

As things turned out, they did not want anything, and I have remained close with many of the friends I got to know there in those two years. That time period was also my introduction to teaching — I had a fellowship, second year, that paid my tuition in return for teaching a couple of undergraduate courses — and I realized how much I loved passing on knowledge to a classroom full of students. So, when I returned to Boston in the early summer of 1976, the initials I envisioned as being associated with my future career were PhD, FBI, or CIA — not P.I. I did have an interview with the CIA that summer, and I did think about filling out an application for the FBI, and I did give some serious consideration to applying for a PhD program with an eye toward becoming a college professor. In the meantime, though, I was living at home and my father's reputation as a private investigator had started to bring in more work than he could handle. It only made sense to help him out for a while.

Like almost everything else that happened in the interface between our family and our family business, my joining the agency was not done in any formal way. I had been home from Saint Louis a couple of weeks when one morning at the breakfast table my mother casually suggested it was time for Johnny to go to work full-time. In all of our minds, I think, it was still a summer job, something to do instead of tending bar, a way to help my dad carry what was becoming a case load he could not manage on his own. The only thing that needed discussion was my salary. After a bit of back-and-forth we settled on $300 a week, to be paid by check, with my mother taking out the appropriate taxes, the way she would later do with our other employees. At that point, my dad said, "If you're gonna come work for me, you're gonna have to get rid of that ugly thing on your face."

So I went upstairs, shaved the stylish black beard I was so proud of, and reported to my new life that same day.

# EIGHT
First Gun

*"This Gun for Hire,"*
- Graham Greene.

I f this book has a central theme, in addition to the inter-
twining of family and work, it is the idea that the television image of investigative work has very little to do with
the reality of the profession. Nowhere is this more true than
when the TV is showing scenes of guns and gunplay. In thirty
eight years on the job, I have taken my gun out of its holster
exactly three times, and never fired it, and this is a history typical of every investigator I have ever spoken with. As my brother Richard says, "If I had to get a gun stuck in my face even
once a year, never mind every week, I would find some other
line of work."

Even so, a handgun is a nice thing to have in certain of the
circumstances we find ourselves in, and, without ever being
fired, mine has surely played a role in some of our interactions.
My father understood that, of course, and one of the first
things he did when I started working full-time was to take me
to get my license. Some fathers go to baseball games with sons
that age; my dad took me to the gun range.

It was early July, 1976. He drove me first to Boston Police

Headquarters, where I filled out the paperwork and made an appointment to qualify at the gun range on Moon Island. At that point the Department ran a criminal background check on me, and my father was required to write a letter attesting to the fact that I needed the license to work with him. He then took me to an indoor gun range in Fields Corner, owned by a former cop and friend of his, Mike Giacoppo, and gave me my first lessons. My father had a 5-shot .38 snub revolver, a Smith and Wesson Detective Special he had used on the force. He borrowed a .38, three-inch-barrel revolver from Mike, because that was the gun I would qualify with at Moon Island . . . and because the longer barrel made it a much easier gun to shoot.

We talked about weapon safety, how to load the gun with the barrel always pointed down and down-range. When the barrel was opened to load, you placed your thumb over it to prevent it from closing. Once the gun was loaded, if the instructor asked for it, you always opened the barrel, unloaded it, and handed it to him. "As part of the test they'll ask for the gun," my father said, "trying to trick you." In the event, the instructor did just that, sending one of the other would-be qualifiers home without a shot being fired.

After my dad showed me how to hold the .38, we "dry fired" numerous times so I would get the feel of the weapon and try not to anticipate the kick. Next, he put two bullets in, spun the barrel and then let me shoot, not knowing when a live round would go. The purpose of this was to teach me to squeeze and not pull the trigger. It's surprising how anticipating the kick makes you fire high.

We had the ear covers, safety glasses, and we set the targets — bulls eyes, not silhouettes of bad guys — in our own bay. It was a new kind of experience to feel that gun fire, a mix of slight trepidation and satisfaction. I do not think I hit anything from thirty feet for the first ten tries.

On that day, we were there a couple of hours and I must have shot a hundred live rounds, and probably another fifty dry-firing. Under my father's watchful eye, I shot one-handed, two-handed, single-fire and rapid-fire. I remember the smell of gun powder on my hand afterwards, and my dad saying, "In real life, most times when a shot is fired, the target is ten feet away or less." Once I was consistently on the paper, my father was comfortable that I knew more or less what I was doing. We returned another time or two before he told me I was ready to take the test.

Driving out to Moon Island with him on test day I was palm-sweaty nervous. But I relaxed when we walked in the door and I saw that he knew the police instructor, and that it was like old home week with the two of them. (It reminded me of when I had tested for my driver's license: By the time we were ready to go on the road, the Registry cop was so involved in conversation with his old friend, my dad, that he seemed to forget I was alive and sweating there, in the front seat.)

There were about ten other guys trying to qualify at Moon Island that day. A score of 270 out of a possible 300 was required in order to pass. We shot from thirty feet, using a three-inch-barrel police pistol we had never fired before, no practice shots. You shot one-handed, single fire, and as I picked up the gun I remembered my father had told me there was no time limit. I should take my time, dry fire, get the feel of the weapon, and then take the first shot, see where it went, adjust my aim if necessary, but take my time.

I think of this whenever I return for the four-year recertification test, and see most of the other shooters standing at the white line, firing briskly away. Usually I have taken only a single shot by the time everyone else has emptied the chamber.

I scored 280 and received my license in the mail the next week. My license was — is — for "protection of life and property" which allows me to carry a weapon concealed, and anyplace. Once the license was in my hand, my dad and I went to a gun shop on Massachusetts Avenue in Cambridge. "Remember," he said, "this thing is going to be on your waist all day. You don't want something too heavy. So I purchased a Colt .38, six-shot detective special, which I have to this day. He also bought me a nice holster, made for a left-hander, and I wore that gun every day at work for many years.

On the way back he reminded me (his law) that I could not stop for a beer when I had the gun, and (Massachusetts law) that I could never leave it in the car, unattended. "When you wear that gun," he said, "it's to protect your life, period. If it comes out of the holster, it's because your life's in danger. No showing off. You discharge a weapon within city limits it better be to save your life or you'll be charged. You shoot somebody and you'll get sued. It's not like TV, Johnny. No warning shots, no winging anybody."

The one time I have ever taken it out of the holster on the job was during an extortion case where I was lying under a blanket in the back seat of a car, making a $5,000 delivery payment to the extortionist. There were other times, in bad neighborhoods, or, later, picking up millions of dollars of diamonds at the airport, when I transferred it from holster to jacket pocket for easy access. But those were exceptions. These days, I rarely carry it at all. And my Walther PPK .380 automatic, a gift from my Uncle Joe and the same weapon James Bond carried in the old films, stays where it belongs, locked and in a safe place.

# NINE
The Bowdoin Street Circus

*"O brave new world*
*That has such people in't!"*
- Shakespeare

Beacon Hill, where our office was located, and where I was now going to work every morning, is a humble bump on the otherwise flat landscape of central Boston. In all, it covers less than a square mile and reaches a couple hundred feet above sea level, but it is the epicenter of political power in Massachusetts, holds a lot of history, and ties together disparate sections of the city.

Most of the hill is criss-crossed by narrow streets with expensive Federal-style brick rowhouses standing shoulder to shoulder. The streets are lit with gas lamps, the brick sidewalks are uneven, the fences are of spiked wrought iron, painted black; the glass windows shine like diamonds, the doors are lacquered, and the flower boxes and shrubs perfectly tended. At one time, there was Beacon Hill and Black Beacon Hill, where famous African Americans including Harriet Tubman, Frederick Douglas, and Sojourner Truth spoke at the African Meeting House on Joy Street. Today, of course, that distinction is long gone, and the hill is a homogenous neighborhood that contains some of the priciest real estate in New England. Secretary of State John Kerry and his wife Theresa Heinz have a home there. John F. Kennedy had an apartment on Bowdoin Street opposite the State House. Jack Welch, the CEO of General Electric had a place there, too, among dozens of less famous but equally well off men and women.

On the sunny south side of the Hill, you have the gold-domed State House that looks out on Boston Common and part of an historical tour called The Freedom Trail. At the opposite end of the compass, only a few hundred yards away, the not-so-sunny north slope of Beacon Hill points to different traditions. A generation ago it fed down into Scollay Square, which, with its burlesque halls and rough bars, was a favorite destination of sailors on shore leave and the haunt of every kind of street criminal. In the urban development craze of the 1960s, the buildings of the Square and of a vibrant nearby neighborhood called the West End were torn down, and huge piles of rubble and memories carted away. In their place, Bostonians now see the twenty-two story state and federal office buildings and Boston City Hall, much less seedy, of course, and yet a stretch of heartless modern stone and steel that should be included in architecture textbooks under the Never Do This section. A few bars remain along Cambridge Street — the northern border of the Hill — reminders of the way things used to be. The tavern where the TV sitcom *Cheers* was set stands on the southwest border, at Beacon and Charles. For the most part, though, modern-day Beacon Hill is a tame, residential section, a place where, especially during the day, you are more likely to see a government worker in suit and tie than a kid in jeans.

For thirty years, our office occupied a storefront on Bowdoin Street, about equal distance from the State House and what had once been the West End, and a two-minute walk from the brass-doorknocker, bay-window town homes. On any given day, you might see the governor out for a stroll, a couple in topcoat and bow-tie and fur, or a drunk wandering up from the Red Hat looking for a place to empty his bladder. It was, in other words, the perfect spot for an operation like ours, a business that would always have one arm in the troubles of wealthy families, and the other in the streets. That is one of the aspects of private investigations that must have appealed to my father, and one that has kept me interested all these years: you are repeatedly given glimpses into very different walks of American life, from heirs of a family fortune battling over an inheritance, or the children of business tycoons lured into religious cults, to the inner-city gang member accused of shooting a rival gang member, or an injured construction worker looking for disability payments.

At first, my dad rented only the windowless back room of the three-room first floor at 45 Bowdoin, a nine-by-nine-foot office with shag carpet on the floor and cheap paneling on the walls. He had a wooden desk that weighed half a ton (and is in our current, much larger office, four and a half miles away), a rolodex, a red phone. Later, we would occupy the whole first floor, but in the early years the room farthest from the sidewalk was used for storage by our landlady Maria and her husband Jimmy, and the larger front section was used by two constables I shall call Freddie and Alex.

Before we took over the whole first floor, Freddie and Alex had their own little storefront business going, and would serve summonses, preside over evictions, and dabble in other ventures not quite so official. Freddie was a full-time court officer at the Suffolk Superior Court House two blocks away. Alex would be in the Bowdoin Street office most mornings, typing up summonses, and then be out the door by 11 a.m. and gone for the day to deliver them. His place would be taken by his partner Freddie, who came over from the courthouse after lunch, until he retired from that job, at which point he tried his hand at other things.

I would step in the door and there would be Freddie, five-foot-eight, bald on top, forever hitching up his pants and checking his collar in the mirror. On the long table in front of him, arranged neatly as if in a haberdashery display, he would have forty or fifty new dress shirts, still in their plastic covers.

"Johnny, Johnny," he'd say, "Pick out a shirt."

"Where'd you get all these, Freddie?"

"Ah, they fell off a truck. Grab one."

"No, thanks," I said, "My dad would shoot me."

The next day he would be selling sweaters, or he would be organizing gambling junkets to Las Vegas. My father and mother went on a few of these trips together. My dad liked Vegas and played craps, and my mother was exceptionally lucky at roulette and slots, and would always share her winnings with her children. (One night many years later, she called my home at 11 p.m., weeping. I expected the worst until she said, "Johnny, Johnny, I hit the number!" She had won $1200; all four kids received a share). They came back telling us that everything — flight, hotel, food, drinks — had been complimentary, except you would have to withdraw $5,000 when you arrived at the casino, and spend that money at the tables. If his guests were inexperienced, Freddie would take the $5,000 and gamble for them.

One day, after what must have been a losing streak connected to one of these junkets, Freddie came running into the back office, waving his arms, "I'm not here," he said. "I'm not here, Johnny. Johnny, two guys after me. Whatever you do, don't tell them I'm here."

I stepped out into the main part of the constables' office at just about the time two hefty guys in black leather jackets were coming through the front door.

"Where's Freddie?" one of them asked me, not in a kind way.

I said I had no idea.

"Really?" he said sarcastically.

"Sure, really. My dad has a detective agency in the back," I hooked a thumb over my shoulder. "We just share the space."

"Right. You tell him we were here and we're fuckin' coming back, and we're gonna fuckin' break both his fuckin' legs."

"Fine, sure," I said. "I'll do that."

When the men were gone, Freddie thanked me profusely, nervously, and disappeared into the city. My father used to like me to do our paperwork out in the front office when the constables were not there. "Good for business if people see somebody at the desk," he would  say. But after that visit, I complained that I did not want to be perched out front like a flesh-and-blood target if Freddie's pals came by to shoot up the place. My dad just waved at me and told me to stay out there, look busy, and not worry about it.

Though we had work from lawyers and insurance companies, and from spouses wondering about the faithfulness of their mate, we were also a kind of walk-in detective agency, open to all worthwhile possibilities. It was common to see passersby catch sight of the sign, put their hands to the windows and peer inside, as if they might see Sam Spade interrogating a bad guy, or Sherlock Holmes studying fingerprints through a magnifying glass. I learned early on that, ordinary as it was to us, something about our work piqued the curiosity of people. They wanted a glimpse into the hidden world; they wanted to see other men and women doing something wrong, and being caught for it. More evidence, I guess, that our troubles are always fascinating to our fellow humans.

This curiosity and our prominent location led to some

strange moments, and, for me, some valuable lessons in how to distinguish between legitimate prospective clients and people who would waste your time. A passerby would walk in, close the door with a dramatic gentleness, and whisper, "I think I'm being followed." One time, a young man came in, sat down across from my father and showed him a matchbook with a telephone number scribbled on it. "I had some drinks last night," he said, "and met this girl. I have her number but can't remember her name to save my life. Can you find out a name from a phone number?" Someone else stopped by to ask us to do a background check on a Beacon Hill socialite. I was there alone at the time, and when I passed the potential work onto my dad he said, "He's a thief. The woman's loaded. He's using us to get her schedule so he can break in when she's away."

Mike Taibbi, a Channel 7 newsman then (now a reporter with a national affiliate) stationed a camera in our office for a special report he was doing on people who used the state office building's garage across the street when they should have been paying to park somewhere else.

A guy who claimed he worked for then-governor William Weld paid us a visit, absolutely positive he was being followed. We followed him ourselves for a while, and when we assured him no one else was on his tail, he got this glazed look in his eyes and said, "They got to you, didn't they? Gave you a hundred bucks or something to forget you ever saw them."

Another visitor plopped $2,000 on the desk and said, "Consider yourself retained. I want to disappear, and I want you to tell me everything you'd do to find somebody who disappears."

It was, for a young man, a Ph.D. course in human oddity.

There was a lot of foot traffic on Bowdoin Street in those days, and, though I do not recall many significant jobs coming from the characters who dropped in to talk to us, I do remember that the street was a kind of circus side-show, all kinds of acts involved. Saint John the Evangelist Church a few doors down from us operated a soup kitchen that attracted a regular crowd of street people. Some of them would visit our offices on their way to or from lunch. One in particular, a tall, lanky, intimidating guy with scabs on his face kept coming in and coming in, putting the fear of God into our almost fearless secretary, Mary, until I had to make it clear to him that he was not welcome.

Only two or three of the buildings on our side of Bowdoin Street had commercial storefronts. These included a sandwich shop next door to us, run by two gay men named Eddie and Chuck, who made the best tuna and chicken salad in the city and kept playbills hanging in the shop for customers to peruse while they waited for their order. I would go in there for lunch and Eddie would look at me and say, "You know, Johnny, I think I can make you jump the fence."

"Why would I want to jump the fence for an ugly old guy like you?" I would reply, and we would go along that way for a while as he made up the order.

In fact, the same Eddie had jumped the fence himself some years earlier — or at least set one foot on the other side — marrying a considerably older woman who owned the corner building. "You want to buy this building, Johnny?" he would say to me, after she had passed away. "I'll sell it to you for $65,000." I did not have anything like that amount of money then, of course, and it never occurred to me to go to the bank and ask about a mortgage.

Today, according to the real estate agents that rent the same space, the building is worth roughly a million dollars.

When our friends the sandwich-makers moved out, in the mid-eighties, yet another Eddie set up shop there, selling Joe and Nemo's hot dogs. ("We'll drag them through the garden for ya," he would say, if you wanted a dog with everything on it.) This Eddie, from the small north-shore city of Revere, was about five-six, and built like a fire hydrant. Whenever the streets were not covered in snow, he would come to work on his Harley. Renowned as a ladies' man, Eddie was continually bragging to us in some detail about his latest sexual encounter, though we never knew to what extent these stories were accurate and to what extent embellished. He was a generous neighbor, always giving kids free hot dogs, and he could afford to be: from that little business, catering to garbage truck drivers and State office workers, he would rake in as much as $5,000 a week. I know this because he would keep the money in his briefcase, all cash, and, some Fridays he would open it, proudly, to show me. I would see the bills, and mixed in with the bills, a pistol. He would then go play cards from Friday till Sunday and usually lose most of his weekly haul.

In the midst of this circus, my father cultivated his connections with lawyers, and did the hard, sometimes monotonous work of tracking down witnesses and photographing accident scenes. It is fairly common for ex-policeman to try P.I. work as a second career, and very common for them to fail. Part of the difficulty involved in making transition from cop to private eye is that the steady paycheck has disappeared. Another part is that the former policeman can no longer rely on the authority of the badge to convince people to talk to him. There is no power of arrest or subpoena, no handcuffs, no threat of jailtime, just the force of one's personality, a talent for reading people, and the ability to adjust one's voice and manner to a wide variety of situations. It is like moving from commercial pilot to the owner of a small plane and suddenly realizing there is no ground crew and no air-traffic controller: you are up there on your own.

Still, after one small altercation with an unauthorized representative of the neighborhood zoning commission who claimed Phil had not applied for the proper permission for the office sign and would have to take it down ("You take it down yourself," my dad said. "And when you come down off the ladder I'll be waiting for you.") my father seemed at home there on Bowdoin Street, and in his new profession. From that first, beardless summer day, he made me feel at home, too . . . after his own fashion.

With him, there was never any question about who was boss — he was too old-school for that. But there was also a way in which he let me, and later my brother Richard, share some of the responsibility, allowed us to grow up. Always according to his rules, however. On that first day, still mourning the loss of my beard, I answered the phone, "DiNatale Detective Agency." And after the phone call he said, "No good. I want you to answer it "4115"," which were the last four digits of the phone number. He and his friend Bill Monahan at the phone company had gone through dozens of available numbers until my dad found one that felt just right.

"That doesn't sound like a business," I told him. "Why do it that way?"

"Because I fucking say so," was the reply.

On the other hand, beginning on that first day, he insisted I call him by his first name, Phil, when we were at work. I thought that didn't make sense either — anybody could see I was his son, same build, same big head and prominent nose and direct eyes and dark hair — but to him it seemed more professional to be there with an assistant than a relative. In time, my siblings and I would all come to call him Phil, which is not exactly an old world tradition.

He had a similarly unusual relationship with my mother. She would cook and clean for him without complaint, do the books, sew torn clothes, and put up with his temper at times, or try to act as a mediator between him and whichever one of us had gotten into trouble. Other times, she would stop him in mid-tirade, hold up a hand and say, "Enough. You don't talk to me like that. That's going to cost you a dress." Next day, she would head into Boston and buy an expensive dress, wear it a few times and give it away, making sure my father knew of the donation. One time my mother was in front of the house in one of those dresses, on her knees in the dirt, weeding her flower garden. She must have known Phil was about to come home. When he saw her, he said, "Evelyn, what the hell are you doing? That's the new dress!?"

"I've just about finished with this one," she said. "I've worn it twice, that's enough."

Big Evie, some people called her, though, physically at least, she was fairly small. Size 10, my sister Jean tells me. She was careful with the family finances, but sometimes Big Evie would show one of my sisters a dress she'd had for a few months and she'd say, "Tell me, would Jackie Kennedy wear this?" And out it would go.

We were an eccentric family, I guess, despite the ordinary looking surfaces of our life. Eccentric and unselfconscious and unafraid of work, and so we fit in well there, on a cobblestone street on the back side of Beacon Hill, as if the other characters on the block had been waiting years for us to show up and fill out the cast of the Bowdoin Street Circus.

# TEN
## Stalking, Lying, Love

*"Love is a kind of warfare."*
- Ovid.

Within weeks of the onset of my full-time presence on Bowdoin Street — this was still the summer of 1976 — my dad and I found ourselves in the midst of a stalking case. I remember it well because it was something I think of as a "TV case", that is, the kind of thing that broke up the not-so-dramatic work of witness location, auto and construction accident investigations — the bread-and-butter of our profession.

The client who contacted us — I'll call him Josh — was a young, successful Boston entrepreneur, owner of a travel agency. He had hired a lawyer, the lawyer had recommended he talk to us, and so my father and I paid a visit to Josh at his downtown office. In his early thirties, Josh was the kind of guy who looked like he would rather be walking around in jeans and a jersey than suit and tie. When we introduced ourselves and sat down, he told us that his girlfriend, Melody — who had her own apartment on Marlborough Street but often spent the night at his place — had recently started receiving upsetting phone calls. Josh had been getting them, too, at home, though he had already arranged for the number to be changed and un-listed. Melody had also started receiving some ugly mail. He showed us a selection of cards with things like, "Fucking bitch, stay away from him," and "You'll get yours" scrawled on them. My dad wondered aloud if we might have the cards dusted for fingerprints, but decided against it: too many people had handled them by then. After studying the cards for another minute or so, he launched into his hundred questions: Could Josh think of anyone who might be doing this? Old girlfriends? Former boyfriends of Melody? Business competitors? Personal enemies? Troubled family members? I sat there, writing down the answers on white 8 x 11 lined paper. When the interview was finished, we went back to the office and set up a file on the case. Phil, as I was learning to call him, put in a call to his friend Bill Monahan, asking him if Josh's new unlisted number might have been leaked by a phone company employee. Bill said he would look into it.

Soon the stalking escalated. After spending the night at Josh's place, Melody went back to Marlborough Street and found that her apartment had been burglarized. Clothes and papers were lying everywhere, and her stuffed animals — childhood mementos — had been hung by the neck from the ceiling.

We drove over there — three minutes from the office — to check things out. Her end of Marlborough Street was a pleasant, old-fashioned Boston neighborhood, and she lived on the third floor of a nice townhouse. My father followed me up the stairs, huffing and puffing and cursing the lack of elevator, immune to the building's quaint charms. He had brought his camera along and took pictures of the front entrance, the stairwell, the door to her apartment. Inside, we sat with Melody at the table in her walk-in kitchen. Before he had taken me out on the case, my dad and I sat down and he gave me a little talking-to about his interviewing procedure, one of the few times I learned things from him in conversation, rather than by observing. During interviews, he said, he wanted me to keep quiet and take notes; if I spoke up, I might break his train of thought, skew the direction he was trying to lead the interviewee. I was also never to change my facial expression because of some answer the person gave. At the end, if he had forgotten something, I could mention that to him; otherwise, my job was just to take notes.

Which I did.

Melody was an attractive young professional woman in her twenties, only a few years older than I was at the time. I felt sorry for her. Even to me, the sight of those stuffed animals hanging by their throats all over the apartment was unnerving; I could not imagine what it must have been like for her to come home to that bizarre scene. I remember a giraffe, a bear that looked like it had gotten a great deal of affection in her childhood, and a small furry menagerie of other creatures hung by white string from the smoked-glass light fixtures.

Phil suggested she speak to the landlord and have him change the locks, and then, as he had done with her boyfriend, he asked a long list of questions — possible enemies, work relationships, daily schedule, habits, that kind of thing — all done more in the tone of a friendly conversation than a formal interview. He addressed her as "honey", which is something he did with every woman he ever spoke to, at the donut shop, in the hospital, or on the job. It may be a measure of his rough charm that none of these women ever seemed to take offense. Despite his stocky build, rough face, and straightforward manner, my dad could be easy-going and amicable when he wanted to be, and, depending on the situation, would alter the tone of his voice, his facial expression, the way he stood or sat. Sometimes he would even sit sideways to the person he was interviewing, taking up the posture of a parish priest hearing confession. He sensed, as I did, that Melody looked up to him as an older man, a representative of the law enforcement world, someone who was there to help her, and he spoke to her the way a father might speak to his adult daughter, quickly putting her at ease. She answered all the questions carefully and thoroughly. Afterwards, Phil got down on his knees and examined the door jamb, looking for signs of forced entry, checking to see if there was any way someone could have had access to the apartment through the windows; and then, we knocked on doors and spoke with several other people in the building, asking if they had seen anyone who looked suspicious.

About a week later, Josh called a third time, saying things had suddenly turned even more serious: Melody had been abducted. Two men hiding outside her apartment door had grabbed her, put a chloroformed handkerchief to her face and knocked her unconscious. She woke up, hands and feet tied, in the breakdown lane of the Massachusetts Turnpike Extension. Unharmed but traumatized. At this point the Boston police became involved; Phil and I met them at the location on the Turnpike extension where she had been found. They were cops from Division 16, my father's former territory, and though I had expected there to be some resentment or competitiveness, I sensed how pleased they were to have my dad on the case, what a natural rapport he had with them. I watched the way he talked and joked and at the same time managed to find out all the information he needed and pass on to them what he knew. I had the feeling that they were happy to let him take the lead in the case, and was a bit surprised at that.

After the abduction, and after giving Melody some time to calm down, we made a second trip to Marlborough Street. This time my dad had his Dictaphone cassette recorder, which fit into a black leather carrying case with a side-pocket for the microphone. Since there was no note-taking to be done, my job was to make sure — on penalty of state prison time if I failed — that the Dictaphone did not run out of tape or batteries. After asking the young woman's permission — without which it is illegal to do a voice recording in Massachusetts — Phil set the microphone on its little stand and said he was going to ask her a series of simple questions. He wanted just a yes or no answer. She acted a bit perplexed about this at first, but, again in his soothing way, my father told her it was going to help in the investigation, and, once someone was arrested in the case, it would keep her from having to repeat the story again and again to the police and in court. He started out with the basics: Was her name Melody? Yes. Did she live at 2 _ _ Marlborough Street? Yes. Was she employed at Boston Aesthetics? Yes. Was she a native of the city? No. And so on. Only toward the end of the interview did he ask if she had any idea who might be stalking her and what they were after.

When we were finished we said our good-byes and went downstairs to the car. My dad always had me drive — his way of helping me learn the city. I pulled out of the parking space and, following his directions, headed toward Route 128 and the western suburbs.

"Where we going?" I asked after a while.

"Dedham. Ernie Reid's house."

"Who's Ernie Reid?"

"Voice analysis guy. Her story don't add up."

"What do you mean, doesn't add up? I feel bad for her. The animals get hung, she gets kidnapped. She looked like she was scared out of her mind."

My father glanced across the seat at me, then returned his eyes to the road. "First off," he said, patiently, "there's no main suspect, neither on her side or his. Could there be some secret admirer kind of thing going on? Sure, yeah. But I don't think so. Second, Bill Monahan says no way somebody at the phone company leaked the new number. He knows the number, the boyfriend knows it, she knows it, that's it. Third, the break-in was phony. Nobody could climb in through the windows unless they climbed three floors straight up the side of the building. And there was zero sign of forced entry anywhere, her door or downstairs. Fourth, and the main thing, the kidnap idea don't make sense. Think about it. What, these two guys are hiding in the alcove outside her door? They chloroform her, and then what? Carry her down three flights of stairs, past all those neighbors' doorways, then across the sidewalk to a car? And nobody sees this? Then all they do is tie her up and dump her on the road, nothing else? Now, there could be something unusual going on here, I'm not saying there isn't. You have to keep your mind open. But if we apply the KISS theory — Keep it Simple, Stupid — she's lying so she gets to move in with the boyfriend."

"So what are we doing now?" I said, still a little skeptical.

"Ernie says she's lying, she's lying."

Ernie Reid was a name my dad had often mentioned, but someone I had never met. He was a wunderkind private investigator in his early 30s, someone who specialized in what we call "pretexting", that is, pretending to be someone he is not for the purposes of getting information. Over the ensuing years, my brother Richard and I would come to know Ernie and his work well, and come to think of him as "Ernie the King of Pretexting", because he could call you on the phone and, in a voice you had never heard before, say, "Son, this is Father Donohue from Saint Mary's. I need to speak with you for a moment about your last confession," and, you would three-quarters believe him. He received particular pleasure out of pretexting people he knew. My brother and me, for example.

Ernie was a P. I. doing business under the name Secret Service Associates (for years he fought the U.S. Secret Service for the right to use that name, and finally won his case), and among other projects, he ran a business called Audio Analysis Laboratories out of the basement of his home in Dedham, a quiet suburb just southwest of the city. We went around back and pounded on the bulkhead door and he let us into his studio. Though he did other kinds of investigative work, Ernie's second specialty, after pretexting, was voice analysis, and he had a piece of equipment called a Psychological Stress Evaluator, or PSE. He also had a full-sized walk-in bank safe, shelves holding five-gallon jugs filled with coins he collected — one jug for pennies, one for nickels, one for dimes, etc. — a wall covered with another of his collections, police patches; and a small armory of guns. Pistols, rifles, machine guns. He was plump, deep-voiced, married, and childless, and he loved what he did.

While he and my father sat by the PSE and ran the tape, I checked out the guns, holding a machine gun in my hands for the first time, working the mechanism on his 30.06, hefting the shotgun shells.

When they were finished running the tape through the PSE, Ernie leaned back in his desk chair and said, "There's stress in her voice when you ask her about the break in, and when you ask her about the kidnapping."

"Lying, in other words."

"Looks that way."

That was all my father needed, the last ounce of evidence to tip his own private set of scales. Before heading back into the city, we called Josh and asked him to meet us at the office. My father sat him down and laid everything out for him, not drawing a conclusion so much as pointing to it in such a way that nothing else seemed possible. The lack of a suspect, the implausibility of the kidnapping story, the reliable information from his friend inside the phone company, Ernie's analysis of Melody's voice. Josh was not happy. "Makes sense," he said bitterly. "I've been thinking of breaking it off, she probably feels that, and this is her way of having a reason to move in. Now what? She's got problems, now what do I do?"

Dump her, I expected my father to say. She's been lying to you all along, cut her loose. But, "Why don't you call up her parents," he suggested sympathetically. "Have a talk. See what you come up with. It's your relationship, but that's what I'd do."

Josh left, furious at having been played like a fish. I do not know what became of his relationship with Melody, but I know how pleased he was that my father had found the source of the phone calls and other troubles. I know because, in addition to paying us promptly (a surprisingly rare occurrence in the P.I. business), Josh sent my father and mother on one of his trips to Paris, all expenses paid. They were there a week or ten days. My mother came back smiling and wearing a new dress, and my father came back telling everyone it was the worst vacation he had ever taken in his life. He did not like the French (and they, apparently, had not liked him.) He did not like the food, did not like the small hotel rooms, which were nothing like the rooms in Vegas, did not appreciate the fact that there were no heated pools or big, fluffy towels. "I'm never going back there again," he said, and he never did.

My father and I did not spend any time rehashing the false-stalker case, never sat around the office with him telling me what to look for in an interviewee, how to talk, what questions to ask. That was not his style, any more than it was his style to apologize and explain the reasons for an angry outburst. Then and in a string of future cases, I learned how to talk to someone by watching Phil do it, keeping my mouth shut . . . and

making absolutely sure there were extra batteries for the Dictaphone.


In a strange postcript to this story, almost twenty years later my brother Richard received a call from a friend — again,
coincidentally, the owner of a small, successful business — saying he was having some personal problems, and could Rich and
I come up to the North Shore and talk to him? This guy's girlfriend was also being stalked; a van had pushed her car into
traffic at Fresh Pond Circle when she was leaving the supermarket parking lot there. Was there a suspect? Yes. A few years
earlier the woman had been sexually assaulted. She had testified
against her assailant in court and he had served time. Now, she
said, she thought he was out on parole and trying to make her
life miserable. Richard and I went to talk to her, asked her in
some detail about the earlier case, and returned to the office
with a few facts. One of those facts happened to be the name
of the prosecutor in the sexual assault case, a man named Vin-
cent Smith. Vinnie was an old friend from the neighborhood,
and now a good client of ours. I called and asked if he remembered anything from the case, specifically if there might be
some information he could give us about the man he had sent
to jail. "John," he said, "the guy was bad news. He's still inside.
We locked him up and threw away the key."

So, I made a tape with the girlfriend, just as my dad had
done decades before — simple, yes-or-no questions. I took it
to Ernie, still in the business. Ernie ran it through a more modern version of his PSE and came to the same conclusion —
more stress in her voice that an honest speaker would exhibit
— and then Richard had the unsavory duty of passing the bad
news on to his friend.

# ELEVEN
Bowdoin Street Circus Part II

*"There is no wealth but life."*
-John Ruskin

Adding to the occasionally eccentric nature of the Bowdoin Street storefront was our landlady there, an Italian woman who went by the not-very-Italian name of Mary Connolly. Maria, as we — and her husband — always called her, had a bit of a checkered past. According to what I heard from Phil, she had once been a stripper in the burlesque bars a few blocks away. She had saved her money and, after retiring, had invested in real estate. By the time I met her, some thirty years after the conclusion of her exotic dancing career, Maria owned a couple of villas in her native Italy, and several properties on Beacon Hill. These included #45 Bowdoin Street, which was officially registered as a Boston rooming house. She and her husband Jimmy — another piece of our entertaining little world — lived on the second floor; they rented the first floor to us, and ten single rooms on the third, fourth, and fifth floors, usually by the week, to an assortment of tenants that would have been perfectly at home in the cast of a Fellini movie.

There was Mr. MacMillan, tall, gaunt, sixtyish, who wore

the same blue suit and skinny silver tie every day. I would see him reading the *Financial Times* at the Kirstein Business Library when I went down there to check their shelves and shelves of phone books. Sometimes we would meet at the mailboxes, where he would be collecting stacks of envelopes Jimmy said were dividend checks from the dozens of companies in which he owned stock. A millionaire many times over, Jimmy insisted, but Mr. MacMillan lived in one of the depressing 8 x 10 upstairs rooms, no refrigerator, no TV, no phone, shared bathroom down the hall. According to Jimmy, Mr. MacMillan's children would call periodically, and Jimmy would bring the message upstairs, but Mr. MacMillan wanted nothing to do with them.

There was Jerry, who, at age sixty, slept on a mattress that was propped up on a wooden box in the dirt-floored basement. Bespectacled and mildly retarded, Jerry would empty the trash for us and the other tenants, and run the occasional errand. I would like to think Maria gave him his meager lodging in exchange for those services but I suspect she charged him rent. If we handed Jerry ten dollars as a tip for washing the front windows, his face would break into such a broad smile you would think he was holding a winning lottery ticket and about to cash it in.

And Charlie, who was badly stooped and legally blind, a third-floor tenant our kindhearted secretary Mary looked after. She opened his mail and helped him with bills, and told me, "He says he goes to bed every night expecting to die." He did die while we were in that building.

And Mr. King, who dressed like a beggar, spoke with a strong Yiddish accent, and had numbers tattooed on his forearm.

Maria ran herd over all of them, though she was afraid of a man I'll call Gene, a lanky southerner who lived on the third floor and could turn loud and violent when drunk. In one un-guarded moment, Maria's accountant, a small man from the south shore named Elliot, told me, "You and five of your friends couldn't spend Maria's money in ten years."

(Elliot did our books, too, and he loved cigars; the papers and tax forms would come back smelling so strongly of cigar smoke that we would leave them out in the trunk of the car for a week before bringing them back into the office.)

But you would never have suspected that Maria was afflu-ent from the way she dressed and acted. For one thing, the building was not exactly maintained according to the sanitary standards of the city health code — roaches and rodents were some of the other residents. For another, if she came to the office to replace a light bulb, Maria would make sure to let us know we owed her 38 cents. (Yet, she was careful in the other direction, too: One time she stood waiting for ten minutes while I spoke to a client on the phone so she could pay me twelve cents for a stamp she had borrowed.) When vandals broke one of the two-foot-square windows that faced the street, Maria tried to charge us for replacing it. Though she eas-ily could have afforded to pay someone to do it, she changed the sheets on the beds upstairs and vacuumed the tattered car-pets herself, and when her relatives visited from Italy, instead of putting them up in a hotel, she would squeeze them into a vacant room on the third floor and let them share the toilet with the rest of the gang.

Some years later, because we were tired of living with the moldy shag carpet and ugly paneling, we had some friends, the Connelly brothers, come in and renovate our office. We paid for it ourselves. When it was done, Maria thought the place looked nice and tried to raise the rent.

We never had a lease, so suggesting a rent increase was more or less a monthly routine with her. One time, when inflation had hit the Boston rental market, I was working in the office while my dad was off on a case, and she slipped quietly through the front door.

"Is your father here, Johnny?" she started out, as if he might have been hiding in the corners of the room, or researching a case under the floorboards.

"No, but he'll be back soon."

"That's okay, I want to talk to you alone anyway, about something. And he's always yelling at me."

"You know he loves you, Maria."

"Well, we're going to have to raise the rent, Jimmy and me, from 500 to 550 dollars a month." She said this in a tone of voice meant to convey the idea that, if they could not take in this extra fifty, she and Jimmy were going to join the band of street people who were served a free lunch down the block at Saint John's the Evangelist.

"That'll probably be okay, Maria," I took the liberty of saying, "No problem. But he'll want some written guarantee that you're going to keep it at $550 for a couple years."

She went away with an expression on her face I could not read. I thought it was because I had asked for a written agreement. But when Jimmy came down — chain-smoking his Lucky Strikes and spitting grains of tobacco on the floor as he always did — and I mentioned the conversation to him, he shook his head. "You don't understand, Johnny. If you don't argue with her, she thinks she's getting cheated. Next time, tell her $550 is crazy. $525 you could do, maybe, but $550 is nuts."

Actually, every other word Jimmy uttered had four letters and began with an "f", so the above scrap of conversation was more colorful than I have depicted it. After an exchange like that, he would sit in the chair in my father's office, spitting tobacco and complaining about Gene, the drinker, who, he said, was going to go too far some night, with his noisemaking. "I had to go up there twice last night. Next fuckin' time, I told him, I'm comin' up here with a fuckin' baseball bat and I'm gonna make your fuckin' brain into fuckin' jelly."

More than once, my father and I tried to advise Jimmy about the legal consequences of turning a tenant's brain into jelly, but he did not seem to be listening. His passion was doing repairs, and they were always done poorly. For some reason I will never be able to understand, my father's term for sloppy work — carpentry, masonry, any kind of bad police work — was "a shoemaker's job." By that definition, Jimmy was the consummate shoemaker. Still, he seemed to take great enjoyment out of going down into Jerry's room, where his tools were kept, and bringing up an assortment of instruments he was going to use to mangle some new project or another. We would complain about the noise of water constantly running in the toilet, and Jimmy would fix it — more or less — by borrowing a part from one of the toilets upstairs. We would mention the smell from a dead mouse behind the paneling, and Jimmy would say, "Ah, don't worry guys. Fuckin' thing will degenerate soon." Anything to save a few dollars. Every day, it seemed, we would see him walking around with his hammer, or heading out to go to the hardware store on Cambridge Street. Maria had all the money in the family, so perhaps this was Jimmy's way of trying to carry his weight in the relationship.

But, I will always remember the crooked, inch-thick, thumbprint-covered beads of caulk with which he sealed one of the front windows.

As I will always remember the expression of disdain on my dad's face when he spat his opinion out the side of his mouth: "Shoemaker's job."


Not unlike Eddie Immanelli, the hot dog king, Maria and

Jimmy belonged to a sector of society I think of as the "rough rich," people who have as much money as members of the upper classes, but — by choice or otherwise — live a life lacking in luxuries they can easily afford. Mr. MacMillan would fit into that category, too, inhabiting, as he did, a roach-infested rooming house when he could have paid cash for a small estate. In some people, for better and worse, money leads to a refinement of tastes: they join a private country club, buy a home in a safe, walled-off neighborhood, drive a nice car, get their suits at Brooks Brothers or hand-made on Savile Row, send their kids to private schools. But in others — and I have friends and clients in both categories — money might provide a sense of comfort, but it does nothing much to change the way they talk or dress, the place they choose to live or the people they choose to spend time with.

Though you would occasionally see her in a fur coat, and Jimmy in suit and tie, Maria made her home in the latter group. Phil told me that, when she went back to Italy to see relatives, she would carry as much as $10,000 in cash in her girdle. Maybe because of her long-gone dancing days, she put a great deal of effort into her physical appearance, and, even all those years ago, in an era when it was uncommon, she would periodically have work done — nose, cheeks, eyes — fighting off the onslaught of age the way she once might have fought off the unwanted advances of bar patrons. We would see her with bandages on and never say anything.

Amusing as it could sometimes be, Maria's legendary frugality had certain less than pleasant side effects. At one point a tenant passed away on the premises — no foul play involved: it was not Gene; Jimmy had not been up there swinging a baseball bat. The body went undiscovered for several days, until the other tenants complained about the smell. Finally, Maria and Jimmy unlocked the door, saw that their tenant had expired, and they called the police and an ambulance. After he had removed the body, one of the EMT's told me the floor was so covered with cockroaches it seemed to be moving. Maria had seen the same thing, of course, but instead of calling an exterminator, she came back later that day with a can of Raid and sprayed it around. As they are in the habit of doing, the cockroaches sought shelter wherever they could. Later, our secretary at the time, whose name was Virginia, called me up and screamed, "Johnny, Johnny! They're coming through the phone, oh my God, Johnny!"

We ended up hiring a client of ours to do a real exterminating job, and sending Maria the bill.

# TWELVE
A Jewel of a Relationship

*"O accurst craving for gold!"*
-Virgil

I t is not uncommon for a business, especially in the early stages, to be blessed with a client that helps it move from one level to the next. In our case, this client was Gems and Luxury Jewelers. Gems and Luxury started out as a relatively small-scale operation, conceived by an elderly Russian émigré couple and run the out of an office in their attic, in the town of Wakefield, half an hour north of downtown. In 1975 the owners had a problem: one of their salesmen was robbed. Until then, the salesmen had been fairly cavalier about things, usually carrying their line of gems in rolling suitcases and storing them in the trunks of their cars. This was an era before Zirconium replicas, so the jewels were real; a suitcase's contents could sometimes be valued at $200,000, and the thieves were aware of that. They would follow the salesmen and wait for their chance. In this particular case, the salesman stopped in to fill up with gas, left his keys in the ignition, and when he paid and came out to the pump, his car, and the jewels, were gone. Gems and Luxury notified the FBI, but after looking into it for a while, the FBI told him they could put in only so much time on the theft. Someone there recommended they talk to my dad.

Warren Derzen, himself a talented salesman and executive, purchased the company from the Russian couple, and had grand plans for expanding it — plans that would soon bear fruit. As a first step he purchased a much larger building in Greater Boston, and hired us to oversee the transferring of all their inventory to the new site. At this point, I had been working full-time for just a couple of months and the only important case I had worked on was the case of Melody, the self-stalker, so it was a thrill to show up at Gems and Luxury on moving day, armed to the teeth.

We were all there — Phil, me, my friend Mark Rose and my father's friend Bill Monahan. In short, the three guys he trusted most in the world. We were packing pistols, shotguns, and 30.06s and we stood around the loading dock like the father and brothers in *Bonanza*, waiting for the bad guys to come riding over the ridge. It was not a game or a TV show, however. That part of Greater Boston was famous for its underworld activity — every few weeks, it seemed, another body would turn up in a trunk — and we were talking about moving several million dollars worth of diamonds, gems, silver and gold about fifteen miles across congested territory, through dozens of stoplights and intersections, all perfect locations for a hijacking. My father had worked on enough big robbery cases in his detective days to know that, where a payload of that size was involved, anyone aware of the date of the move, anyone with refined tastes or a gambling debt, might be tempted to sell the information to people who made a profession out of grand theft. So we kept the schedule as quiet as we could, planned an unusual route from point A to point B, and armed ourselves for battle.

Of all of us, I think my dad was the only one who had ever

fired a gun on the streets (and most of the time he was shooting up into the air to get a fleeing suspect to stop), so I now shudder to think what might have ensued if someone had actually tried to make off with the merchandise.

To complicate matters, it was a raw, rainy, early fall day. We arrived at Gems and Luxury at 6:00 a.m. Warren Derzen had arranged for riggers to come and move the half dozen heavy safes onto a flatbed truck. These were not small wall-safes — one of them was a ten-foot cube, big enough to fill half a room — so the movers used wooden rollers that looked like six-foot sections of telephone poles. We stood under umbrellas and overhangs, weapons at the ready, perusing the city streets for any suspicious-looking characters, and watching the burly riggers ease the safes off the loading dock, roll them onto the back of the flatbed, and secure them there with straps and clips. They were capable and experienced guys, but it was clear that the rain and slippery surfaces were making their job more difficult.

In a small caravan — one car ahead of the flatbed, two cars behind — we made a crooked, fifteen-minute trip through the back streets of Malden, Chelsea, and Everett. We ended up at the new Gems and Luxury headquarters, a squat, sprawling, former supermarket building on the busy parkway. It was a good location for an expanding business: a two-minute walk to a couple of donut and sandwich shops; a ten-minute drive to Logan Airport. Between the triple-deckers and large, wood-frame houses on the other side of the Parkway you could see the office buildings in downtown Boston; if traffic was light, you would be able to get a delivery truck there and back in under half an hour.

Pa and the other *Bonanza* boys took up positions in the chain-link-and-barbed-wire-enclosed parking lot. The rain came down in earnest. The riggers muscled the first of the smaller safes onto the loading dock without trouble, but as they were in the process of sliding the large one along the flatbed, one of the rollers slipped on the wet surface and turned sideways. The safe tilted. I saw it and yelled. Other people were yelling, "It's going! It's going!" There were two riggers on the truck, one on the loading dock, and a fourth standing on the ground guiding the safe from below. But once two tons start to slip, it takes more than six or eight strong arms to halt the momentum. We were all screaming by the time the safe tipped sideways and went over the edge of the truck. Everything seemed to happen in a strange kind of speedy slow-motion, dreamlike on the one hand, but so quick I could not move on the other. The man standing on the ground just managed to dive into a protected spot against the wheels of the truck as the safe crashed down. It hit on one corner, then flopped down flat with a loud *Boom!*, leaving a triangular crater in the asphalt exactly where the rigger had been standing. After a couple of beats, as if he expected another safe to come crashing down on top of its brother, or as if he had been frozen in place by the narrow escape and needed a minute to thaw out, the lucky man emerged. He must have dived right into a puddle because he was soaked from the waist down. Refusing to so much as glance at the safe, he walked to the cab of the truck, took out a bottle of Seagram's, and, without coming up for air, gulped down what looked to be at least half a pint.

The riggers had to arrange for a crane to be brought in; there was no other way to get the safe up onto the loading dock. This meant hours of standing around in the cold rain, trying to keep our guns dry and passers-by from wondering what was going on around the unmarked building. (Later, when people asked, I would tell them it was a lingerie factory.) By 10 p.m., we finally had the place locked up tight, all the alarms working, and we were able to go home.

That first day had not gone exactly as planned, but it was the beginning of a relationship between Gems and Luxury Jewelers and DiNatale Detective Agency that lasted twenty-two years, resulted in as much as $250,000 a year in billing for us, and, despite the complexity and pressure of the work, went about as smoothly as any business relationship could possibly go.

My father understood right away that the larger Gems and Luxury, a place that would have between $40 and $60 million in inventory on the premises most days, was going to require not only alarms, but security guards to protect from outside thieves and employee pilfering. If we let another company handle the security guards while we focused on investigations and inside theft, we would lose out on the guard contract, and run the risk that the other company would take over the rest of the work, too. So when Warren asked us if we wanted to handle all the security for the new operation, all the guards, all the cameras and metal detectors, all the investigations, we were happy to agree. More than any other single event, that contract turned our fledgling Beacon Hill storefront operation into one of the largest P.I. firms in New England.

We started off by staffing the company with security guards, armed, but in shirt and tie, not uniforms. It was because we wanted them to blend in and look professional, not draw attention to themselves every time they went out for a sandwich at lunch. We made sure the fence and barbed-wire were in good repair and had two dozen cameras installed in smoked-glass domes in the ceiling, with the lenses hidden so workers would not know when they were being watched. A check-in system was developed, an audio system to scan visitors. We also installed an electronic gate and made sure every visitor to the building was escorted from front door to office and then back again. Amelia Scondrizzo, chief of operations, arrived at the gate at 5:30 every morning. One of our guards would meet her there, and, while she waited in her car, he would go in and check the building and make sure no one had been hiding inside since the day before, or had somehow managed to gain entry while the place was closed. Amelia had a duress code she could punch into the keypad if, say, an intruder was holding her at gunpoint, and this code would alert the alarm monitoring company. Once all was clear, she would head for her office, and the three other security guards would go to their stations.

It might sound simple, but it was not. Pay is notoriously poor for security guards, and even if that relatively low-income area had offered a workforce brimming with educated, skilled, motivated people, we would not have been able to attract them. On more than a few occasions, a guard would get his or her paycheck and decide to celebrate for the next two days, as if not only the pay period but the entire era of work for money had ended forever. This meant that someone — too often I was the someone — had to go over to Everett and fill in. It was not my favorite work. I was twenty-four, eager to learn the business, and standing around a jewelry company for eight hours was not exactly the stuff of my dreams.

Still, there were times when I had to make a trip to Logan Airport as an armed guard for a multi-million-dollar shipment of gems coming in from Asia, or going out to markets around the world. We were always heavily armed, always tried to vary the route, and come or go on an unpredictable schedule. And, though I never did more than stand guard for eight hours, ride shotgun on the airport runs, and bring checks to the bank and deposit them, it certainly was not difficult to understand the effect that Gems and Luxury was having on our family finances.

And then there was Dorothy.

For a full-service company like Gems and Luxury, where the jewels were brought in by buyers from overseas, cut — mostly by Armenian-born experts — set, polished, and shipped, all from the one location, there was obviously at least as much concern about inside theft as about gangland characters crashing down the fence and storming the loading dock with AK 47s. More concern, in fact. From its earliest days, even before the onset of our relationship with them, the company had been dealing with employee theft. But as the business expanded, that problem grew worse, and we were asked to place someone undercover full-time.

These were the days before computerized inventory, so an employee could make off with a set of ruby earrings or a diamond wedding band and it could be weeks before the missing piece would show up on any report. There was a place we referred to as the Gold Room, where the finished product was stored, and where four-foot-wide drawers lined the walls from floor to ceiling. All through the work day employees were going into and out of this room, filling orders. A thieves' paradise. And a place where we needed to keep a constant stream of undercover agents.

Dorothy had come to Boston from New Jersey to attend Boston University, and she had stayed around after earning a degree in sociology, with a minor in criminal justice. She would become friends with the daughter of my father's cousin, Babs DiNatale, a Wheaton grad and a Quincy police officer. Phil called Babs and told her he was looking for someone to work for him. Babs knew Dorothy was interested in the law enforcement field. The result of this chain of blood-relationship and friendship was Dorothy being hired, in the fall of 1976, to go undercover at Gems and Luxury.

There is a whole complicated procedure to putting someone into an undercover position, and we are justifiably proud, I think, to be able to say that, in thirty-four years of doing that, in a wide variety of circumstances, we have never had one of our agents discovered. Part of the reason for that is we never rush things. Clients like to think we can place someone undercover and have the information they need in a couple of weeks, but we insist on a three-month minimum. The process of getting co-workers to trust you is a gradual one; a new employee who asks a lot of personal or leading questions is bound to make thieves suspicious. Starting with Phil, and continuing with Richard and me, our policy has always been that no undercover agent we hire should ever have to confront a thief or cheater face to face in the workplace or in court. On television, it does not work that way. You see the *U.C.* agent making a dramatic entrance into the interrogation room and confronting his or her co-worker with a pointed finger while the cops close in with handcuffs. We never wanted to put our people through something like that, we knew it would ruin our U.C. work there forever, and we felt that, if we could not prove guilt independently, albeit with help from the undercover agent's reports, then we were not worth hiring. During the initial interview, we would not say it was undercover work we were hiring for. But if the candidate seemed right — smart, brave, good with people, able to improvise, willing to make a suitable time commitment — we would talk about an undercover position, and we would assure the candidate they would never have to make a difficult accusation face to face.

Once the person was hired by our agency, we needed to get them hired by the company where they would be working undercover. We would contact friends — sometimes in related businesses, sometimes not — and have them help us make up a resume for our agent. Usually we would have rehearsals in which the person going undercover would have to memorize a made-up work history and details of tasks performed at another company. This was not merely a workshop in deceit, our way of putting one over on people and encouraging friends to lie. It was based on my father's often-stated belief that no one can keep a secret, and it was the best method of inserting someone into a company while keeping his or her real status known to the fewest number of people. Even the personnel department would not know. In the case of Gems and Luxury, the information would be given to Warren Derzen and Amelia Scondrizzo, the agent herself, Richard (in later years), my father, and me. The fact that we were always easily able to place people via the regular application process speaks partly to the care we took in preparing a candidate and a resume, and partly to the lack of care many personnel officers take in conducting background checks.

Dorothy applied for an opening at Gems and Luxury and was hired. She would do her regular job there, sorting merchandise in the shipping room, or packaging it for delivery from the Gold Room, and be paid their regular wage. On top of that, she would be paid our regular wage, including hourly compensation for any time spent socializing with her co-workers. And on top of that, we would add a fee for our services for every hour she worked. My father considered her "a billing machine," and liked her from the start.

It is lucrative — for the agent and for us — but stressful work. Over the years, more than one of our employees has had difficulty with it. You are, after all, assuming a false identity for a large part of the week, playing a role, and often these jobs go on for quite a long time (six months to two years is a common tenure). On top of that, our employees would occasionally feel guilty about befriending someone they would later have to turn in for stealing. Honestly, though, that part has never bothered me. It is the same way I have always felt about being hired to catch cheating spouses or people on phony disability. We never hurt anyone who did not deserve to be hurt, never accused anyone of anything until or unless we had solid evidence. We never lured anyone into cheating or stealing, only did what we could to protect the victims of those acts. In many cases, the reports filed by our undercover agents served purposes other than simply catching an employee doing something wrong: often, the employer or business owner received valuable information about the efficiency of a certain type of process, and was made aware of smart suggestions or festering complaints that might never have reached the front office. It was also common for the U.C. agent's report to contain information on employees who were doing particularly good work.

Dorothy's job included handing in a written report every Monday. Because my father was having heart troubles at this point, I would spend part of Tuesday morning reading the report, then take it over to Amelia's office, deliver it personally (the fewer people who saw it, the better), sit down and have a talk with her. After studying the report, which was two or three pages, Amelia would usually have a few questions, some things she wanted Dorothy to look at in particular during the coming week, and I would then go back to the office and call Dorothy up and let her know. As time went on, we started to have these conversations in person, over a beer at Charlie's Eating and Drinking Saloon at the Chestnut Hill Mall, or at a bar in Dedham not far from where she was living. One beer turned into two beers. Two beers turned into dinner. Two beers and dinner turned into a friendly walk. The evolution of our personal relationship was a steady, but gradual one. As she likes to put it now, "it took me a while to become aware of John's charm."

These dates involved another kind of undercover work, because the last thing we wanted was to be out at a bar together and have one of her co-workers at Gems and Luxury see us and make the connection. This was made a bit easier by the fact that there exists an invisible dividing line that runs east-west through the middle of Boston. It is one of the quirks of the city that people from the North Shore, even if they work in downtown, tend to do their socializing north of that line, and people from the South Shore stay south. There are exceptions, of course, and now that the Big Dig has complicated all the traffic routes that used to make it so hard to cross from south to north and vice-versa (now it is just hard to go anywhere), maybe it will change. But since Dorothy and I lived just south of that line, and Gems and Luxury was five miles north of it, we felt we were relatively safe. We spent a lot of our together time indoors, in any case.

Once, though, after we had become something of an official couple among friends and family, we were invited to the wedding of one of my many cousins. As we were driving up to the reception — held on the North Shore — Dorothy spotted, among the other guests, a co-worker from Gems and Luxury. She turned her face away and I swung the car out of the parking lot. All dressed up and ready to party, we had to make a change of plans. I called my father and explained, and, later, called my cousin and apologized. Dorothy and I went south and had dinner instead. After twenty-four months at Gems and Luxury, she retired from undercover work, and became part of the cast of characters at 45 Bowdoin.

Two years later we were married.

Thirty-four years and three children later we still are.

# THIRTEEN
The Speed Typist

*"High thoughts must have high language."*
- Aristophanes

It was Maria's husband, Jimmy, who introduced us to Mary — they were both members of the Sons of Italy. Once my father realized he needed someone to handle the increasing load of paperwork, we had a succession of part-time secretaries and typists, but for one reason or another, they had not worked out. The ones from the temp agency took a long time to train. Others started out in a burst of enthusiasm but quit after two or three days. One of them, I'll call her Gina, used to aggravate my brother Richard by constantly correcting his pronunciation and grammar, and he was happy to be able to let her go when he found out she was discussing our cases during her bus commute into the city.

Business was going well, Jean had four sons by then and was retired from her unpaid typing position, I was busy with surveillances and interviews, and we found we really needed a permanent person to answer the phone, type up letters and reports, and deal with the potential clients who walked through the front door. Jimmy suggested a friend of his named Mary, and Mary came to see me about the job. She was a tough-looking young woman, solidly built, with shoulder-length dark hair, and a rough way of talking that was common to the near northern suburbs. Later, when she came to work in a low-slung, sleeveless T-shirt, we discovered that she had a huge tattoo of a bird of prey on her left shoulder blade. Talons spread, ready for the kill.

"So how fast do you type?" I asked her, during what passed for her job interview.

"Fast," she said. "Supah fast. As fast as you can talk."

"How many words a minute?"

"I'm fast as a fiyah engine."

"All right, what do you think you need for a salary?"

"Three-fifty or fouah bills a week."

"That's high. I'll have to give you a typing test if we're going to pay you that much."

"I'm not takin any fuckin' typing test," she said.

"All right, then we'll start you at 350 and see. If you type as fast as you say, you do, I'll give you the extra fifty fuckin' bucks next month."

She typed like lightning, our Mary, and was as kindhearted with the tenants and the needier street people as she was no-nonsense with the ones who stopped in to give us a hard time. As a bonus, we sometimes sent her to Martha's Vineyard, where we had a client who owned several bars. Mary's assignment was to pay a couple of daily visits to each of these bars, sit and drink, and watch to make sure the bartender wasn't cheating his boss. She enjoyed it.

Mary also had a couple of interesting friends. One of them, Lorraine, worked the door at a Combat Zone bar called the Naked i (not the kind of place even the owners wanted to capitalize), and was so lonely, or so devoted to Mary that, after she woke up from her morning rest, she would call her ten or fifteen times a day. We still had only the one line then, and every time the phone rang, we would be hoping for a new client, only to hear Mary say, "Oh, hi Lorraine." We mentioned it to Mary, who either could not convince Lorraine not to call so often, or never tried. This was another situation that drove my brother crazy, so he told Lorraine, "Listen, Lorraine, from now on you get two calls a day to Mary, one in the morning and one in late afternoon. We're trying to run a business here."

"Well then fuck you guys," she said.

Mary's boyfriend, Richie, was not much more cultured. On one occasion she came to the office with a black eye. "What happened to you?" We asked her.

"Richie hit me."

"How? When?"

"We were down at the Red Hat havin' a few drinks. He said somethin' I didn't like and I fuckin' smacked him."

"And that's when he hit you back?"

"Yeah," she said. "Aftah he got up."

Some years later, Richie died of a drug overdose. Mary stayed with us for almost a decade, taught school for a while, and then became one of the first female police officers in Winthrop, Massachusetts (I gave her my father's Boston Police Department handcuffs to mark the occasion). Years later, after a long hiatus in our relationship, Lorraine would end up giving us some help in a difficult case.

# FOURTEEN
Delivering Ian

*"It is certainly no part of religion to compel religion."*
- Tertullian

I sometimes think of human life as an enormous, complex painting filled with a variety of characters and colors, something you can look at for years without fully seeing. By this point in my more-or-less partnership with Phil, I was only in my mid-twenties, but already I had spent many hours in front of the canvas, studying the cheaters and the thieves, seeing the kinds of things people do for money, and the kinds of things that can happen to them because of greed or lust or pure bad luck. What I had not yet had a chance to study, though, was the part of the painting that had to do with religious feeling. Or, at least, that part had always been monochromatic for me. Like so many of our neighbors and friends, we were Roman Catholics, and we lived by the rules of that faith. Mass on Sunday, no meat on Friday, fasting during Lent, confession, communion, rosaries, novenas. Some of us took the rules and rituals very seriously, others less so, and, of course, we all had friends who were Protestant, Jewish, or claimed no faith at all.

While I had seen plenty of people who were devoted to

their faith, until Ian, I had never encountered anyone whose life had been taken over by it, turned upside down and inside out. I had never before paid attention to the part of the painting where religious feeling bulldozed family relations, career, education, and threatened to bury sanity itself. Meeting Ian was to be another of the life-lessons the family business would offer me in my formative years.

The Ian case — which is how I think of it — was another time when Mark Rose and I worked together. Our clients were the parents of a young man named Ian Masterville, who had moved to Boston for college and ended up being converted by one of the less-well-known religious cults. We would later have similar cases that had to do with the Moonies and Hare Krishnas; this was a smaller group. In addition to being the first time that religion brought people to our office, it was the first time I dealt with a professional psychologist, and I have to say that, if nothing else, the experience taught me there were at least two legitimate ways of coming to understand the puzzle that is human behavior: you can study it in the regulated environment of a classroom, clinic, or therapy session; and you can study it on the streets, by seeing how people behave in moments of duress.

Not surprisingly, my father — who had no college degree and no formal training in the workings of the human mind — possessed an eerily accurate radar when it came to the more eccentric aspects of biped behavior. Sometimes, in the midst of a case, he would take a minute to point out to me some rule of human interaction — why people resorted to stealing or lying, for example — underscoring it with his theory that, if you followed your instincts, you were usually going to ascertain the true motivation. The famous KISS theory was something he lived by, and, though it is not always the wisest path, it seemed to work for him.

In this instance, the object of our attention was a junior at Boston University, a young man who had abandoned his studies in favor of this out-of-the-mainstream spiritual path. It was not so much his motivations we needed to unearth, as his buried sanity. Seeing the trouble his son was in, the young man's father, a Justice Department lawyer, had hired Attorney Bill Homans — someone with whom we already did a lot of business — to secure temporary guardianship. Bill went into Probate Court and made the case that the young man — Ian, we are calling him — was not capable of taking care of himself. In order to support this contention, Ian's parents had to sign affidavits and testify in front of the judge. This gave them, and by extension us, the legal right to go to Ian's apartment and transport him to a private hospital in Jamaica Plain where, his parents hoped, he could be deprogrammed.

Ian was living in an apartment complex in Brookline — typical for Boston University and Boston College students in those days because the schools did not have sufficient dormitory space. I was renting in Roslindale then; my father called me at the apartment on Thursday night and said it was going to be a straightforward job: we would pick up the young man and drive him to the hospital, which was only about five miles away. It would take, my dad guessed, no more than an hour. After that, Mark and I would be free to head to Cape Cod for a long weekend. Some friends and I had rented a cottage there for the summer.

The next morning at 9:00 a.m., we rendezvoused outside Ian's apartment. Ian's father and mother were there, my dad, and a psychologist armed with the guardianship papers that had been obtained the day before from Norfolk County Probate Court. The psychologist gave us strict instructions that when we entered the apartment we were to do nothing without his okay. It was especially important to avoid making any move toward Ian that might upset him. He, the psychologist, was going to do all the talking; Ian would most likely leave with us voluntarily.

When Ian's father used his key in the lock, we stepped into a filthy kitchen. The psychologist looked into the half-sized refrigerator and found nothing but mold and a few soda cans. "This will help substantiate our guardianship," he told me, in a way that made me think he felt unsure about the whole operation, and guilty about having Ian temporarily lose power over his own life. From the looks of the apartment, though, I was confident Ian's parents had made the right move. There were clothes strewn around, dust and cobwebs everywhere, that dead sense some rooms get when no one has done anything in the way of cleaning them for months and months.

At first, we thought Ian was not there. He hadn't answered our knock, hadn't come to the door when we opened it. We searched the living room and the first bedroom, and saw only a stained mattress in one corner, no sheets. Then I heard Mark say, "Jack, what's this?" pointing to what seemed to be a pile of dirty laundry in the middle of the second bedroom. Phil walked over, lifted up a crumpled sheet, and there was Ian, lying on his side, either deep in meditation, or trying to convince us that he was. The psychologist instructed my father not to touch or disturb him. He was obviously in a trance state, he said, and if we were not careful we could do him irreparable harm. The psychologist approached Ian, speaking in low, soothing tones, calling out to him gently, looking at us knowledgeably and nodding as if to say: this is the way it has to be done. His crooning and supplicating went on for three or four minutes. "Ian, Ian, we need you Ian," he cooed. "We need you to wake up now, Ian." And so on.

My father was looking at the psychologist and pointing to the sides of his own head. The psychologist did not understand; neither did anyone else. So Phil went over, reached down, and gently removed the plugs from Ian's ears. Ian looked up and saw his father and mother and a group of strangers, and he understood right away what was going on. The psychologist spoke to him in the soothing tone, telling him what we were trying to accomplish, that it was for his own well being, that it was all temporary, that the best thing now would be for him to come along with us and let us get him some help. Ian refused to move and threatened to call the police if we did not leave. He and the psychologist went back and forth for a few minutes like this, until finally my father crouched down next to Ian, with a certain look on his face that I recognized from my own days of stubborn battles with him, and he said, in a matter-of-fact voice that had a lining of something else to it, "Ian, look, this is how it is. Either you're gonna stand up and walk out of this room, or I'm gonna pick you up and carry your ass out the door and lock you in the trunk of my car and drive you to Jamaica Plain. We have the papers. Your choice."

Ian saw the light and stood up. He was wearing a pair of gym shorts, no shirt and looked as if he had not bathed in the better part of a week.

"And you're gonna have to clean up before I let you in my car," my father added.

So we waited in the messy apartment while Ian showered, shaved, and got dressed, and then Mark and I and my dad and Ian climbed into my dad's car and made the trip to Jamaica Plain with Ian's parents and the psychologist following. By the time we pulled up in front of the hospital, it was about 10:30. Ian, his parents, the psychologist, and my dad went inside. Anxious to head off on our long weekend, Mark and I waited in the car. Forty-five minutes later, my father came out the door and said, "Boys, we got problems."

The hospital had made a determination that Ian was not a

danger to himself or anyone else, and therefore they could not admit him. At that point, Ian's father — who had some political clout and a good amount of money — made a phone call. He arranged for his son to be taken by private plane from Logan Airport to another hospital, outside Philadelphia, a place with a reputation for treating just this kind of patient. Phil told us we were going to have to accompany Ian on the plane, fly him down there, see that he was admitted, and then fly home on the same plane. The weekend at the Cape was shrinking by the minute, but there was no real option. We drove to the airport with the same seating arrangements, in two cars.

At the time, there was a small company at Logan called Butler Aviation. It was housed in a blue building, set off to the north side of the airport's main terminals, no more than two hundred yards from the airport fence and the triple-decker neighborhoods of East Boston. There was some delay in catching our flight — probably because the arrangements had been made at the last minute — and we were all standing around outside the Butler terminal waiting for the plane when Ian jumped up and made a run for it. Seeing him sprinting across the tarmac in the direction of the houses struck us as such a bizarre sight that, for a few seconds, we all just stood there, watching. My father gave Mark a nod; Mark took off after Ian, caught him about halfway to the airport boundary, and marched him back by the scruff of his neck.

"Can't believe that took you so long," my father said.

For the better part of another hour, we waited outside the hangar. It began to rain. Mark and I were not dressed for the rain, so we stepped inside the door to wait. He left to use the bathroom. My father had to do the same. I was standing there with Ian and his parents when he took off again. Not as fleet of foot as my partner, I did not give Ian as much of a head start, and did not catch him until he was at the very edge of the terminal property. This time, I had to tackle him to stop him, and Ian wrestled with me on the wet tarmac for a while until Mark came over and we led him back.

"Try that again," my dad said, "and we handcuff you to the door."

Another uneasy bit of time passed before the plane taxied up to the terminal. It was a prop plane, three steps to get in, a curtain between the passenger section and the cockpit, then two seats to either side, and a small fold-down rear seat. Phil gave me his old Boston Police handcuffs — a prized possession and the same ones I would eventually give to Mary — in case I needed them, and made sure I brought the custody papers with me. We left him at the terminal, crossed the runway, and started up the steps, Ian's parents, then me, Ian, and Mark. Halfway up to the door, Ian balked and started yelling. I was pulling him, Mark pushing him, the pilot turning around and wondering what the hell the problem was. "No big deal," I said. "My brother here just doesn't like to fly." We got Ian up the steps, pushed him to the back and seat-belted him in.

Ian's parents were in their fifties and very distinguished looking people — somewhat intimidating to me at first, in fact. I remember his mother's high-pitched voice, and that his father looked dapper in his suit and silver hair. Clearly, all communication with their son had broken down by that point, because, while we had been waiting, and as the plane sped down the runway and lifted off, they did not exchange a word with Ian. The rain was still falling, the first couple of minutes were bumpy, and I was thinking that the Cape Cod weekend was not starting off on a very good foot.

We had not quite reached cruising altitude when Ian tore off his seatbelt and bolted for the door.

His distinguished mother yelled, "Don't let him open it! Break his fucking arm if you have to!"

Mark and I did not need any encouragement; we were ready to break both arms. I was sure the door was going to fly open and we would all be sucked out, but we managed to subdue Ian, to convince the pilot that things were under control, and Ian's mother that no, we wouldn't let him do that again, no matter what. As my father had done, I told Ian I was going to handcuff him to the seat the next time he so much as took off his seatbelt, but he seemed to have quieted down. He pulled his legs up beneath him, closed his eyes, rested his hands on his knees with the thumb and index finger forming a circle, and began to meditate. This would have been fine, except that the meditation consisted of Ian letting out this low hum for about sixty seconds at a stretch, and then yelling "Hah!". Every time he yelled, Mark and I were sure he was about to make another dash for the door.

It was the longest two and a half hours of my life.

We didn't land in Philly until late afternoon. I got off the plane and immediately put a cigarette in my mouth, and the pilot said, "You'll blow us all up if you light that thing, the plane is still running."

The pilot agreed to wait — I imagine those two flights cost Ian's parents a sizeable sum — and the five of us walked into the main terminal, which was crowded with weekend travelers. Ian was going along quietly between Mark and me when suddenly he jumped up on top of a ticket counter and started screaming, "These people are trying to kidnap me!" Mark and I pulled him down, but he struggled with us. "They're kidnapping me! They're kidnapping me!" People were yelling at us, "Let him go!" Mark yelled back. I yelled at Ian, the parents were yelling. In the midst of this craziness, the airport police showed up, arrested all three of us, and marched us outside to the cruisers and then off to the airport jail. At that point, I was deeply thankful that my father and Bill Homans had made sure

I took the court papers with me. After a lot of questions and a few phone calls, the police let us go.

It was closing in on the dinner hour, and the pilot had come to find us to tell us he could wait only another fifteen minutes. If we couldn't finish up whatever it was we were doing in that time, then he was heading back, and we would have to take a commercial flight the next day. Mark and I hadn't packed any clothes, and were not particularly interested in a night in Pennsylvania when we had friends expecting us on Cape Cod. I convened a quick conference with the parents, and told them it was a ninety minute drive to the hospital. The best thing to do, in order to save themselves more trouble and the expense of our night's lodging and tickets for two on a commercial flight, was to hire a private ambulance, and deliver Ian to the hospital that way. They agreed.

The ambulance showed up, and, not knowing how else to make sure Ian made it there, I decided my only option was to handcuff him inside the ambulance, one hand to a metal rod just behind the back seat. He did not like that, exactly, and I cannot say I blame him, but I felt he had given us enough trouble for one day. I handed his father the key, and made sure he promised to mail the cuffs back. The ambulance headed off, and Mark and I sprinted to the private plane.

We gave the pilot the story of what had really been going on, and he told us he would have never have taken off if he had known. When we were airborne, I asked if there was any water on board. "Do you one better," he said. "You see that couch back there, where the crazy guy was sitting. Open it up and flip it over and you'll find something to drink." We did: gin, vodka, whiskey.

The next day, when I called my father from Cape Cod, a bit hung-over and not happy about having missed all that time with our friends, I started to complain about how Ian had gotten us arrested, and almost gotten us killed. My father listened to this with a fair degree of patience . . . until we arrived at the part of the story that had to do with his handcuffs. Phil was a funny guy that way. Generous to a fault, if you needed ten thousand dollars he would be first in line to give it to you, but if you took some small object that belonged to him — a comb, his Parker pen, or especially his handcuffs from his BPD days — he would start in on a mini-tirade about *my things*, and promise to bury you six feet deep if you failed to return them. Fortunately for me, the client mailed us back the handcuffs a couple of weeks later.

About two months after that, Mark's brother, Kevin, and I had a similar assignment — securing temporary custody of a young woman who had joined a different cult, and driving her, with her parents, to the same private hospital outside Philadelphia. We were at the admitting desk, the young woman was all taken care of, when I thought to ask the admitting officer if Ian was still there.

"Sure is," the officer told us. "Doing great, too."

I asked if we could say hello, and the officer said we could. I didn't know why I did that, curiosity maybe. Or maybe I just wanted to see Ian in a better frame of mind and know that our efforts had been worth something. Unfortunately, when Ian saw my face at the door of his room he had a huge fit, which set his recovery back several months, and Kevin and I drove back to Massachusetts with another lesson in the mysteries of human psychology in our portfolios.

In time, because we did not always have enough work to keep him busy, and because he really wanted a career in a different aspect of law enforcement, Kevin's brother Mark moved on to become a prison guard at Walpole (the same maximum security prison where Albert DeSalvo ended his days). One small story will paint a picture of him: During the famous blizzard of 1978, a storm that dropped three feet of snow on the city and clogged the highways with thousands of stranded vehicles (I remember going by cross-country skis to Dorothy's house to bring her cigarettes, and skiing over the tops of cars on route), Mark knew the prison would be understaffed. So he packed a suitcase and walked to work — twenty six miles through several feet of snow — and stayed at the prison for seven nights until things in the city returned to normal.

# FIFTEEN
The Man Who Found a Violin on the Beach

*"Music oft hath such a charm*
*To make bad good, and good provoke to harm."*
- Shakespeare

B y the summer of 1977, half a year before the famous
February 9th blizzard, and a few months before the
world would be turned upside-down at DiNatale Detective Agency, I had pretty much abandoned my other options
— the CIA, FBI, graduate school and teaching — and was becoming comfortable with the idea of making a career out of
private eye work. Without ever pushing me, my father had welcomed me into the business and started treating me like a partner . . . more or less. He introduced me to his many contacts,
instructed me, almost always by example, in the different aspects of the work, and often gave me the sense that I was making a contribution. Thanks, in large part, to Gems and Luxury
Jewelers, the agency was thriving. The relationship between
Dorothy and me was blossoming into something more than I
had ever felt with past girlfriends. I was making a good
paycheck every week, driving a new maroon Camaro with a
buckskin interior, living on my own with a friend named Bernie
in the second-floor apartment in Roslindale (Bernie's deaf

121

Dalmatian lived there with us. The dog's name was Bumper, he obeyed hand signals, and would sleep on the couch even if we put chairs there to stop him: he would simply sleep on top of the chairs. We always knew when Bumper was coming home, because we would hear the screech of brakes outside in the street, and then the sound of him bumping his muzzle against the screen door).

Most of all, I felt challenged: there were so many different aspects to the average work-week, everything from following wayward spouses to rescuing brainwashed kids, helping exonerate an innocent client, trying to establish liability in a civil case, or finding evidence against someone who claimed to have been hurt at work but really had not been. I consulted with high-priced lawyers and rubbed shoulders with some of the toughest people in the city (like the character in the Chelsea produce market, who, after Phil presented him with the bill for getting a close-up photo of his wife's boyfriend — no easy task — told us, "Shit, Phil , for another hundred bucks I could have had the fucking guy killed.").

I had seen Robert Redford play a CIA analyst in *Three Days of the Condor,* and knew I did not want a career poring over Russian language documents in some fluorescent-lit library basement outside Washington. And I had spent my high school and college years working part-time and summers at New England Life Insurance Company. It was a perfectly good company, and a perfectly good job, but I had seen some older men and women there who had spent their whole career sitting in an office cubicle doing some repetitive task. I knew that was not the life for me. Whatever insecurity and risk private investigations involved, I knew I would never die of boredom, or move into my later years in a kind of sad hypnosis brought on by decades of monotony.

Some investigation agencies choose to specialize, but we

have always stayed with our Bowdoin Street roots, operating what I think of as a "walk-in" business, doing any kind of work that pays the bills and meets our ethical standards. In the early years, my father had a fair amount of civil and criminal investigations, working for attorneys and insurance companies. Sometimes this meant — and still means — catching people who are claiming to be injured but really are not; and sometimes it means making sure a truly injured worker receives the compensation he or she deserves. In the 1970's especially, we had a rash of cases similar to Ian's, where a young man or woman had been absorbed into a religious cult (the Moonies were especially active in Boston in those years), or run away or disappeared, and we had been hired, by the parents usually, to find them and bring them back into mainstream life. There were always surveillances to be done, many of them not only having to do with cheating spouses, but with child custody cases, background investigations, personal injury cases, and the uncovering of evidence to help in criminal defense cases. We would occasionally find ourselves involved in a murder or rape investigation. But a significant piece of our billing had to do with another of the ancient vices, one that I had been exposed to at Gems and Luxury — stealing.

One of our more memorable theft-related cases came to us via the lawyer for a very wealthy couple who owned a town home on Marlborough Street in the Back Bay. While they had been at their summer house, thieves had broken in and basically emptied out the Boston residence, carrying away, in the process, a Louis XIV desk. I do not know exactly what transpired between my father and this client, but we took an unusual route to recover the desk. Phil had an acquaintance who was familiar with some of the city's unsavory criminals. He called up this friend, and asked if any of his less than upstanding associates might have heard something about Louis XIV. A few days later, the friend called our office and told my dad, "$15,000, and you can get the desk back." My father and I went to the home of this wealthy couple and told them about the offer. The woman blinked, once, and said, "Let's go to the bank." Phil had spoken with the BPD detective as well as the insurance company that was more than happy to get the desk back for $15,000. The next day, the friend came to our office, accepted the payment, stuffing the bills down into the top of his calf-high sock, and a day or two later he called and said, "Room 132, Town Line Motel."

So my father and I drove up to the motel in his Ford L.T.D. We already had the key to room 132, opened the door, and there was the enormous Louis XIV desk, sitting there as if the motel owners had decided to splurge on furnishings and charge extra for room 132. Somehow, Phil and I worked the huge thing out the door — just as a State Police trooper was driving into the parking lot. He had other things on his mind, I guess, and did not even look at us. We hoisted Louis XIV up onto the roof of the L.T.D., secured it there with ropes and blankets taken from my father's trunk full of hardware supplies, and brought it back to our wealthy clients.

They were so pleased that they insisted on inviting my father and me up to their summer home for a day. During a tour of the house, which was right on the ocean, the woman pointed to a grandfather clock and told me it was one of five Napoleon had ordered made for his five top generals. After the tour, the couple's daughter, an attractive young woman in her 20s, took it into her mind to invite Phil and me out for a sail in her new boat. We felt that we could not refuse. Out we went, far from shore, with the inexperienced young woman at the tiller. The wind came up, the boat capsized, all three of us went overboard. Unfortunately for my father, he went overboard on the side of the boat where the sail had fallen. I could see that he was stuck there, banging his fists up against the canvas again and again, trying to create an air pocket, struggling for breath. I worried he would have a heart attack, so I swam under the boat and grabbed his legs, hoping to turn him in another direction, but he must have thought he was being attacked by hungry fish, and he kicked me away. Eventually, we managed to right the boat and bail it out, and the young woman, somewhat abashed, brought us back to shore. Our clothes, of course, were soaked. I sat in that extravagant summer house with Phil, both of us in borrowed bathrobes, waiting there as our pants, shirts, and underwear tumbled and clicked in the dryer. After a long silence, my father looked at me and said, "This is *not* somethin' we talk about back home."

A somewhat similar case came to us via a man named Morris Rand, an extremely successful real estate developer and someone for whom we had worked in the past. Morris was in his sixties, but his hair was jet-black, his Rolls Royce pearly white, and his attractive girlfriend less than half his age. Among other projects and holdings, Morris owned a building of luxury apartments at 1501 Beacon Street, Brookline, a place with a concierge and indoor pool. When it was being built, we had supplied the security guards for 1501 Beacon (in a pinch we would sometimes use my brother-in-law Ed, who was in medical school at the time and would sit at his guard post all night with his textbooks open on the desk). My brother Richard would handle most of this account in later years, and I think he enjoyed trying to sneak into the underground garage close behind the car of a resident, or trying to get into the back of the building via the pool entrance without the proper I.D., anything to keep the concierge on his toes.

One of the lucky tenants at 1501 Beacon was a concert violinist. The musician had a Stradivarius violin — which, these days, can be worth as much as $200,000. The instrument need-

125

ed some work, so he sent it out to the repair shop via DHL. A few weeks later, the repaired violin was sent back to him by the same shipper, but when our client opened the package it was empty. No Stradivarius. No explanatory note. He called DHL, but before they could even begin tracking the package, the violinist had his explanation. It came in the form of an anonymous phone call. The caller claimed he had been out for a walk on Revere Beach, five miles north of the city, and found the violin in the sand! Just by looking at it, he had figured out it was not any ordinary violin, and he thought that, since he was being decent enough to call the owner rather than try to sell the instrument and pocket the cash, he deserved a reward. For a very reasonable finder's fee of $15,000 — as I remember it — the man said, he would be happy to see that our client got his Stradivarius back. But, naturally, he did not want the police involved.

*If you ever want to see your violin alive again* . . . that kind of thing.

To the musician, of course — more accustomed to the instructions of an orchestra conductor than the directions of an extortionist — the Stradivarius was at least as important as a beloved family member. Not knowing what else to do, he went to his landlord, Morris Rand. Morris told him to call us. My father had gone over to interview him, and had started to work on the case, when the musician decided he wanted to contact a law enforcement agency after all. Since it was a matter of extortion, he ended up being referred to the FBI. The FBI consulted with my dad, and they agreed the best approach would be to work on things together. Since he had already been in contact with the extortionist, my father arranged to act as middleman and deliver the cash.

I was excited when he asked me to be part of the staged delivery. Though I had been working on surveillances for the previous six or seven years, and though I had done some undercover work in bars and helped out in difficult situations like the one with Ian, there was still a way, in 1977, that my father held me at arm's length. Often, my work would be to drive him to various appointments around Greater Boston. Lawyers' offices. Courthouses. The Secretary of State's archives. The Registry. But there were times, usually when he was going to meet a contact, when he would say to me, "I'm going in, you stay here," and at those times I would feel like I was being pushed back into my adolescence.

I would ask why. He would say he didn't want me to hear certain things, didn't want me to have to testify in court about them if the case went that far. Those explanations always left a little angry residue on the pride I felt at having become a full-time part of the company.

But I was going to be a significant player in the Stradivarius case. On a sunny early fall day in 1977, my father and I made the fifteen-minute drive north, over the Mystic River Bridge, to the working-class city of Revere. In accordance with our instructions, I was carrying an envelope containing $15,000 dollars in small bills — twenties, fifties, and hundreds. My father seemed as calm as if we were driving north for a walk on Revere Beach, a crescent of sand that had once been Greater Boston's equivalent to Coney Island.

We drove slowly along through the busy streets, past triple-deckers and large wood-frame houses that had been home to Irish, Italian, and Jewish immigrants for more than a century. We swung around a death-defying traffic circle and into the parking lot of a fairly large strip mall. At the far western end of this mall was a Howard Johnson's Motor Lodge and Restaurant. We parked seventy or eighty yards from the door of the restaurant and went in. I had stuffed the envelope into the back of my pants, and covered it with the tail of my sport jacket.

Even with my relative inexperience, it was a simple matter to determine which one of the lunchtime customers was our guy: he was sitting by himself over against the window, smoking nervously and eyeballing everybody who came through the door. I'm sure my father saw him even before I did, but instead of going over to him, Phil sat at the counter and ordered a coffee and a hot dog. "And could you toast the bun for me, Honey?" he asked the waitress.

It took about thirty seconds for the extortionist to approach us. "You ready?" he asked my dad. "Let's go."

My father looked calmly up at him. "Yeah, I'm ready. But I just ordered a hot dog."

"So what? Let's go."

"So I want to eat my hot dog," my father said, and the man looked at me as if to say, "Is your partner crazy, or what?" I shrugged. The man went back to his table and his chain-smoking, and my father — who was just engaged in a little game in order to have the exchange play out by his rules — sat there calmly drinking coffee. When the hot dog was served, he ate it in a relaxed way, wiped his mouth, took the last sip from his cup, paid, and stood up. The man followed Phil out into the parking lot. I stayed in the restaurant.

Our plan was that my father would go sit with the man in his car and once he had seen the violin and verified that it matched the client's description, he would signal me by opening the passenger door and putting his right foot down on the pavement. I watched them from a distance of a hundred feet or so, waited, saw the door open and my father's leg swing out. On that cue, I left the restaurant, carried the envelope over to the car and handed it in through the driver's window. The lucky guy who had found a Stradivarius while strolling along Revere Beach — and who actually worked for DHL — had just enough time to glance into the envelope when two unmarked cars came speeding across the lot and screeched to a stop a few feet away. Four men jumped out. One of them had a bullhorn. The others had drawn guns.

NO ONE MOVE! THIS IS THE FBI! PUT YOUR HANDS WHERE WE CAN SEE THEM AND DO NOT MOVE!

In a moment, the three of us had our hands against the roof of the car, legs spread. As we were being patted down and handcuffed, my father started to curse the violin-stealer out in the most unflattering terms. "You motherfucker, you little piece of shit! You called the FBI on us, you little — ". This made no sense, of course; it was just another mind-game: my dad wanted to say these things to the extortionist before he could say them to us.

Even as he was being led away, the guy was protesting his innocence. When he was safely out of sight, the agents removed our cuffs. My dad made a little smalltalk with them, and then, not wanting to attract any more attention than we already had, we got into the car and went back to the office.

All had gone well. I had studied another corner of the painting, as it were, collected another type of experience to remember and learn from. And I had seen the FBI in action, which, for another few hours at least, only reinforced the exalted view I always had of them. *Supercops*.

In the apartment that night, having a beer with Bernie, waiting for Bumper to come home, and still basking in the pleasure of a new job well done, I had a phone call from my dad. This was not an unusual occurrence. For all his gruff professionalism around the office, Phil had a sentimental side. He would call, sometimes more than once a night, ask how his boy was doing, what I was up to, and let me know what we had planned for the next day. That night, though, the tone of the call was a bit different. "You son of a bitch," he said, in an admiring way, "you kept the fifteen grand, didn't you."

"What?"

"The FBI just called me. They think you palmed it and still have it."

"No way, Dad. I gave it to him, he looked at it and slipped it under the seat."

My father was laughing. "Sit tight. I'll call you right back." Ten minutes later he called again. "I just talked to the FBI agent. I told him the money was in the car under the front seat."

"No problem, then."

"Guess what?"

"What do you mean, guess what?"

"The guy posted bail and they let him go, along with the car. Nobody ever searched the car. He drove right out of the FBI garage with the money . . . the stupid bastards."

# SIXTEEN
Almost Losing Him

*"Here are the tears of things; mortality touches the heart."*
- Virgil

You didn't have to have a medical degree to look at the history of my father's family and understand that he was a prime candidate for heart trouble in middle age. His mother died of heart disease. His oldest brother, Tony, died of heart disease. Two other brothers, Joe and Tommy, had heart problems. Another brother, Billy, and his only sister, Phyllis, both underwent bypass surgery.

My father was, unfortunately, not an exception to this genetic pattern. Though he had always worked hard — or maybe it is more accurate to say *because* he had always worked hard — he was not much into exercise. In his generation, it was uncommon for working men to have gym memberships, unheard of them to know their cholesterol numbers, and unusual for people to pay attention to what they ate. Most guys like Phil worked to pay the bills not fatten the investment account, ate what they liked and could afford, and considered it exercise if they got a parking space at the far end of Saint Theresa's lot on a Sunday morning and had to walk a hundred yards. But most people did not have the ticking genetic time bomb my father had.

He had gone through some troubles before — a mild heart attack while he was working on the Strangler case, another small attack at home in 1974 — but the heart attack he suffered in the fall of 1977 was of a different order of magnitude entirely, and destroyed so much heart muscle that, even bypass surgery was never an option after that.

At the time, Phil was working on another theft case with me, at the River Shoe Company. But his main focus was a complicated murder trial with a defense lawyer named Gerald Alch, who was in practice with F. Lee Bailey. Alch was a dapper man, late forties, tanned year round; he would later become a respected judge in the Dedham District Court. My father often referred to their case as "a modern-day Sacco and Vanzetti" because two Italian immigrants — Arthur Graziano and Rocco Facente, had, he said, been railroaded into a murder rap. Probably not the kindest and gentlest of men, possibly with underworld connections, they had been accused of first-degree murder in a drug deal gone sour, found guilty, and sentenced to life in prison.

After an appeal process that lasted five years, the Massachusetts Supreme Judicial Court overturned their conviction, based partly on closing remarks by District Attorney Matty Ryan that included, "Let's get the mafia out of Springfield." Graziano and Facente were out on the street again, but Matty Ryan wanted to retry the case.

Eddie Corsetti, a reporter at the *Boston Record American,* and a man whose information for a series of Strangler articles, I now know, came secretly from a Deep Throat named Phil DiNatale, was following the case closely. He mentioned it to Jerry Alch, and said Frank Sinatra had taken a personal interest and was willing to pay some or all of the legal fees and make an appearance in court. Alch immediately became involved, and hired my dad to help prepare a defense.

They worked together for a year, putting together their argument, convinced that the men had been wrongly accused. For Alch, the motivation was probably the straightforward challenge of winning a complex trial and seeing the innocent go free. For my father, I suspect, there was another dimension to it. His father had been one of the first Italian American plainclothes detective in Boston history, and in the process of doing his job, had endured a steady stream of insult and ethnic prejudice. Phil had encountered a lot of that, too: we often heard the stories at home. That kind of thing leaves an open wound, and I am sure it was part of Corsetti's motivation, and Sinatra's, too, and part of the reason my father involved himself in something so far from home.

In between visits to the River Shoe factory with me, Phil had been up in Springfield — about an hour and a half west of where we lived — three or four nights a week for months. He would make trips back to Boston to work on other cases, but most of his energies were expended on behalf of Graziano and Facente. Once the trial got underway, my father and Jerry Alch basically lived at the Sheraton Hotel in West Springfield, working night and day. The trial lasted three weeks, and, even though Sinatra never ended up sending any money or making an appearance, it seemed, from Alch's point of view, to be going along very well. Jerry administered a lie detector test to his two clients. They passed. The DA asked to have his principal witness polygraphed, too; the witness failed. There were, as Alch tells it now, some withering cross-examinations of prosecution witnesses.

One night, my dad returned to his room "breathless" as Alch remembers it now, saying he had found a woman who had been present at the drug deal and was willing to testify that another man, not Graziano or Facente, had done the shooting, and had then fled to South Carolina. Jerry and Phil stayed up much of the night interviewing this woman and putting her through a mock cross-examination. The next day, under direct examination by Jerry, she did just fine. But a day later, the District Attorney called to the stand an elderly man with a big book in his hands. The man was the keeper of the records for the Hamden jail; the book held all those documents. According to one of them, on the day the killing took place, the defense's new star witness had been behind bars awaiting trial on prostitution charges.

She had perjured herself. D.A. Matty Ryan, whom my father came to despise, started talking about charging Phil DiNatale with suborning perjury, which carried a thirty-year jail sentence. But, even without that unlikely consequence, my father felt ashamed at having been so easily duped. He came home for Thanksgiving, then went back to Springfield the next morning. Early on the following day, as he was getting ready to attend a Saturday court session and what would be Alch's successful closing argument (despite the defense team's embarrassing mistake with the lying, so-called witness, the jury took only about fifteen minutes to find Graziano and Facente not guilty), Phil collapsed in his room at the Sheraton. He managed to crawl to the telephone and call for help.

In Boston, on that late November Saturday it was overcast and in the low forties, but I was about to join Mark Rose for a game of golf. I was a fanatic for the game then — still am — the George Wright course was a one-minute drive from my front door, and Mark and I had a tradition of playing on the two days after Thanksgiving. As I was getting ready to leave the house we had a call from my sister Jean. "Phil's had another heart attack," she said, and I could hear in her voice that it was different this time. "We have to get up there. I think he's going to die."

Richard was visiting our uncle Tommy, hunting with him near Bangor, Maine. I sent them a message and went to pick up my mother in West Roxbury. She was waiting at the door when we arrived; the fact that she had her bag packed was a good sign I thought. It meant she expected to be in Springfield for a few days, which indicated that someone had told her my father had at least a chance to survive. We met Jean and her husband Ed — a surgeon by then, and cool under pressure — outside their house. Ed got behind the wheel of my Camaro and we drove to Springfield through such intense snow squalls in the Worcester Hills that I did not know who would die first that day, the four of us or my father. I remember the tension of that ride, Ed driving, my mother praying under her breath, the white-outs and wind, all of us wondering if Phil was going to make it.

When we finally arrived at Providence Hospital in West Springfield, we found him in Intensive Care. A doctor came out and told us they had given him all the morphine they could at that point, but he was still having a lot of chest pain, and they were not sure he would survive to the next day.

Though I was accustomed to my father's health troubles, I was more accustomed to seeing him as a robust, energetic, middle-aged man, five foot seven inches, two hundred and thirty-five pounds, with a barrel chest, a big head, big hands and arms and a look in his eyes that made it seem like he had never encountered a person who intimidated him, or a situation he could not handle. It is always the case that we show the less savory aspects of our personalities at home. I was used to that — my father's short outbursts, personality quirks, his low threshold for frustration. But now that I was working with him, the side I saw most often was the side he showed the working world — not exactly easygoing, but supremely calm and confident. On days when I was in college at Boston State and Jean was working as a secretary at New England Life, we would all commute into the city together, along with a neighbor, Detective Sergeant Frank Haugh, and it seemed like every cop at every intersection knew my dad and had a smile and a friendly wave. Though I am sure he had enemies — police commissioner Edmund McNamara comes immediately to mind — whenever we worked with cops, or with lawyers, it would always be clear to me that my father was held in high esteem, known and respected for his work on the Strangler case, the kind of man you could count on in a tough situation, the kind of person who carried himself with just the right mixture of physical confidence and sense of humor about things. The kind of man who seemed to control events, rather than letting them control him.

But, when we were at last allowed to visit my Dad in that hospital room in Springfield, what we saw, really, was the beginning of the end of him. He was unconscious, his skin as gray as the November sky, and he was hooked up to various machines and I.V.'s

He would live another ten years, and would fight back hard against his severely damaged heart. But, though we would still work on cases together, and though he would continue to be the lynchpin of the agency, at least into the mid 1980's, he had finally met an opponent he could not wrestle to the ground or pin up against a wall with one forearm. It is always difficult for a child to see a parent age and grow weaker, but when that parent is a force of nature, the way Phil was, it is particularly hard.

My mother found a washcloth and wiped the perspiration from his face. We kept that visit short, then stayed in Springfield several days. My father remained in the hospital there for three weeks, slowly regaining his strength. We would go up to visit with him on weekends, and, once he was strong enough, he would call me every day and give me advice about ongoing cases. But the doctors had told him that if he wanted to recover he should avoid excitement, and my mother was always reminding me of that, and telling me not to get him upset. Shortly before Christmas, he was taken by ambulance back to the house on Sherbrook Street. My mother and my sisters Jean and Evelyn, were nursing him, which was not the easiest of jobs; he was not used to being sick, and did not like it, and could be demanding and moody. After their heart troubles, my father's older brother and sister had changed their lifestyles dramatically, and both ended up surviving to their late 80's. But Phil was not the type of person to be content sitting in an armchair with a blanket over his lap, moving peacefully into his golden years. He didn't really believe he would grow old, couldn't accept it, wouldn't let it happen, would rather flame out than wear away. Even then, I think we all knew that.

# SEVENTEEN
Everybody Wants a Good Running Shoe

*"I get by with a little help from my friends."*
- Paul McCartney

Fortunately for me, with my father disabled by the heart attack, the income from our guards and undercover agents at Gems and Luxury provided a steady stream of income. We had such a solid relationship with Amelia Scondrizzo that — from a business standpoint — my father's absence did not worry them much. There were other active cases, too, most of them relatively small and uncomplicated. The one that needed immediate attention was the troubles at River Shoe.

The late '70s was a time when jogging and running had seen a surge in popularity (and a time when shoes and sneakers were still being manufactured in America). River was making a running shoe called the Speedster that was selling as fast as they could be pulled off the assembly table and packed into boxes. The company had a factory and offices on the Cambridge-Somerville line, a few miles west and a little ways north of downtown Boston, and a ten-minute drive from Bowdoin Street. That summer the controller at River had called and said they were experiencing major theft problems, and asked us to do some investigating. My father and I had good cameras then, Nikon 35 millimeter with a telephoto lenses that went from 40 millimeters to 240 millimeters. We would spend time parked across the street from the factory, watching and photographing employees as they stepped out during coffee break and lunch and deposited small packages in their cars. From time to time we would also see a vehicle drive up to the back side of the building, one of the tall factory windows would swing open from the bottom, and what looked like a mail sack would come flying out. The people in the car would collect the sack, we would photograph them, follow them as far as the housing project on the same block, then come back and continue to stake out the factory.

With all those photos, plus the evidence from River's own inventory discrepancies — they had no inside cameras, but they did have a lot of empty boxes that should have been full — we were close to being able to finger the thieves and confront them in what my dad called "an interview" (though "interrogation" might have been a more accurate term). But, we were not quite there yet, and it is always a huge mistake to take things to that level too soon.

Complicating matters a bit was the widely accepted but technically unofficial policy at River Shoe that, when you signed on to work there, you could take a pair of shoes off the assembly line and keep them. Unofficial, as I said, but understood. One pair. A few of the workers had started to abuse that policy. They would take a new pair of running shoes, push the heel support down to flatten it out, and tie one shoe to each calf. Wide-bottomed pants were in style, which made things easier. At break time, they would step outside, sit in their cars, drop off the stolen shoes, and head back in to work. Some employees we photographed were doing this three times a day. The most brazen among them were on the other end of the mail sack before it came flying out the window.

We knew this and were fairly sure that we knew at least some of the employees who were stealing. But, when my father suffered his heart attack in Springfield, we were just at the point where we needed a last key bit of proof to seal the case.

Richard was helping out around the office and with surveillances then, but mainly concentrating on his college classes. I had two years of full-time work under my belt, but, as is obvious in the cases I have talked about, my father was the main player and I had mostly gone along as a supporting actor. By then, I had watched him do dozens of interviews with suspects — at Gems and Luxury, in the false-stalker case — but had never done one myself. Given his fragile health, and my fragile sense of being a fully-developed private investigator, high on the list of things I did not want was to have to drive up to Springfield, stand next to my father's sickbed, and say, "Sorry, Phil, I screwed up the River case."

Nice as it is to successfully complete an investigation single-handedly, I have never been afraid to ask for help. "I know what I don't know," was always one of my father's favorite sayings, and both Richard and I have inherited that attitude. In November of 1977 I was aware of the fact that I had not quite mastered the art of calling thieves into a room and getting them to sign a confession. My dad was healthy enough — barely — for me to ask about this. He encouraged me, told me he was sure I could handle things, and, from his hospital bed in Springfield, looking pretty beaten-up, he added, "Call Tom Calabrese. Detective. Cambridge P.D."

So I did.

I met Tom in Cambridge, and told him what had happened to my father and where we were with River Shoe, and I let him know that I was not sure how, exactly, to proceed from that point. Were the photos of the workers with bulging calves really going to be enough to get them to admit to stealing? Did we have a way to link the two ends of the mail-sack toss? I did not have anything like my father's interrogation skills, was I going to be able to convince the thieves we had the hard evidence and get them to sign a confession? Or was I going to invite them into the interview room and try to win the poker hand with two 10s and a jack?

Detective Calabrese was a large man, thin nose, ruddy face, hands the size of hockey gloves. After listening to what I had and what I did not have, he pondered for a few seconds and said, "Let's go." We climbed into his unmarked car and made the short trip to the factory. It was late afternoon and the River employees were just getting off their shift. Tom and I watched until I saw the three people — our main suspects were apparently friends, or at least part of the same car pool — emerge from the building and get into one car. They pulled out of the lot and headed toward the Lechmere train station. Tom followed for a few blocks and then said, "Let's pull them over."

"Pull them over?" I had visions of him making me go up and confront the three thieves and I was not quite ready to do that, not in River's conference room, and definitely not on the street.

Tom put the light on top of the car and turned on the siren. When the three River workers pulled to the curb, he told me to wait, then got out and approached them. I saw him leaning down to speak to the driver. Next thing I saw was the three guys standing outside the car, resting their hands on it, legs spread in the kind of criminal's yoga pose no one ever wants to practice. Detective Calabrese started patting them down. He turned his face to look at me, and though I doubt he actually winked, that was the impression I had. "Oh-oh, what's this?" I heard him say, in a stage voice. "What's this, now?" He had patted his way down to the driver's lower legs. He pulled up

141

the pant leg, revealing the tied-on, brand-new, flattened-out Speedster, and he posed there as if I might want a photo, then hooked a finger at me.

When I was standing near the trio, Calabrese said to the driver. "See this guy here?" he pointed to me. "This guy's been doing a little investigating for the company that employs you. Taking photos and so on. Following certain cars. For some reason, they feel they've been having thievery troubles. Could that be?"

No one said a word.

"Well, I'm going to do you gentlemen the big favor of letting you go instead of arresting you. On the condition that you go into work tomorrow and you talk to Mr. DiNatale here, my friend. It's important to remember that I have your names and the license number. Do we have an agreement?"

Nods all around. Calabrese did not even bother collecting the running shoes; he just let the guys go. The next day, nervous as I have ever been in my life before or since, with the possible exception of my wedding day, I walked into River Shoe, met with the vice president and the controller, and said, with all the confidence I could summon, "We're all set. Here are the names of the employees I need to talk with."

Miraculously, they had all come into work that day. Part of that had to do with River's relatively easygoing policy: the worst they could expect was to be fired, and they probably had hopes of talking their way out of even that consequence. Even if they were fired, background employment checks were rare in those days, so it was not like they would have trouble finding another job.

Sitting behind the controller's desk, I interviewed them one by one. From the waist up, I kept things together; under the table my toes and legs were shaking. The first member of the trio, a young Hispanic man who spoke English well but not as a first language, did not seem very calm himself. From watching my dad, I knew a couple of tricks. For one, I kept the surveillance photos on my desk but didn't show them to the suspect, leaving him to wonder just what kind of information we had. For another, after I had introduced myself, handed over my card, and laid out the case against him, I gave him a way out. "You seem like a good guy," I said. "Probably the first time you've been involved in something like this, right? You have a chance here to give us the information we need — who else was involved, how many pairs were stolen, and so on — and I think that would probably be the best way to go about it now, given all that we have on you and your pals."

I had been careful to tell him I was not a policeman, and that there was no obligation to talk to me — he could always go hire a lawyer. There was a moment when he seemed ready to tell me to shove my evidence and walk out but he decided against that route and admitted everything. I copied it all down and wrote out one of our official statements, a carefully worded document that begins this way: "My name is _ _ _ . My date of birth is _ _ _. I am giving this statement to John DiNatale from the DiNatale Agency, who has properly identified himself and is working on behalf of River Shoe. Etcetera. (Taking care with those written statements makes the lawyers' job easier — in cases where there is a lawyer — and it reduces the risk of us being sued at a later date for things like false imprisonment, intimidating a witness, or intentional infliction of emotional distress. Lawyers also like to have P.I.'s take these statements for them in case a witness later decides to change his or her testimony. In those instances, the lawyer can put the P.I. on the stand; without that option, they would have no objective way to convince judge or jury that the witness's earlier statements had been different.)

The shoe-stealer's two accomplices made the same decision. The whole thing took several hours, and, once the confessions were signed, I turned them over to River and let them decide what the punishment would be.

That wasn't the end of our involvement with River Shoe, or the end of the stealing there — various kinds of stealing. Later, we would have an undercover agent named Dana, who enjoyed jogging, apparently, and who put a drop of poison into what was an otherwise harmonious relationship between us and the sneaker-makers. River fired him for repeated tardiness and other transgressions. I ended up paying for the shoes he lifted — saying it was part of his undercover job. But in the fall and winter of 1977, at least, River was happy with our work, and I was happy to be able to tell my dad, next time we made the drive up to Springfield, that we had gotten a confession . . . and had been paid.

It was only a day or so after his visit that Tom Calabrese revealed what he had done to get the three thieves out of their car. "Somebody dropped a dime on you guys," he told them, when he was leaning down near the driver's side window. "'Said you were carrying a weapon without the proper permits. I'm going to have to ask you to step out of the vehicle."

Which, generously interpreted, was a slight bending of the rules in order to help the son of a friend in need.

# EIGHTEEN
Richard

*"Am I not a man and a brother?"*
-Josiah Wedgewood

My siblings and I all had different relationships with Phil. Evelyn stood up to him when he was angry, and, later, felt he was gruff and remote around the house. As a young girl, she would go into the bathroom and wrap herself in his bathrobe just to smell his scent and feel he was close to her. Jean wished that, as adults, they had been able to have a glass of wine together, or have a real conversation; she wished he had chosen another line of work and never had anything to do with Albert DeSalvo. Both of them, though, saw him mainly in the role of *pater familias* whereas my younger brother Richard and I saw another side, all business on the one hand, and yet somehow easier to get along with. We had a common language — our work — and common concerns connected with keeping the agency afloat. Still, even between Richard and me there were differences in how we related to our father. If the relationship I had with him was a complicated and somewhat unusual one, then the relationship between Phil and Richard fell into a category beyond description. There was plenty of respect and affection there, too, but much more conflict.

It did not start out that way. As the youngest child, Richard was given a measure of slack I never knew. It was not so much that the strict family rules had changed by the time my brother — six years younger — came along, as that the enforcement level was different. The best example would be that, even at an early age, he would sneak upstairs and fool around with my father's gun. For the rest of us, the .38 Phil kept in the top drawer of his bureau might as well have been radioactive material. We were not to open the drawer, we were not to even think about touching the gun; Richard went up there on the *Q.T.* and played with it.

Though he was only six years old when the last of the stranglings occurred, only nine when Albert DeSalvo escaped from Bridgewater, my brother has strong memories from that time, like all of us. He remembers our father working on the diagrams at the kitchen table, the edges of the drafting paper held down with masking tape, his flat carpenter pencils sharpened with a chisel, rulers and erasers arranged neatly at his side. Without any of us knowing it, Richard would sneak into my father's Strangler files when he was not home. The files included graphic photographs of the crime scenes, of women strangled and stabbed, left in sexually provocative poses, nothing a kid that age should ever see. But, maybe because of his three-generation connection to police work, Richard seems to have taken the sight of them in stride. There were no nightmares, no teary admissions to my parents. It was just part of Dad's work, just a part of our life. When DeSalvo went over the wall at Bridgewater, Richard remembers being driven to my aunt's house in Somerville, and spending three days there, sharing a bedroom with his cousin Bob, and wondering if DeSalvo was intent on finding and taking revenge on the man who had played such a key role in fingering him as a serial killer. But it did not traumatize him as it did his oldest sister.

In later years — unlike me — he grew tired of talking about DeSalvo and my father's connection to the story. Part of that was just the tediousness of telling the same tale again and again, and part of it, most of it, had to do with the disconnect between others' curiosity about the exotic, hideous crimes and the fact that they had simply been part of our lives. Gruesome and sad beyond mentioning, but in another way just part of the family routine.

As a seventh grader, Richard was already sitting in the car with my dad on surveillances, keeping him company (our mother would sometimes come along too), and eating at Pewter Pot restaurants from one end of Greater Boston to the other. My mother would check out the cleanliness of the ladies' room, my dad would be watching to see if the cashier charged customers for items sold at the front counter or if she pocketed the change. Richard would be mainly interested in the licorice strips and lemon drops, but he enjoyed riding around the city, and enjoyed the feeling of being a young undercover agent sitting beside more ordinary families who were just out for a sandwich or a muffin.

By the time Richard turned eighteen, my dad had already schooled him thoroughly in the art of surveillance, and was comfortable sending him out on his own. They would go deer hunting in Vermont together. (My brother had a passion for fishing, too. As a very young boy he would catch foot-long carp from the Charles River and sell them for twenty-five cents each to the Mayers, a couple of Holocaust survivors who lived next door.) They would go to the Holiday Inn gym and work the heavy bag with the Stivaletta family and their Golden Globe boxing sons. Rich remembers riding in the car with my father, and Phil saying, out of nowhere, "You're not doing drugs, are you? Because if you were it would kill your mother."

In my brother's twenties, however, this bond began to fray. Richard was, in his own way, as headstrong as our father, and seemed constitutionally incapable of apologizing. He balanced this with an incredible generosity, once painting our sister Evelyn's ten-room house, for free. As he grew into full maturity, though, his freewheeling personality began to clash with my father's sense that he knew what was best for all of us. Somehow, and this was a mystery to everyone involved, Richard and Phil were able to draw a clear line between the personal and the professional. Whatever friction it was that caused the regular heat between them simply ceased to exist the minute Richard was on the clock. He respected my dad's abilities, and my dad respected his, so much so that there was little question in Richard's mind as to what kind of work he would end up doing.

After finishing Catholic Memorial, he enrolled in the criminal justice program at Northeastern University. College was, for him, a mix of intimidation on the one hand — law professors teaching classes held in 200-seat auditoriums, females beside him in class for the first time — and, on the other, the sense that he already had more experience in the law enforcement world than even the oldest students he came to know.

As it does to this day, Northeastern offered something called a "co-op" program, which meant that there was a blending of school work and field work. Naturally enough, Richard did his co-op at 45 Bowdoin Street. He had his gun license by then, and filled in for other security guards on the unpopular closing shift at Gems and Luxury, often riding shotgun on the post office runs, with hundreds of thousands of dollars worth of jewelry in boxes in the unmarked van. Or he would take the overnight shift at 1501 Beacon Street when the apartment building was under construction, sitting at a desk watching TV and making the rounds every hour between 7 a.m. and 7 p.m. All this bred in him a certain kind of toughness, the ability to go without sleep, to risk being caught on a surveillance, to stand toe-to-toe with some executive at Gems and Luxury who was failing to follow the security procedures.

But, he has more of a comical side to him than I do. In fact, I sometimes think he looks like a taller, more handsome version of Henry Winkler, the "Fonz" TV character. He gets the same devilish glint in his eyes sometimes, even now. As a young man, he would play tricks on our father — looking out from an upstairs window of the building next door (he was dating a law student who lived there) and watching, amused, as Phil called his name out the front door, again and again, searching for him.

In something like the same way that graduate school in the Midwest opened my mind to a different aspect of American life, Richard's summer in an Outward Bound program in northern Minnesota introduced him to the world beyond West Roxbury. He made friends with the sons and daughters of wealthy families there. Only a few months out of college, he was a guest in mansions on Martha's Vineyard and near the ski slopes of New Hampshire. He was introduced to competitive sailing, to parties in Newport, Rhode Island, to a level of life he had not even been able to imagine as a boy in the house on Sherbrook Street. By twenty-four he had bought a piece of land on Nantucket, sold it for a handsome profit, and purchased another piece of property there which he still owns.

In the midst of all this — the tony parties, the Marblehead racing scene, the legions of fun-loving friends and girlfriends, the increasing personal troubles with Phil and increasing professional responsibilities — my mother fell ill with cancer. She and Richard had always been particularly close. It is impossible to try to measure and compare suffering and grief, but Richard still lived at home, and was incredibly devoted to our mother in her long illness, and the sorrow and trauma of that time was at least as intense for him as it was for me and Jean and Evelyn and Dorothy.

He would bathe her, take her to the bathroom, make sure he was home in time, after weekend dates, to get her out of bed and feed her. Others helped, too, but Richard's contribution was not matched by anyone else's, and perhaps his sorrow was not either. From the day she died, he has not been able to shoot a deer or kill a fish.

After our mother's death, his troubles with Phil intensified. Phil's relationship with another woman — something I will get into a bit later — did nothing to make things easier. Richard ended up leaving the house he had grown up in and coming to live with Dorothy and me until he bought a place of his own.

Well into his thirties, he enjoyed the bachelor life, fending off the advances of a particularly amorous secretary who worked with us for a while ("You couldn't go into the back room when she was there," he says now with a half-smile, "or you risked being sexually molested.") enjoying the camaraderie of the various Eddies, and Jimmy, going out on the town in his new BMW.

In those years, there was an acute nursing shortage in Boston. Richard had a friend whose mother was in charge of recruiting medical workers, from Ireland mostly. Dropping off this friend after a weekend of partying in Newport, Richard saw that the backyard was filled with attractive young Irish women and felt it was his duty to stick around and help them make the transition to American life. "I remember picking out the prettiest one," he says, "and helping her with her luggage." A few years later he ended up marrying her, a Dubliner named Siobhan. In a toast I wrote for their wedding, I said, "We do not have in-laws in our family. Siobhan is now the younger sister, and she will always be my sister."

For Richard and me, while the business occupies much of

our lives — including late-night phone calls from clients on weekends and our vacations — we have always kept the emphasis on family first. From the time of Phil's major heart attack, I was really running the business, but I had seen enough of family squabbles over money to know that was something I never wanted to happen between us. As soon as Phil retired, Richard and I decided to split all the profits from the business strictly down the middle, and, while we have argued about things, money has never been one of them. Over the past twenty-three years, we have developed an uncanny telepathy. This was most apparent on surveillance cases in the days before cell phones and walkie-talkies. If we were both working on a case in separate cars — a particularly effective strategy — we would somehow know when the other person was going to fall back and we had to pick up the trail. We both drove Camaros for a while, both joined the Charles River Country Club, both lost a son. My two daughters and his three children joke that some days we even come to work dressed in identical shirts and pants, like the karmic twins we seem to be.

We have formed a rare bond, I think, over the course of working together all these years. Our strengths complement each other's: Richard can reconstruct an auto accident scene like an expert, can draw up diagrams as well as my father used to, and knows more about surveillance than probably anyone in America. I am good with clients, placing undercover agents and developing covers for them, and wrestling with billing procedures. He has a way of being able to deal with those lawyers I cannot stand, and vice-versa. The fact is, over the past thirty years, we have spent more time with each other than with our wives and children, and we are still the best of friends. Putting this book together without giving him his own chapter would have felt like a crime . . . and would have been something he would never let me forget.

# NINETEEN
The Fireman with the Diamond Earrings

*"But man, proud man,*
*Drest in a little brief authority,*
*Most ignorant of what he's most assur'd,*
*His glassy essence, like an angry ape,*
*Plays such fantastic tricks before high heaven*
*As make the angels weep."*
- Shakespeare, *Measure for Measure*

All through the late seventies and eighties, as Richard came into the business full-time and traveled along the same learning curve I had known, Gems and Luxury Jewelry continued to be the backbone of our business. As time went on, in place of the periodically unreliable security guards we had used at first, we started to hire graduates of Richard's alma mater, the Northeastern University Criminal Justice program. This worked out well for them — many of them went on to become officers in local or state police departments — and for us, too, because we used the guard work as a kind of trial period. If people proved themselves at G & L, we would often end up hiring them as a regular at the agency, to do undercover or surveillance work, or other kinds of investigations. It was through this route that two key employees, Tim O'Callaghan and Cal Kenney, came to us.

Among the other security measures we implemented at G & L was a forty-five-minute seminar I presented to the salesmen, educating them on the intricacies of surveillance so they would know if they were being followed. I had done a certain amount of work in the defense of armed robbers, and they would let me in on some trade secrets, telling me how they cased a bank job, studied the route of an armored car, or watched a jewelry salesman for a while to figure out his routine. I passed on some of that to the G&L salesmen, telling them, for instance, that if they suspected they were being followed down the highway, they could make the person behind them commit by pulling to the side of the road about 400 yards before taking an exit, and watching to see if anyone stopped behind them. At home, they should keep their car in the garage, if possible, and use automatic timers on lamps so it would be more difficult for someone to know when they were home. Run every call through an answering machine. Use a route out of your neighborhood that lets you check to see if you are being followed. We even had them go to a special mechanic who drilled holes in the trunk of their car and installed a thick chain that kept the trunk from being opened all the way — which made it a little more difficult for thieves in a hurry to pull the suitcases out.

We kept current on the latest technology in security equipment, too. Although what mattered most was the skill of the guard using them, those systems were continually evolving and improving. The first-generation metal detectors we had used at the company had been designed for finding knives and guns, not small pieces of jewelry. A zipper or an underwire bra could set it off — and, realizing that, some thieves hid gems in those places — but even the old machines paid for themselves in ways that had nothing to do with thievery. Like most big jewelry manufacturers, Gems and Luxury could have lost substantial sums every year from gems and precious metals accidentally thrown out in the trash, so all G & L's refuse was sent through an x-ray machine before making it to the dumpster. Those first-generation machines were not any good, however, when it came to revealing a diamond or sapphire hidden in a more creative way, or a small stash of gold dust collected by a gem polisher and carried out in a pocket.

Our second-generation detectors were state-of-the-art systems. When they were first installed, we had to see that every employee had a base reading — without watches, belts, or jewelry — to determine the amount of metal already in their body. This could come from fillings in teeth, surgical staples or pins, pacemakers, and the like. If your base reading was, say, .004, and one day you swiped your personalized card into the reader and walked through and it registered .010, there would be a conversation with the guard and perhaps a hand-held scan. Certain employees tried to find ways of getting around this. One young lady dropped a ring into a can of Coke she was drinking, then casually set the can just on the other side of the detector as she was being screened. We caught her — that time, at least. One of her co-workers nestled a pair of emeralds in her cigarette pack; another tried to walk out with a diamond in her mouth. Eventually, we even ended up catching the manager, a well-liked and otherwise dependable guy who had resorted to stealing to cover his gambling debts.

It was often that way, at least when it came to jewelry theft: the thieves had a gambling habit and were in debt to a bookie; they had a girlfriend on the side and needed extra money for gifts; they had gotten deep into drugs and did not have the cash to support their habit. On occasion, I have encountered people who steal simply for the thrill of it, or out of pure greed. They have everything they could possibly want, but they like the feeling of putting something over on a boss, or they get turned on by the risk, or they need to acquire more and more things as a buttress to their flimsy self-esteem. Usually, though, in our experience at least, it was addiction first and stealing second.

In time, we had such a thorough system of checking at Gems and Luxury that I liked to tell the employees there to "dress for express, not to impress." The less metal they wore (with the exception of wedding bands, they were not allowed to wear jewelry), the simpler shoes, the fewer belts and buckles, the easier it would be to get them through the detectors, the faster the line would move, and the greater the general happiness. Eventually we purchased X-ray machines that could pick up a sliver of gold in a lead pipe, we always locked the dumpsters at night and unlocked them in the morning, we had employees carry their personal belongings in and out using transparent plastic bags, and allowed them single cigarettes, not packs, when they stepped out on breaks. We had different undercover agents in place at different times, and Phil's brother, Joe, an ex-cop and the most reliable person on the planet, doing guard duty there in his retirement.

Still, things happened. A woman who worked in the sample room figured out a way to get around all our anti-theft measures. She was lifting things — diamond bracelets, if memory serves — and giving them to her boyfriend, a firefighter. The fireman managed to sell them for her, but he made the mistake of bragging about their operation to friends — or people he thought were friends — in the station house, and using one of these pals to help him fence the stolen material.

We unraveled this chain of deceit and disloyalty only after Amelia, the director of operations at G & L, received a phone call from a man — probably the fence — who said he knew there were employees who were stealing, and he knew how they were getting the gems out of the building. Like the friend-

155

ly guy who had found the Stradivarius on the beach, he offered to share his knowledge for an honorarium: $5,000 and a set of one-karat diamond stud earrings for his wife.

Phil was just returning to work at this point, mostly recovered and participating in a rehab program at the Faulkner Hospital. Through his friend, Bill Monahan, at the phone company, he was able to trace the calls made to Amelia's private phone line, and the next time the man called we had his number, so to speak. And then, using the reverse directory, his name and address. A quick registry search told us what kind of car he drove. Mark and I started to follow him. We followed him so closely, in fact, that at one point we were in a bank of pay phone booths on Revere Beach, with the firefighter standing in a booth next to us, and we could hear him talking to Amelia about setting up a drop.

After consulting with my dad, Amelia — a brave woman — agreed to make the drop at the bottom of one of the off-ramps from the Northeast Expressway. The drop was to take place at midnight; Amelia herself would deliver the money and earrings. Once he had received his payment, the man would call and give her the thief's name and his or her method.

Long before midnight, Phil and Mark set themselves up in the bushes alongside the exit ramp. Fortunately, it was a warm night. Unfortunately, a skunk had made its home in the brambles at the side of the highway there. It is difficult enough to sit quietly in the dark for a couple of hours; harder still when you hold your breath wondering how the skunk will feel about your presence. But the skunk held his fire.

My part in the operation was not much more comfortable. My father had instructed me to lie down on the floor between the front and back seats of Amelia's big Buick station wagon, and keep a blanket over me. "When you get there, take your gun out of the holster and have it ready," he had said. "We don't know how this is gonna play out, and I don't want you having to fish around for your weapon if you need it."

That made things easier.

We drove north on the expressway and took the Sargent Street ramp. Exactly at midnight, Amelia stopped the car, left the money and earrings in a box the guy had left there, a few yards off the road. She flashed her high beams twice, and we drove off. The fireman, it turned out, lived half a mile away on the north-facing slope of a hillside; he could see the flashing lights from his kitchen window. He came and picked up his package. Phil and Mark watched him from the brambles, waited until he was out of sight, and then drove to a convenience store (no cell phones in those days) and notified a detective friend of Phil's in the local police. The detective was waiting for the call. Together with Mark and my father, he and other officers drove to the fireman's home, surrounded it, and made their presence known. There was an amusing moment when, realizing he was caught and trying to get rid of the evidence, the fireman tossed the envelope with the money and earrings out one of his windows. The envelope landed at my father's feet.

The firefighter was arrested. He "sang", as the saying goes, naming names and providing details. In our experience, this is almost always the way it plays out. Once the evidence against them is clearly established, only a very few hard-core criminals keep to the honor code of silence, and even then it is almost always in their own interest to do so. Just about everyone else — whether it is a murder case and a life sentence or several years for stealing and extortion — is eager to give any information that will reduce the time behind bars. It is unsurprising, I suppose, but maybe if potential criminals understood this aspect of human nature, it would act as a bit of a deterrent.

The next day, my father and I confronted the actual thief in a conference room of Gems and Luxury. She started weeping uncontrollably and giving reasons why she had been forced to resort to stealing — again, a perfectly typical reaction. That time, though, there seemed to be real desperation to her tears, and I felt sorry enough for her that, once she was taken away, I was on the verge of telling my father I thought we might cut her some slack, just this once. But Dorothy was undercover at G & L then, and had befriended the woman, even "stolen" a few things herself in order to be accepted. A few days later, the woman met Dorothy and some other co-workers in a bar, had a couple of drinks, and started bragging about how she had fooled the detectives with her fake crying act. She thought, because of it, that she might get off. She did not — a lesson for her, perhaps, in the limits of deceit.

A lesson for me, too: that experience has put a damper on my sympathies to this day. Maybe it is similar to the way cops feel when they pull over a driver who has been speeding and the driver starts making excuses or begging for a break or naming highly-placed acquaintances in state government. We are always catching people in the act of doing something they should not do. Half the time they confess, sometimes they cry and ask to be given a break. Strangely, in my experience, it is the big guys, the tough guys, who break down and admit everything, and the little old ladies with blue hair and light fingers who look straight at you, with a mound of evidence against them, and admit to nothing. As Richard and I like to say to each other: we have seen the man behind the curtain, and it is not the all-powerful Oz. Either way, I have been privy to so much of this over the years that a kind of film has formed over my naturally soft heart. Again and again, I have watched thieves and cheaters beg for forgiveness, ask for a break, pour out a sad story of hardship and stress that forced them to do what they did. In the early days, my first instinct was to believe them, but time and experience have shown me that most people who cross that line are sorry about it only because they got caught. Given a second chance, they would most likely use it to steal or cheat or manipulate all over again, only more carefully. These days, I reserve my compassion for those with stress and hardship who do not use it as an excuse, and do not pass that hardship onto someone else.

In the late '80s, Warren Derzen took Gems and Luxury public. The stock offering raised a huge amount of cash, and he went on a buying spree, snapping up prestigious companies from a Massachusetts-based firm with a long history of making trophies and rings, including World Series rings — to a prominent New York wedding ring manufacturer. This meant more work for us, trips to Texas and New York, among other places, to supervise the shipping of merchandise, or the designing of security systems. Eventually, though, the debt incurred by this spate of acquisitions ran up hard against an economic downturn. Zales, one of their best customers, declared bankruptcy. G & L had trouble making timely payments to their bond holders, and in the mid-1990s, Warren was forced out by a new Board of Directors.

We had a twenty-year relationship with him, mutually beneficial, but with his departure Richard and I could see the handwriting on the wall. We continued to work with Gems and Luxury for another few years, but by early 1997 the company was barely keeping its doors open, and in order to protect the jobs of our security guards there, we ended up making a deal. G&L would hire our guards as regular workers, moving them from our payroll to theirs; we would step away. This stepping away was not easy for us, however. For more than twenty years, Gems and Luxury had been our biggest client, a steady source of income in good times and bad. As a type of bittersweet cherry on the many-layered cake that had been our business with G & L, the Board agreed to pay us a severance fee, which softened the blow somewhat. Three years later they declared bankruptcy, but the building is still there. I drive by it sometimes on other jobs. There is only a single bit of remaining evidence of the years of jewelry-making: one corner of the parking lot is still guarded by the old, barb-wire-topped fence.

# BOOK THREE
## Personal Challenges

# TWENTY
Binding of the Family Book

*"Men are what their mothers made them."*
- Emerson

In other books that focus on the world of business and law enforcement, the personal dimension is often left out, and this has always troubled me. It is as if the business dealings exist on a plane untouched by human relationship, as if the big deals and bankruptcies, the dramatic crimes and investigations are done by machines who have no wives, husbands, or children, none of the pain and joy and worry that always gets carried into the office or along a dark city street. The period from the late '70s to the late '80s included the height of our work with G & L, the growth of my sense that I could handle most things that came down the line, and Richard's full involvement of every aspect of the business. But, I remember it more for the personal side of things than for the cases we worked on. The two are inextricably linked, of course, in any life, and I have tried to link them here in this story. In a family business, especially a small family business, one in which the family is close-knit, as ours was and is, the shocks and symphonies of household life reverberate and sound in the office with a particular force.

Once my father was back on his feet after the major heart attack, he and my mother decided they wanted to sell the small house where they had raised us and buy a more comfortable home a few miles farther from the city. Their timing was not good — at this point, the school busing controversy and violence associated with it had driven home prices down in most Boston neighborhoods — but, in their late fifties and early sixties, respectively, my parents felt it was time for them to make the move.

After searching for a several months, they found a piece of land on a quiet cul de sac in Dedham, eight miles to the south and west. They hired a builder, a man named Charlie Zacarias, and my father immediately began to torment him. Any carpenter's worst nightmare is building a home for another carpenter. The only project with more headaches is building a home for a client who has the skills, but has spent his working life doing something else. This client was my dad.

To make things worse for Charlie, my father — still recuperating from the heart attacks in the late '70s — had an abundance of time on his hands. His contribution to the agency was essential, but, in terms of time, only about a quarter of what it had once been; at that point, I was really running things. Routinely, my dad would drive over to Dedham to see how the house project was coming along, and he would make Charlie's life miserable.

That was not his intent; he was not a mean man (though he would, unfortunately, badger the cooks and waitress at IHOP to put more filling in the cheese blintzes, sending the dish back so often that the rest of us would be cringing with embarrassment in the booth), and, having done so much of it himself, he had a full measure of respect for people who worked with their hands. It was just that, from police work, to the Strangler investigation, to building stone walls, my father was a sometimes troublesome mixture of perfectionist and workaholic. He did everything three times as thoroughly as it needed to be done. If the doctor said take two aspirin, Phil would take six; if he could have left at 6 a.m. for our trip to Miami, and driven ten hours, he left at 2 a.m. and drove sixteen; where someone else might have taken a shortcut and accepted another investigator's work, Phil did the job all over again, himself. Probably the best example of this is something I mentioned earlier: long after Andrew Tuney and Jim Mellon and even John Bottomly had abandoned the Strangler Bureau, my father hung on, doggedly putting the last pieces together, stubbornly trying to get the murder convictions and close the case. That was the way he did everything, crossing every 't' and dotting every last 'i'. And, he seemed to think it was self-evident that everyone else on earth ought to have the same attitude.

He would go over to Dedham with a red magic marker and tromp around the worksite marking pieces of wood with big red X's. These pieces were not to be used in his new home. "Too many knots," he would say to Charlie. "Too bowed. What the hell are you doing usin' wood like this to build my house?! What kind of shoemaker are you?"

Charlie would yell back; the two of them would stand there shouting at each other on the quiet suburban cul de sac. It got so bad that, whenever my father said, "Hey, who wants to take a ride over and see how the new house is comin' along?" we would scramble around looking for an airtight excuse. Gee, Phil, I'd like to, but I have to go over to Gems and Luxury today. Or, I need to get the oil changed in my car. Or, I want to watch the end of the football game. The Patriots are only four touchdowns behind."

Eventually, despite these small wars, the new home was completed, a roomy, two-story raised Cape with a two-car garage beneath it, and a bay window my mother liked. There was a backyard big enough for all the grandchildren, a flower garden, and a feeling of privacy and spaciousness my parents had never known in West Roxbury. I thought something was missing, though. For months I badgered my dad about putting in a swimming pool, turning the backyard into a place that would be fun for the grandchildren. We would be sitting in the new house having lunch and I'd say, "Hear that, Phil?"

"What? I don't hear anything."

"That splashing sound, don't you hear it? It's your grandchildren enjoying the pool you put in."

"Will you stop!" my father would say.

Or, I would go out and pace off a rectangle in the yard, making sure he was watching from the back door. "Now what are you doin'?"

"About sixteen by thirty-six would be nice, I think. You could put the diving board at this end."

He would wave a hand, tell me to cut it out, resist for a while. But eventually he relented, and, once the hole was dug, the concrete poured and the whole thing filled up and filtered, he probably ended up spending more time in the water than anyone else. There was a short set of stairs leading up from the main section of the yard to the pool area, and we bought a couple of big concrete lions and had them positioned at either side of the top step, a grand touch that Phil seemed to appreciate.

Like our business situation at that point, our family life seemed to be sailing along smoothly. Dorothy and I had been married the previous fall and were living happily in Hyde Park. (Yes, a drug dealer lived in the modest house next door, and yes, he broke into our home and stole many things — including food from our refrigerator — and yes, I went through his trash and found the evidence, and yes, I ended up cramming some of the trash into his mailbox to let him know that I knew, and yes, a few months later, I took a lawn chair and sat out in the front yard with a beer and watched as he was led away in handcuffs; but still, we had a nice little home of our own, Dorothy and I; it was one minute from the golf course, and we were in love.)

Thanks to Jean and Ed, there were grandchildren in the picture. My dad had slowed down a bit. He and my mom, married thirty years by then, still had their regular date-night on Fridays at the Howard Johnson's 57 restaurant in Park Square. Some of my warmest memories have to do with meeting them there when I was out and about in town. My dad was relaxed and happy with his plate of prime rib, my mother with her baked stuffed shrimp, both of them pleased to have me sit down with them, both of them interested in what I was doing, each sharing some of their meal.

And then one day, this calm, happy period of our lives came to an abrupt end. My mother was working out on an exercise machine my father had bought when he was rehabbing from his heart attack, and she felt a sharp pain in her lower back. At first she thought she had just pulled a muscle. She went to see her regular doctor — who had always been a kind of god in our neighborhood — and he agreed that it did not seem to be anything serious: she had a physical six months earlier, she was in good health. A little rest, heat, some massage, and the lower back pain would go away. But, our local god had missed something. Shortly after that appointment, my mother had dinner in the North End with her sister, Ruthie, they went for a stroll in the waterfront park there, and she tripped and twisted her ankle. A lump formed, as suspicious-looking as it was painful. She made an appointment to see an oncologist named Doctor Cady at Deaconess Hospital, and I happened to be sitting on the couch in the new home in Dedham when she returned. My mother walked through the door and limped into the living room. She came over, put her arms around me and said, "Johnny I've got cancer, and it's not good."

The kind of cancer she had — "chordoma" it is called — manifested itself at first in painful, unsightly lumps in her arms and legs and on her back. Dr. Cady tried surgically removing them, but they were metastasizing too quickly. She changed her diet. She underwent chemotherapy. With my father and sister and me, she attended a ceremony at the Mission Church, at which Father McDonough, a noted faith healer, laid his magical hands upon her and prayed for a miracle. At his touch, my mother fainted. My sister, Evelyn fainted, too (for her, the experience led to a life of devotion to Jesus Christ).

For a while after that, my mother seemed to feel better, but then the disease attacked her body in earnest and we could see that she was failing. Everyone chipped in. Richard was living at the new house; on weekends he would be out with his friends until two in the morning, then come home and make himself stay awake until five, because he knew my mother would wake up then and would need help getting out of bed. He would get her up and washed and make sure she had breakfast, before he finally went to sleep. Evelyn was at the house for so many hours every week that her marriage suffered and eventually broke up. Dorothy, who had become close friends with my mother, cooked and tended to her, as did Jean. I spent many nights there. Ed arranged for her medical care. That time was so stressful for all of us, that I stopped being able to eat and lost fifteen pounds in a couple of months.

After a procedure called a "spinalectomy" in which, in order to remove a tumor pressing against the spinal cord, several of her vertebrae were taken out and replaced with artificial ones, my mother was confined to a wheelchair. Phil bought a special hydraulic lift with a swinging arm (it had a sheepskin seat) to help get her into and out of bed. Even as the pain and inconvenience steadily increased, though, there was no complaining, never a hint of *"why me?"* That simply was not my mother's style. She said the rosary and watched TV; she greeted people with a smile when they came into the house, apologized for not being able to make them something to eat. Richard had a dog then, a brown and white Springer Spaniel called Kojak, who loved to hunt the way some cats love to catch mice (so much so that Richard would sometimes tease Kojak by coming out of the bedroom in his orange vest on days when there was no hunting trip planned; the dog would start howling and sprinting in circles), and Kojak became my mother's best friend. He would spend hours sitting on her toes or her lap.

Death came to my mother with a terrible slowness. "She died by inches," is the way Dorothy puts it. We watched her slowly waste away, suffering to a degree that seemed monumentally unfair for a woman of her generosity and warm heart. Near the end, she could not get out of bed, could not talk, could not swallow. Her veins could no longer accept the morphine needle, so all we could do for her was to call in the good Hospice people, and occasionally moisten a washcloth and touch it to her parched lips. On the night she died, just hours before she took her last breath, Kojak let out such a piercing, pitiful howl that we all felt it in our bones.

It would be impossible to overstate the effect that my mother's death — June, 1983 — had on our family. Although the agency was my father's business, and though his was the more forceful personality in our family, my mother had really been the binding that held the book together — home and office both.

She could wear the disguise of quiet wife and homemaker, submitting to my dad's authority, yet my mother would stand up to him if he got too loud with her. It was she who nudged him toward accepting me into the business, my mother who did the books and cooked the meals, my mother who took the car to the gas station at 6 a.m. during the oil embargo — sometimes waiting in line an hour to ensure that my dad started the day with a full tank; my mother who went to work on a factory assembly line for a time after my father's first heart attack when we needed the money, and my mother who, when I planned to move my belongings from Roslindale into their house during the two-week gap between the end of my apartment lease and the wedding, said, "Just move in with Dorothy, John." Which was not what Catholic mothers said in those days, and was testimony both to the love she felt for Dorothy and the confidence she had in her own understanding of what was right and wrong.

"You can do it as well as anybody," she told Richard a hundred times in his first shaky weeks at college. When my sister Jean was living nearby, with her husband Ed working the long hours of a medical resident and with two young boys in the house, my mother — who was always up for her prayers and solitary walk at 5:30 in the morning — would leave a bag of hand-cut donuts from Anna's and two small cartons of orange juice on Jean's front step. On rainy days, she would go over there and help keep the boys occupied. Later, when Ed and Jean moved to Vermont, my mother would sometimes call me up on a Friday and say, "Johnny, your sister's lonely. I want you to go up and get her and the kids and bring them down here for the weekend." And I would make the four-hour drive to Burlington, collect Jean and her rambunctious little ones, and bring them back to Boston for a few days of pasta and affection.

In the family, we sometimes referred to her as "Big Evie," to distinguish her from my sister, "Little Evie". In fact, though she was not physically large, there was a huge spirit shining out from within her, a strength so full of warmth and generosity that her passing left an enormous and unfillable hole in our lives. "There was a light that was transferred from my mom to us," is the way my sister Evelyn puts it.

It was months and months after her death before the rest of us could get back to anything like a normal schedule. The binding of the family book had been broken. There is no way to fix something like that, no way to measure what she gave us, and no way to tell the story of our work and our family without giving my mother this small acknowledgement.

# TWENTY-ONE
Do Not Go Gently

*"Rage, rage against the dying of the light."*
-Dylan Thomas

My dad retired two years later, a gradual process that was nowhere near as physically painful as my mother's passing, but had almost as much tension and angst associated with it. Knowing Phil as we did, it was probably too much to hope for that he would move smoothly into old age without kicking and screaming. Whatever lack of calm acceptance he might have shown us in this regard was only intensified by my mother's protracted suffering and death. I know there were problems between them (how many long-married couples can claim otherwise?) but I also know that there were plenty of gifts and good times (Jean remembers Christmas Eve shopping trips with our father; he would go to Leeds, a dress shop on Beacon Hill that was out of his price range, buy a dress he thought would look nice, and load up the box with tissue paper so my mother had a little extra thrill, opening it on Christmas morning). It was a relationship typical of an older generation, with the husband considering it his duty to bring home a paycheck, and the wife considering it her duty to support him in that, to keep the house and feed the family.

When she was gone, when, at sixty-four years old and the veteran of four heart attacks, Phil could clearly see the evidence of old age gaining on him, he was not exactly a textbook example of mellowness.

After the series of heart attacks, my dad was religious about his rehab program — I would go to the health club and work out with him three days a week. Still, he never regained his strength, and that was a wound to his pride. "Look at these arms," he'd say to my brother-in-law. "Look at me, I'm rotting. I used to be so strong." He seemed to be constantly on one medication or another, including something called Lasik which regulated the fluids in his body and which he referred to as "the water pill."

At one point, pulled over for speeding on Route 3 north of the city, he protested so vehemently that the State Cops handcuffed him and charged him with three criminal counts. The whole thing was a mess, an ugly confluence of my dad's inflated pride and the Staties inflated sense of entitlement. They charged him. He sued them. Eventually all the charges were dismissed and the suit dropped, but it was another sign that our father was not going gracefully into his sunset years.

The most difficult aspect of this late-life crisis, for us, was that he took up with a much younger woman. In one sense this was not so surprising. For the past fifteen years, he had been something of a celebrity in Boston. People remembered seeing George Kennedy on the screen, holding out his hand and saying, "I'm Phil DiNatale." His name had been in the papers a thousand times. He was a good-looking, outgoing man, with plenty of friends and plenty of opportunities to meet women. Rich and I and our sisters might have been happy for him . . . if we had liked the woman (I'll call her JoAnne), if we had not had the sense she was just milking my father for every dollar he was worth, and if he had not tried so hard to get us to accept

173

her — too soon, in our opinion, after our mother's death.

At this point in the life of the agency — the middle '80s — my father did not work on cases much, but his name still counted for something in attracting clients, and he maintained a list of friends and contacts, in Greater Boston and elsewhere, that proved invaluable to us. "Phil," I would say, "we just got a murder case in Maine, who do you know there?"

"Bucky Buchanan."

Or, "Phil, we have to go to San Francisco to track down the daughter of a client. Anybody there we can call?"

"Eddie Bigorino."

He knew investigators from New York to Los Angeles, cops in Western Massachusetts and New Jersey; he was made an honorary captain of the New Orleans P.D. It was next to impossible to name a part of the country where he did not know somebody in law enforcement, and these contacts were always willing to help "Phil DiNatale's boys" out of a tough spot. Rich and I were comfortable in the business by then. I had been at it full-time for almost ten years, Rich for more than five. But my father's experience stretched back four decades, and we were never shy about asking his advice.

But he was not good at taking ours. "Phil," one of us would tell him, "you've had four heart attacks, you're on sixteen different medications, what are you doing staying out till midnight?"

None of our well intentioned pleas, not even the professional advice of Ed, the doctor in the family and a man Phil respected and liked, could budge him out of his determination to burn the candle as fiercely as he could. Once, in the hospital for what he called a "tune-up", he became so frustrated at his condition that he ripped the I.V. out of his arm. Back in the social whirl he loved, he and JoAnne would be out until the small hours, drinking martinis and carrying on. He would get up in the morning and drive her to work, then come by the office, have coffee and hang around with us for a while, ask questions about what we were working on, offer to help. He would go over and talk with Eddie for a while, or ask to be driven to the Arch Street Chapel so he could say his prayers. He would have lunch, go home for a nap, then be out with Jo-Anne again in the evenings. A nice schedule for a thirty-year-old; for my aging father with the half-destroyed heart, a prescription for disaster.

Frustrated as we were, there was not much we could do. JoAnne was working him, and we knew it, and he did not, and when he came to the office one day and said he wanted us to take care of her when he was gone, that was the spark that set off a full-scale battle. Richard and I said: *Look, you've spent your whole life telling us to pay attention to how people behave, showing us the guys who ruined their lives because they fell crazy in love, made bad decisions, threw good things away chasing something better. We have no problem with you dating her, we want you to be happy. But that's your life, not ours, and we're not going to be saddled with her. If push comes to shove, we'll get our own licenses and start our own business.*

After so many years of working together harmoniously, that was a very painful afternoon for all of us, two hours bursting with raised voices and hurt feelings. Blinded by infatuation, my dad could not understand why we didn't want to give Jo-Anne a piece of the company we had all worked so hard to build. Much later, I found a handwritten will he composed on the night after that big argument: in it, he said he wanted to leave everything to Saint Jude's Children Hospital, nothing to his sons. He had second thoughts and never filed it, but the lines of careful printing stand as a testimony to the depth of his feelings on that day.

Eventually, Eliot our accountant prevailed upon him. As families often do, we put the argument behind us and, while we never did warm up to JoAnne, we did eventually agree to have a dinner with her one night at Jean's house — which pleased my dad. In accordance with Eliot's professional advice, Phil sold us his stock in the agency, at the rate of $500 a week, started collecting Social Security, and made a graceful exit, with no provisions for Jo Anne other than ones he might have arranged for privately. We made sure he could accomplish this transition without worrying about finances and without losing his dignity. He had a car, a credit card, the $500 a week, and the sense that he could stop by the office the way he had always done, and he would always be welcome there. He lived with that . . . for two years. At some point in this period he came to me and said, "Johnny, I want the license to be in your name now." It was a real gesture of love, because having his name on the wall had always meant a lot to my father. It was also, I thought, a sign that he was ready to move on.

One afternoon he came by and went into the bathroom and did not come out. After fifteen minutes I called — no answer — then knocked — no answer, then opened the door. I found him passed out standing up, leaning against the wall. Despite the fact that alcohol did not agree with one of his medications, he had been out for a lunch with JoAnne and had a couple of drinks.

From there, it was a not-so-slow downhill slide. He had developed congestive heart failure. Because of the big heart attack in Springfield, there was not enough muscle left to support any kind of a repair job, bypass surgery or anything like that. Ed helped get him the best medical care in a city known for great medical care, but he could not convince Phil to change his lifestyle — the late nights and martinis, the Oreo cookies, the five-times-a week pasta dinners — and Phil could not understand why the doctors couldn't just patch him up like corner men tending to a boxer, and send him back out into the swirl of the city for another round.

Near the end of Phil's days, Ed and Jean were generous enough to take him to live at their home. Jean made meals for him and put up with his moods; Ed helped with the medical advice. The youngest of their four sons remembers him mostly as "a grouchy old guy who lived with us", and it hurts that he did not know the more vibrant man we grew up with. On the morning of Superbowl Sunday, 1987, Phil complained of chest pains — a daily occurrence in those hard days. "Just eat your grapefruit and don't worry about it," Jean said, at first, but then Phil let out a sound that was like a drawn-out moan with some words mixed in. "Do you want me to call an ambulance?" she asked.

"No," Phil said. But then, as Jean was leaving the room, he changed that no to a yes. She made the call. By the time the ambulance arrived, he had taken his last breath.

Hundreds of people attended the funeral service at Saint Susannah's in Dedham. After the burial, many of them came up to me and Richard and told stories about working with Phil, reminded us again what a good cop and detective he had been, what a decent friend. We had, as all children do, a thousand memories of our own. Despite some tough moments in the later years, we had what a lot of sons never have: the chance to work with our father and have a first-hand appreciation of his skills. Along with so many other traits — physical and otherwise — he handed those skills down to us. Now the long apprenticeship was over.

# TWENTY-TWO
Death and Life and Death

*"I have known sorrow and learned to aid the wretched."*
-Virgil

Maybe it is true that part of children's purpose in the world is to compensate their parents for other losses, to fill the void left by the death of a mother or father. Though the noisy rides back and forth to Burlington had given me pause about the idea of having children, and though Dorothy had suffered a miscarriage early on, as if in compensation for the loss of my mother, we were blessed with a daughter, Lindsay, in early 1985. And, as if in compensation for the loss of my father, we were blessed with another girl, Jackie, in 1990. Partly because of the people we are, partly because of what we have seen in our work — the fragility of life is made clear to us on a daily basis — and partly because we both grew up in close-knit families, Dorothy and I have made family life the sun around which everything else orbits. The girls are our treasures, and through the ordinary difficulties of daily life, we have tried always to make them aware of that.

There have been some extraordinary difficulties, as well. A little more than a year after Jackie was born, Dorothy became pregnant again. In July of 1991, she gave birth to a son, who we named John Drew, and nicknamed *J.D.* From his first breath, it was clear that J.D. was going to have more than his share of physical troubles. He had trisomy-21, Down Syndrome. He required a feeding tube. In his second day of life, he was taken to the Boston Floating Hospital for surgery to repair holes in his heart. Dorothy was recovering from the Caesarian section birth, but she insisted — against her doctor's strong objections — in getting out of her bed and riding across the city to be with him. The care J.D. had at that hospital was enough to restore your faith in human goodness forever, and the courage the little guy showed, the good nature with which he endured his suffering, has inspired me every day since.

One-year-old Jackie was having some serious physical problems at the same time — she had started having febrile seizures eight months earlier, and had suffered through a long series of them. As I sat with a doctor and listened to him go into detail about the cardiac catheterization he was about to perform on J.D. and the potential of death because he was such a high-risk case, he stopped and said, "Do you have to be somewhere? You seem like you're barely listening."

"I'm listening," I told him. "It's just that I have a one-year-old daughter at the other end of the hall. She's been having seizures and they're doing an EEG, and my wife can't hold her because she's just had a C-section, and I need to be there to get her to calm down enough to keep the electrodes on." And, when the doctor was finished, I literally ran down the hall to get to Jackie's bedside.

Jackie soon came home to us and later became famous as the girl who sneaked away under the backyard fence every chance she got. J.D. survived the various surgeries and procedures, but had breathing troubles, was prone to infections, and ended up spending eighty eight days in the hospital before he was allowed to be discharged. Dorothy wore the same perfume, Obsession, every day for those months so that he would recognize her when she came into the room and know she was not a nurse. I held him and sang him to sleep ("Home, Home on the Range", for some reason) every night. Even after he was allowed to leave the hospital, J.D. needed constant attention. We hired a nurse to come in and care for him at night, so we could get some sleep. And we had a wonderful nanny named Josephine Madden, who had just arrived from Ireland and cared for sixteen-month-old Jackie like a mother, gave her tea with three sugars in her bottle, and taught her to sing "Danny Boy". Josephine had a strong brogue, and for a while we would come home to the strange and wonderful sound of our little girl showing off her small vocabulary in the accents of County Cork.

One night in October, when he had been home less than three weeks, J.D. was so miserable that even the nurses could not keep him calm. We listened to him crying into the small hours of the morning, then got up, saw how much distress he was in, and called the doctor. The pediatrician told us to bring him to the office in Needham, so we bundled him up, sat him in the front seat between us, and headed off. It was only a fifteen-minute drive, but halfway there J.D. started to cry in a terrible way, and then he let out an awful-sounding gasp. His face turned blue. We didn't know whether to stop and call an ambulance, or speed on to the doctor's office. Dorothy was pushing on his little chest and breathing into his mouth. She rushed into the medical building with J.D. in her arms, and then two doctors strapped him onto a board and ran him across the lot to the next-door hospital, working on him the whole way, and then for another forty-five minutes in the emergency room before they finally gave up.

No doubt the hardest thing we have ever had to do in our life was to go to Saint Joseph's in Needham, Lindsay's school, and tell our six-year-old daughter that her brother was gone.

I remember, most vividly, the sense of gloom that descended over all of us then. For weeks, I was not able to work, and Dorothy was able to do little besides feed and care for Lindsay and Jackie. It was not easy for a six-year-old and a one-year-old to have a death in the family (though, in truth, Jackie did not understand what had happened, and her innocence and energy helped to keep the rest of us functioning). Everything was a reminder — every TV commercial with a baby in it, every stroller we saw on the street, the clothes and stuffed animals in J.D.'s room.

Our family — Jean and Ed and Evelyn, Richard and Siobhan — and our many generous neighbors were a source of tremendous comfort in those dark days. We did not cook a meal for month. Diane Moynihan and Carol Flaherty were angels more than friends. Another close friend, Liz Manning, whose husband owned The Stockyard restaurant, brought us whole cooked roast beefs. Other neighbors would come by and take Jackie and Lindsay out for dinner, to give Dorothy and me a couple of hours alone. We received notes and letters from people whose lives had been changed by the example of J.D.'s joy and courage in the face of near-constant suffering. (We have only a single photo of him without a feeding tube in his mouth. We snapped it while the tubes were being changed, and caught his radiant smile.)

After the funeral, contributions to his memorial fund poured in, including donations from three classy twelve-year-old boys who had won money in our golf tournament and handed it over to us before it ever reached their pockets. We ended up using the donations to buy chairs, a crib, toys, and a stroller for the other sick children to use at the Intermediate Care Nursery of New England Medical Center's Floating Hospital.

In the eulogy Dorothy and I wrote, and Ed was able to read for us, we promised that, from that day forward we were going to replace our mourning with a celebration of J.D.'s life.

But, that was easier said than done. He was buried along-side my parents on the last day of October, 1991, yet it was six months or more before we were able to dismantle the crib and give it away. For at least that long, we slept with the knitted blue and white blanket one of our employee's mothers had knitted for J.D. as a welcome-to-the-world gift. We could smell his scent on it. I still sometimes come home to find that Dorothy has taken a nap and draped the blanket over herself. We planted a Japanese Red Maple in his honor in our back yard, and for years I would go out and shovel the snow away from it to make sure it survived.

In a sad irony, a few years later, Richard and his wife, Si-obhan, would also lose a son. Their Harry, born with a number of problems they knew about in advance, lived only two days. It was particularly painful for Siobhan, a labor and delivery nurse, to go back to work after that tragedy.

I include this story here, not for sympathy, but because this is a book about both family and business, and J.D.'s short time with us left a profound mark on our professional as well as our personal lives. Many times in the course of our work we have been called upon to interview parents who have just lost a young child. The causes of death have varied — drownings in a backyard pool, car crashes, household accidents, chokings, ba-by blanket fires, gas explosions, accidental shootings — and of course, at those moments, Richard and I cannot help but think of our own sons. In the faces and voices of the devastated par-ents we see a reflection of our own bottomless grief. Probably it is the most difficult thing we ever have to do — sit down with these men and women and ask them to go through a de-tailed recitation of the events surrounding the death of their child. It is not a time when they want to talk at length to a stranger about the most intimate tragedy one can experience. I like to think that, because of our own understanding of that grief, we bring a human dimension to the process that makes it one small degree less awful. And perhaps, for us, that is another part of the healing.

# TWENTY-THREE
The Other Way of Losing a Child

*"It almost looks as if analysis were the third of those "impossible" profes-
sions in which one can be quite sure of unsatisfying results. The other two,
much older-established, are the bringing-up of children and the government
of nations."*
- Sigmund Freud

I t is possible to look at our business — probably any business — as something that grows out of the infinite complexity of human relationships. People are made up of a
million needs, urges, quirks and attitudes, some of them
healthy, some destructive, some out in the open air, some secret. Almost any time a transaction is involved, even something
as simple as having breakfast at the local diner, there is a meeting of two personalities. These encounters always contain the
potential for friction or affection. When the relationship is
more complicated — employer/employee, say, or broth-
er/sister or husband/wife — then the potential stored inside
each personality can begin to look something like the force
stored inside an atom. In every case I can think of, our work
has had its roots in this territory, the dark, fast-moving atomic
world where previously invisible needs and dissatisfactions spin
and collide for a time before bursting up through the surface.

Thinking about it this way, I can understand why a husband or wife wants proof of a mate's infidelity. Maybe the unproven weight of it is just too heavy a load to carry through the days. Maybe the photos of the theater manager walking hand in hand with his girlfriend, painful as it must have been for his wife, was finally a visible, tangible confirmation of the loss of his love. (Or maybe, as had happened with a few of my father's domestic cases, the unfaithful mate was shocked to see his or her behavior captured on film, and that shock led to a sincere repentance and gave the marriage a second chance.)

Someone stealing diamonds from the jewelry company where they work, someone collecting disability for a bad back that is not really hurting, someone being betrayed by his or her spouse — at first, these transgressions grow in the hidden soil of an individual's thoughts. And then, at some point they move out into the open air. They bear fruit, and cause pain, whether that pain is financial or emotional, tiny as a husband sneaking a cigarette, or enormous as a man compelled to rape or murder. When someone calls our office or walks through the door, there is almost always some trouble involved, some human interaction that has borne bad fruit. Occasionally it has a comical aspect. More often, it is a glimpse into a deep pit of anger, dishonesty, mental illness or betrayal. Sometimes it is all of the above in one package.

The relationship between two people who are married or living together is certainly one that holds a tremendous potential — for love or for trouble. I have had scores, maybe hundreds, of conversations with betrayed wives and husbands, and I am acutely aware of the wound infidelity inflicts. But from what I have seen, during almost forty years of working in the heat given off when people come into conflict, that pain takes second place to what can happen between parent and child. Obviously, the death of a child reaches a place in the surviving loved ones that cannot be touched by anything else in human experience. But the parent-child relationship has many other dimensions to it, and, even when death is not involved, we have seen the power of that.

In addition to smaller troubles (like Jimmy O'Malley hanging out with hippies on the Common) during the Sixties, Seventies, and Eighties we had a large number of cases that involved young people — college-age, mostly — becoming involved in religious cults. Most of these young men and women were well educated and healthy, though they seemed to be looking desperately for a sense of belonging that they were not able to feel from their own family. Ian, whose story is related in Chapter 14, was only one of many examples of this.

During those years, you could hardly walk the streets of downtown Boston without being accosted by a member of some sect who wanted to hand you a piece of literature, talk to you about God, or invite you to come live in a group home and convert to his way of looking at the world. For most passersby, this was a relatively harmless aspect of city life, an annoyance. For a few people, I suppose, it led eventually to a true spiritual path. But the late teens and early twenties is a particularly vulnerable time in our society, the delayed transition to adulthood, and the cults that were active in Boston in those years were not hesitant about taking advantage of a young person's uncertainty, resentment, or mental problems. As a result, it was fairly common for us to have parents come into the office with a particular kind of distress on their faces. Their son or daughter had gotten involved with one of these groups. Could we help them?

There was one such case that had an easy solution: Richard looked at a photo of the missing girl and realized she was living in a boarding house two doors down from our office.

Another time, my father sent Mark Rose and Richard —

then only a college student — to infiltrate a group home owned by a religious cult in Marblehead. My mother was furious. "What if he goes in there and doesn't come back out?" she cried. "Nothing will happen, he's with Mark," my father said. In later years, that became an amusing family story, but for so many parents and young people then, it was all too real a possibility. The son or daughter might eventually leave the cult, but in some cases they would be damaged forever.

Sometimes it is emotional friction that causes a child to break contact with his or her parents. Sometimes, as was the case with Ian, it is involvement in a religious group. And sometimes it is love. Once, I flew to Los Angeles with a client who lived not far from us, a mason — Italian born — whose sixteen-year-old daughter had run away with a black co-worker she had met at a discount clothing store called Filene's Basement.

The dad — I'll call him Vito — was a giant of a man who spoke broken English. He lived with his wife in an exquisitely cared for colonial a few miles from where I had grown up. From conversations she had with one of her daughter's friends, Vito's wife knew their sixteen-year-old had gone to L.A. with her boyfriend, and knew the part of the city where they liked to hang out, though not exactly where they were staying.

So Vito and I boarded a plane and made the long flight, then rented a car and drove to the local police precinct. For whatever reason, even when I showed my investigator's I.D. and talked a bit about my dad and his years on the police force, the LAPD was not interested in lending a hand. If we had any trouble, the desk officer told us, give a call; if not, we were on our own. So Vito and I drove a few blocks, parked in the commercial center of that neighborhood and waited. Without knowing the man very well, I worried that his old-world prejudices might add a layer of volatility to what was already a difficult situation. Not only had his daughter run away at age six-teen, but she had run away with a young man of a different race, and here we were, two white guys sitting in a black section of a city we did not know, waiting for the couple to appear. "Listen, Vito," I said, "when we find them, you're going to have to control yourself. You lay a hand on this guy and we'll end up in jail."

Vito assured me it would not be a problem. Once she saw him, he said, his daughter would come along without a fuss. From similar cases I had seen in the past, I had my doubts. (In one of those cases, we arranged for a father and son to meet in the bar of the Boston Ritz Carlton, and when the son realized his father wanted him to leave the cult, he became enraged, threw a chair through the plate-glass window, and sprinted away across the Boston Public Gardens.)

After only an hour of waiting, Vito and I saw the young couple walking up the block with several friends, and got out and approached them. You could read the surprise on the girl's face, and also, it seemed to me, something else: some kind of half-hidden pleasure or relief that her father cared enough about her to come all that way. She was, after all, only sixteen. At first, the boyfriend started to give us a hard time, but I sug-gested he and I go for a walk, let father and daughter have a private moment, and, albeit with some reluctance, he came along. When we had put a little distance between us and his friends, I told him, "Look, she's a minor. You have to know that, at the end of the day, she's going to have to go home with her dad. If you want, I'll pay for you to fly back with us, but there's no chance she'll be staying here."

By the time we had made a short tour around the block, Vito and his daughter had worked things out. From what I could see, there had not been so much as a raised voice or hurt feeling, so perhaps the prejudice I had worried about had been my own. Vito, his daughter and I took a red-eye back to Boston — I got to know her and like her on that trip — and the boyfriend rejoined her a couple of weeks later. A year after that I bumped into her in West Roxbury and asked her how everything was. "Fine," she said, "We're all set. My parents and I worked everything out."

It would be wonderful — and surprising — if all the parents who hired us were that calm in those situations, and if all the children were so willing to return home, and so glad they did. More typical was a case that came to the office about a year and a half after my father passed away. It was late on a Friday afternoon, Richard was there by himself. The phone rang and on the line was a soft-spoken man with a bit of a Texas twang in his voice. The caller identified himself as Randall Brighams, said he needed to find a young man who had gone missing, and asked if he could meet with someone from the agency and talk about hiring us to find him.

In those years, though my brother was an expert on surveillance cases and had plenty of experience with missing persons work (and everything else that came our way) he was not yet comfortable meeting new clients. This was understandable to me. The initial meeting can be a delicate moment: you hope to inspire confidence in the prospective client, but at the same time you are sizing them up, getting a sense of their truthfulness and reliability, figuring out if it is the kind of situation you want to be involved in, and the kind of people you want to be involved with. And then, there is the question of payment — how much to ask for in advance, what kind of estimate to give about anticipated costs. This is complicated by the fact that there are times when a case does not lend itself to hourly billing, when getting results is not so much a matter of time and employee hours, as of contacts that have been developed over years. I learned all these things at my father's shoulder, watching him in scores of first meetings, questioning him and some-times arguing with him about billing procedures. Richard had not had that opportunity.

He arranged to meet Mr. Brighams at one o'clock on Commonwealth Avenue, near Boston University, and wanted me to come along. I had several things on my plate that day, and so, when one o'clock and then one-fifteen came and went, and Richard and I were still standing outside the car, waiting, I was ready to write off Randall Brighams and get back to busi-ness. The phones we had then were not hand-held cells but ones that were installed in the car itself. Richard asked me to be patient, he sat in the car and made a call. Randall Brighams, it turned out, had gotten lost in Boston's famously confusing criss-cross avenues (Beacon Street, for example, starts off north of Commonwealth Avenue, and ends up well south of it, though both of them run east-west from the center of down-town). He soon arrived — fiftyish, well-coiffed, as soft-spoken in person as he had been on the phone — and we walked up the block and sat in a nearby Burger King.

Randall, as he asked us to call him, had been at a wedding reception in Boston a week or two earlier. He happened to be seated next to Jack Connelly, a friend of Phil's, and a long-time neighbor of ours. They had gotten to talking about Boston, and when Jack said he was the Chief Juvenile Probation Officer in Norfolk County, Randall asked if he knew anyone who did in-vestigative work. Jack gave him our name.

Randall told us he had been involved in the oil business, mostly in the Middle East, for all of his working life. He now ran a company called Two Shore Management, which acted as a kind of general contractor for countries with significant oil reserves. The company did everything from finding the oil, to arranging for drilling experts, to advising the government on locating the most favorable markets. As part of their contract they arranged for young men and women from the client country to attend college in the U.S. and perhaps learn the skills they would need to take over the management of oil reserves when they reached a certain age.

"One of these young people," Randall told us, "is at school here in Boston, a sophomore at the University of Massachusetts. We found an apartment for him at Harbor Point, near the school, just off the expressway. The problem is, he apparently hasn't been back to the apartment in over a month. His parents haven't been able to contact him. The other problem is," he paused and took a sip of his coffee, "his father's the Prime Minister."

We told him we would like to have a look at the apartment, and we all took a ride over there. Harbor Point had recently been renovated, and was then a sprawling complex of townhouses with views of Boston Harbor, the Kennedy Library, and University of Massachusetts. We met the manager in his first-floor office. Since the lease was in Randall's name, we assumed he would be able to get a key and look at the apartment. The manager agreed, more or less, but said he would have to speak to his boss first, and the boss was not around that day. Harbor Point was way over on the eastern edge of downtown; not being able to get into the apartment that day meant we would all have to make another trip, which would have cost everybody money. So I did what I had seen my father do dozens of times — asked the manager to speak with me privately, put a $100 bill in his shirt pocket, and was happy to learn that the boss's approval was no longer needed.

Upstairs, we found the usual living room-bedroom-kitchen-balcony arrangement, though the place had a musty, unlived-in smell. There were books, clothes, and newspapers strewn about, a mattress on the floor. Richard and I started to go through the drawers. It looked like the young man — we will call him Ricky — had taken some clothes along with him. We found a photo of him with a blue and white-striped racing bicycle. The bicycle was not in the apartment or on the balcony so we thought the odds were good he had not been abducted and probably had not jumped into the harbor or otherwise done away with himself. A closer look at the bedroom brought us the pleasant discovery of several used condoms mixed in with the sheets, and then some pornographic magazines, all showing nude and partly-nude men in various provocative poses. Ricky had a cassette answering machine attached to his phone. It was filled with messages — mostly men, but one woman with what sounded like a French accent. Richard and I wrote down the date and time of those messages, and any other information we could gather. One of the voices on the tape belonged to someone who identified himself as Roberto and who said, "I miss you. I've been trying to reach you for two weeks and I get nothing but the machine. Call me." Roberto left a number.

We sat there for a while with Randall, coming up with theories about where Ricky might be. I knew that, with the small amount of information we had been able to harvest from the apartment search and phone calls, and the fact that Randall and his people had already been looking for Ricky for weeks without success, it would probably not be a simple matter to find the young man. He might still be in Boston, he might not. Obviously, he was not eager to get back in touch with either his parents, Randall, or his friends. He did not have an American driver's license, birth certificate, or relatives living nearby, so we were not going to be able to track him down via the usual methods. And, because he had been living in Boston only a year and a half, he would not have decades of friendships we could try to pursue as leads. We did have Roberto's phone number, but Ricky had not seemed too interested in calling him back, either. Clearly we were going to have to go under-cover in the gay community and hope we found someone who knew Ricky and was willing to help us find him.

I asked for a $10,000 retainer fee, and tried, as we always do, to get a sense of how much Two Shores Management was able to spend. Randall wrote out the check right there, and, handing it over to me, said, "When you get to $50,000, call me. On the one hand, we don't want to spend that much. On the other hand, nobody, least of all me, wants to go to the Prime Minister and tell him we put a limit on how much we spent looking for his son. Or that the son is homosexual, for that matter. . . . I should probably tell you that, before becoming Prime Minister, Rick's father was head of the Secret Police."

We had other jobs going then — we always do; sometimes as many as seventy-five open cases at once — but given the length of time Ricky had been missing, the money involved, and his father's position, we decided to concentrate our re-sources and try to locate the young man as quickly as we could. I followed up on the few scraps of information we had found in the apartment — made phone calls, talked to people at the University and the apartment complex, tracked down names. There was no such thing as caller I.D. then, so I used reverse directories to get the full names and addresses of those people — Roberto included. Cal and Timmy began staking out the city's gay bars and meeting places. In a nice coincidence that took us back to the earliest Bowdoin Street days, we had some help from Lorraine — the friend of our fast-typing, tough-talking secretary, Mary (who had become a Winthrop police officer by then). Lorraine was still working the door at the Na-ked i Lounge, and she looked at Ricky's photo and offered to check with her Combat Zone contacts.

When I knocked on the door of Roberto's Savin Hill apartment, introduced myself, and said we were worried about

Ricky's safety, he was not particularly forthcoming. He did give me the names of some gay meeting places, and he did tell me, with some reluctance, that his first encounter with Ricky was in the men's room of the MBTA stop at the Back Bay train station, so I sent Richard over there to stake it out. I remember getting a call from my somewhat provincial brother, who was shocked that there were so many homosexual men in the world, and that so many of them happened to be at the Back Bay station just then. Every Thursday, Friday, and Saturday night for two weeks, Cal and Timmy went undercover in the gay community, holding hands to keep other men from asking them to dance, trying hard to appear comfortable and at home . . . with no results. They never saw Ricky. If any of the men they spoke with knew of his whereabouts, they were not saying so. Every couple of days I would call Roberto and talk to him for a while, making sure he understood we were not out to hurt his friend, or him. Gradually he gave us tiny bits of help. Yeah, he thought he might know where Ricky could be found. But he had not seen him in quite a while, and he was not sure about passing that information on to a private investigator. Ricky's parents' concern for their son's well-being did not seem to make much of an impression on him.

Roberto was not unusual in this respect. It was not the first time we met people who were reluctant to cooperate in missing persons cases. For one thing, it is always a tender matter to choose to break contact with your parents. If you are gay and they do not know it, the tenderness factor goes up by a factor of ten. We were used to reluctant friends, but we also knew that, sometimes, if you are persistent enough and eventually gain their trust, they come to see the situation in a different light and try to help.

At this point in the investigation, Richard followed up on another piece of information: Ricky was engaged to a female physician who lived in Guadeloupe; the phone messages and French accent belonged to her. Given the type of magazines we found in his apartment, and what I had been able to glean from conversations with Roberto, this relationship seemed somewhat unlikely, but Randall had mentioned it to us in our first meeting, and when we brought it up again, his response was: "How soon are you going down there?"

When Richard tells the story now he admits that, in those days, he might have heard of Guadeloupe but had no idea where, exactly, it was and was not particularly eager to go. At first, we tried to find a private investigator on the island. When that failed, we tried to locate someone nearby who might take the job. No dice. And so, armed with nothing more than the woman's name and address, he flew to Puerto Rico, hopped over to Guadeloupe, and took a taxi from the airport to the island's best hotel. The route, he says, brought him through one huge slum, mile after mile of tin-roofed shacks and flimsy apartment buildings, the puddled streets choked with bicycles, the humid air seeming to hang, like the heavy curtain of poverty, over thousands of lives. We worked in some of Boston's poorest sections; this, to his eyes at least, was another dimension of life entirely.

At the hotel desk, Richard asked about hiring a driver/translator. By the time he had gotten up to his room and started unpacking his suitcase, there was a knock on the door. He opened it to find a thin black man, dressed in white shorts and a floral shirt. With a heavy French-Caribbean accent, the man said, "I can to translate to you. And drive." The translator gave his nickname: "Speedy." Richard offered him $200 a day for his services — paid in cash, every afternoon — and Speedy was more than happy to accept.

Because of the tropical heat, Richard learned, Guadeloupians were in the habit of starting their workday before the sun came up, and finishing it about noon. At 5:30 the next morning he met Speedy in front of the hotel. They drove to the other side of the island, to the doctor's home address, and, to their surprise, found it to be an apartment in a broken-down building with laundry hanging on the balconies and people already riding off to work on their bikes. Richard and Speedy sat there and waited. For the next seven hours no one went through the apartment door, coming or going. They returned the next day and spent another seven hours sitting there in the heat. You get to know someone fairly quickly under those circumstances, and by the end of the second day, Richard felt he could trust Speedy enough to tell him who this woman was and why they were watching for her. "You should look on her phone calls," Speedy suggested. "See if she call him in the States. If he call her back."

"I'd love to," Richard said. "But it's not like I can go into the phone company here and ask them to show me her records."

This remark brought a smile to Speedy's face. "I come for you tonight. Midnight twelve. At the hotel."

True to his word, Speedy appeared in front of the hotel at midnight. The streets were quiet and dark. He drove Richard to the outskirts of town, pulled into a large parking lot next to a warehouse, told him to wait in the car, and said he was going in to get the records. My brother watched him disappear into the building, and thought there was a good chance he was being set up, the rich white American spying on a good Guadeloupian woman. Now he was going to be robbed, beaten to a pulp by the woman's relatives, or worse.

But in a quarter of an hour Speedy reappeared with a triumphant smile on his face and a sheaf of papers in his hands. He handed the papers across the seat and, pointing to the warehouse, said, "Telephone company. My brother work the third shift there."

They were, in fact, the doctor's phone records for the previous month. But they showed only the calls she had made to the United States, the ones we had heard on Ricky's answering machine, nothing more.

On the drive back to the hotel, Speedy said that the woman was probably leaving for work before they arrived in the morning, and not returning home until late in the evening. He suggested they arrive at the house even earlier the next day, which they did. Instead of risking the waste of another hot seven or eight hours, Richard went up and knocked on the woman's door. It was 4:30 a.m., the doctor did not know Richard and she did not know Speedy, but she let them in, made them tea, and told Richard everything she knew about her fiancé. Which was not very much. He had not called in two months, had not sent her even a postcard in response to several letters. My brother thanked her, spent the rest of the day driving around the island in a last attempt to find anyone who knew Ricky, paid Speedy, and prepared to leave.

The next morning he arrived on time for his flight only to find that the airport baggage handlers had gone on strike. So he did the sensible thing and went to the beach. Not long afterwards, he was joined there by the Air France flight attendants. The women among them did what European women sometimes do on tropical beaches, they took off their bathing suit tops and got some sun. Happily married by then, Richard nevertheless felt that this bit of visual pleasure was a kind of bonus, a reward for having spent four fruitless days so far from home.


In the meantime, I was keeping the conversation going with Ricky's friend, Roberto. After several frustrating phone calls and another in-person visit, he admitted he had seen Ricky again, recently, and knew where he lived. "Look," I told him over the phone, "we're going to find him eventually, with or without your help. I have five new hundred-dollar bills here, your payment for helping out."

Roberto came in and collected his money, then rode with me to the Mission Hill section of the city. His information was helpful, but inexact.

Pinched between the hospital and medical research district of Longwood Avenue, surrounded by Roxbury, Olmstead's Jamaicaway, and Brookline, the three-quarter-square-mile neighborhood of Mission Hill was named "One of the twenty-five best zip codes in Massachusetts" in 2008: artists, bistros, swelling property values, view of the city and diverse population. But it was not that way in the mid-eighties. If Beacon Hill, at the eastern end of Tremont Street, was an enclave of wealthy Brahmins and politicians, then it seemed a proper symmetry that Mission Hill, at the far western end of Tremont Street, would be a neighborhood ravaged by various "urban redevelopment" programs (read: destruction of old buildings) and crime. The well-known Mission Church (where my sister Jean had gone to pray with our grandmother at a very early age, where we had gone with my mother for the healing ceremony, and from which Senator Ted Kennedy would be buried in 2009) gave the area its name, but in early years it had been orchard and quarry land. Later, it was known for a brewery and an orphanage. Later still, it became famous for the place where a young man named Charles Stuart shot his pregnant wife and tried to pin the crime on a nonexistent black man. Harvard University had bought up some of the residential properties and demolished the old red brick buildings. In their place — after protests by local residents — they built the Mission Hill Towers, a trio of twenty-story brick apartment houses with balconies and nice views. Ricky, Roberto said, was living with a friend in one of those towers, sleeping in one of the probably five thousand apartments. He just couldn't be sure which one.

The four of us — Richard, Cal, Tim, and I — staked out the area for another few days, but didn't see anyone matching Ricky's description. At one point I went around the back side of the buildings with a pair of binoculars, and, after searching the balconies for a while, spotted a blue-and–white-striped racing bicycle that seemed to resemble the one we had seen in the photo. Another day of waiting and watching and at last we caught sight of the elusive young man — walking to the corner store with a friend, and then coming back with sodas.

I was on the phone to Randall Brighams before Ricky had disappeared inside the apartment lobby. "Okay, good job," Randall said. "I'll send somebody over to your office, a large gentleman named Mr. John. It's going to take two or three days for him to get here, but I'll call you when he arrives in Boston. You and Mr. John can go over to the apartment building together. When Ricky sees Mr. John, he'll come along without any trouble, I'm sure."

"Who is he?"

"Mr. John? He took Ricky's dad's place as the head of the Secret Police."

Three days later, looking fresh and rested even after his trans-Atlantic flight, Mr. John stepped out of a cab in front of 45 Bowdoin Street. He was the size of an NFL tackle. He had to duck to come through the doorway and squeezed himself four different ways to get comfortable in the front seat of my car. "You are sure he is at this place?" Mr. John asked me.

Yes, I was sure. But when we went to the apartment and rang the bell, no one answered. Mr. John and I sat in my car for at least an hour before Ricky and his friend came strolling up the street. We caught up to them at the front door. In a calm, polite voice my companion said, "Ricky. It is Mr. John, you are to come with me now."

The expression on Ricky's face, when he turned around, was an expression you might expect to see on the face of someone who just came home to find an Ultimate Fighting champion in his kitchen, fists raised. There was not the tiniest bit of protest. Mr. John and Ricky went upstairs, Ricky collected his things. I drove them back to the office, Mr. John used our phone to call a cab, and they headed off for Harbor Point, Logan Airport, and then home. Back, as I imagined it, to a less than comfortable father-son conversation.

# TWENTY FOUR
Going Undercover

*"In every city where there is a discrete and tightly knit gay community, it is much more difficult for straight policemen to go into the gay world than for gays to come out."*
Boston *Globe* April 6, 1980

For heterosexual Americans the gay community can seem like an alien nation. Clearly, there is love, heartbreak, and relationship trouble on both sides of the sexuality fence, but, not so many years ago, homosexual Americans inhabited a world that was almost invisible — bars with no signs over them, meeting places hidden off in the woods, a kind of disguise worn in the working world, held in place to prevent ridicule, discrimination, and worse. In modern times, some of that still exists, but with celebrities stepping out of the closet, gay advocates appearing on talk shows, and various states voting on their preferred definition of marriage, the questions of sexual preference and lifestyle are at least more openly discussed.

It is absurd, of course, to think that, because it has only recently come out into the open air, Boston's gay community is a feature of the modern age. In the days of the Strangler, for reasons a bit difficult to understand now, the authorities, including Attorney General Brooke, suspected a gay man might be doing the killing, and my father and other detectives spent time in gay bars and meeting places and brought a lot of homosexuals in for questioning. For years, the easternmost end of Marlborough Street — one of the better-off sections of the Back Bay — was a known cruising strip called "The Block". Young gay male prostitutes would stroll the sidewalk there, attracting such a line of unwanted automobile traffic that the neighborhood's well-heeled residents managed to get the traffic turned — just for that block — in the opposite direction. To this day it causes out-of-town drivers no end of confusion.

For young men like Richard and me, who had come of age in the close-knit, insular, rigorously Roman Catholic environment of West Roxbury, Massachusetts, being introduced to the gay community through the family business was probably the greatest shock of our professional lives. It was particularly challenging for me the first time I had to go undercover in Boston's gay bars. As often happens, this job came to us indirectly: something happened that set off a series of events, and some person, lawyer, or organization within that series found it useful to hire us.

In this instance, the first domino in that line was the discovery of a prostitution ring in a small city in Boston's metropolitan area. A man with an entrepreneurial spirit and a record of sexual crimes decided to make some money by pimping for homosexual businessmen, some of them from as far away as the west coast. This man, I'll call him Earl, came up with the idea of befriending some of the adolescent boys in his working-class neighborhood, having them to his apartment (located on the middle floor of a large triple-decker) for cookies and milk, for a little beer, or marijuana, for movies and cards, and then making their presence known to men who were interested in sex with underage males. The boys' ages varied from nine to sixteen, and they earned five or ten dollars for allowing themselves to be used sexually. The men might give them presents or money, would pay Earl a fee, and everybody — at least as far as Earl's warped mind was concerned — would go away happy. The fact that these boys might not want a grown man having sex with them never seemed to dawn on Earl; or, if it did, the financial considerations and his own urges outweighed whatever moral qualms he might have felt. (Judging by articles written at the time, the case was, in fact, the source of some controversy in the gay community. Some members of that community saw it as a voluntary arrangement between younger and older men; some saw it as rape. The police had no such ambiguous feelings.)

After he had been in business for two and a half years, Earl was arrested by members of the Suffolk County District Attorney's task force in a sting operation that made the front page of all the Boston papers. Authorities searched his apartment and discovered, among other items, a cardboard box of photos of boys. The local police went to various schools in the area, and, without saying exactly what they were after, showed pictures of these boys to school administrators until several of them were identified. The police took the boys in for questioning, and in the police station, looking at a number of photographs of those the police suspected of being involved, one of these boys — I'll call him Anton — pointed out several men. The police tracked down all of them and pressed charges.

One of these men was H.H., an eccentric, wealthy businessman who lived on an estate in a western suburb. H.H. vehemently proclaimed his innocence, contacted his high-priced lawyer, and the lawyer hired us to see if we could find any solid evidence that would prove H.H.'s innocence. "I've done a lot of things in my life," H.H. told my father and me, with his lawyer present, "but I wasn't part of this ring and I never even met that boy." In fact, in a statement he wrote out for his lawyer, H.H. described himself as "asexual", a term that baffled me at the time.

Prior to this case, my father had never met H.H., but he was well acquainted with his lawyer, Bill Homans, so he believed H.H. was telling the truth. Since Anton was refusing to talk further to the police, we decided to try to find him, and see whether or not his story held water. I was tapped for the job.

H.H. had put me in touch with a friend of his named Nicholas, who agreed to accompany me to Sporter's, a gay bar on Cambridge Street, and then to a nameless bar on Boylston Street, near the Common. Nicholas was an oversized gay man who lived with his young lover in Chelsea, and he was friendly with Anton's foster mother — whom he referred to, for no apparent reason, as "The Indian Woman." He said the Indian Woman had told him that Anton had lied, pointing to men in the photographs simply to get out of the police station as fast as he could.

When Nicholas, his lover, and I stepped into these bars, I was given another glimpse into the limitlessly varied world of human behavior. It was no small shock for a young man like me to stand a few feet away from two burly construction workers passionately kissing and fondling each other. More than that, I was worried I would be seen by an acquaintance, that the word would spread, people would start saying things about me that were not true, and that kind of thing, in my circles, in those days, was not exactly a ticket to popularity. "Nah, don't worry," my father said, when I told him why the assignment worried me. "If anybody you know is in there, they'll be more worried about it than you are."

That was little comfort. Nicholas and I went twice to Sporter's, and once to the bar on Boylston Street. I made the acquaintance of Anton, we talked a bit, and that was the first step.

For the second step, Nicholas arranged for me to meet the Indian Woman, who was straightforward and intelligent and immediately agreed to provide me with a signed statement that repeated what Anton had told her privately: H.H. had not been involved.

Still, we wanted to have that information from Anton himself. Nicholas arranged an invitation to Anton's house one afternoon. The environment there was, if anything, almost as wild as what I had seen in Sporter's, though in a different way: kids running around everywhere, Anton's foster mother seemingly overwhelmed and acting like a high school friend instead of suggesting that her son pick up his clothes, or stop smoking in the house with little kids around, or stop swearing. We found a less riotous corner of the living room and talked for a while. Nicholas worked the conversation around to the prostitution ring and the charges, and then I said, "Anton, listen. You know me. You know I'm a good guy. But I'm not gay. I'm working undercover for a client of ours, H.H."

Anton shrugged, so what?

"I'm here to try to get you to tell me if he was really involved in the prostitution ring, or if you just pointed to his picture that day so you could get out of the station."

Another shrug, more noise from his siblings shrieking and yelling and running around in the rest of the house. But Anton's foster mother seemed to be suddenly paying attention to the conversation. "I don't want to be involved in any more of that shit," Anton said quietly.

"I know. But you're already involved, and here's the thing: H.H. is looking at jail time for what you said about him. And if he did what the other guys did, that's fine. Let's put him away. But if you just saw his picture at the station and pointed to him because you wanted to get the hell out of there, that's not fine.

This guy's going to do some hard time because of that, and he swears up and down he's never even met you."

Anton looked at me for a few seconds, looked away, took a drag on his cigarette and blew out the smoke. His foster mother moved a step closer, suddenly an adult again. She said, "Anton, tell them what you told me."

"Just the truth, that's all," Nicholas prompted.

Anton turned to look at me, blinked, shifted his eyes. "I don't know him."

"Will you write that down?"

Anton had another drag from the cigarette and nodded. I handwrote a one-page affidavit, Anton signed it, the case against H.H. was dropped, and that was the end of my career as an undercover agent in gay bars. (Though, in later years, working with gay clients and trying to find witnesses to an auto accident that had happened in front of a gay bar, I realized that the experience with Nicholas and Anton had given me a certain level of comfort in that community, something I might not otherwise have had.) Earl was sentenced to twelve years in Walpole State prison but cut that time in half by testifying against other child predators he knew. He is currently back out on the streets.

Our agency was not quite finished with H.H., however. Through his attorney, word reached us that, as he had done in the past, H.H. was hosting lavish all-night parties at his estate, inviting friends, acquaintances, and strangers, and that the local police, and State Troopers assigned to the D.A.'s Office were convinced he was up to something illegal — drug dealing, perhaps even murder. Though I knew H.H. well enough to realize these suspicions were groundless, the police were determined to pin something on him. They sent some of their officers to the parties, supposedly undercover, and my father and H.H.'s lawyer both warned him he was taking a foolish risk. Somebody he did not know could make another charge against him and, this time, it would be harder to deny. But H.H. was tall, powerful, very wealthy and not a mild mannered guy. What he did, instead of discontinuing the parties, was to find out who the undercover police were and arrange to have them overhear a conversation that included the lines, "My private investigator, Phil DiNatale, knows the cops are trying to pin something on me. They're following these undercover guys. One little screw-up and we're gonna be all over them."

Which wasn't true, just H.H.'s idea of fun. But the police officers did not know that.

Nothing happened, except that, during our annual license renewal — usually a formality — we were called in to speak with a colonel in the State Police. This colonel had obviously gotten wind of H.H.'s remarks, and he made the mistake of accusing my father of tailing police officers (something we had not done, but which is not illegal) and advising him to be careful what kind of clients he agreed to represent. Phil let him have it with both barrels.

Years went by. We had no further contact with H.H. or Anton. My father died and left me a little money, and I joined a private golf club where I had caddied as a boy, The Charles River Country Club. On my first day as a member I felt some hesitation about walking into the men's grill, approaching a crowd of people who had probably been playing golf with each other for years, and asking to join up with a foursome. I was hanging out at the driving range, practicing, waiting for I do not know what, when an older man named Joe Pascione came over and said, "You know, John, you'll never get a game if you stay down here." So I went up to the Grill, where the pro put me together with three older members just heading out. We had not played three holes when the skies opened — lightning, thunder, torrential rain — and we had to head back to the

207

Grill. Soon the pro announced that, because of the wet turf, no carts would be allowed out onto the course, even if the storm passed. This emptied out the place. Dorothy was away at the time, and I had nowhere better to go, so I ordered something to eat. I was standing at the bar, waiting for the food, watching a golf match on TV, when I heard a voice coming from the direction of the one other person who had stayed around. "You still following me, DiNatale?"

This was Joe McCain, one of the cops who had been assigned to the D.A's office and who would have seen the undercover agents' reports. Six-four, built like a linebacker, he had retired from the MDC police force after being shot in the chest in a drug raid, then opened a private eye business in the North End. Before that day, I had heard of him — he had a reputation for being close with Secret Service agents and other Federal cops — but had never really gotten to know him and had certainly never followed him anywhere. We sat and had a drink and talked, and when the sun came out at last, we headed out onto the course and played nine holes together, the start of a good friendship.

# TWENTY FIVE
The Irreplaceable One

*"Work is love made visible."*
- Kahlil Gibran

In the earliest days of the agency, my father did all the field work himself, made all the calls, wrote up the reports, hustled back and forth across the city interviewing people, following people, talking with lawyers. But even then the success of his new enterprise depended, in part, on Jean and my mother, who edited and typed the reports and handled the money. As the agency grew, there were more people — myself included for a while — who worked in small supporting roles or behind the scenes, but who were nevertheless essential to the smooth functioning of the whole show. Any business works this way. A writer gets credit for his or her books, but not much is ever said about the editor's assistant or the agent's bookkeeper. A famous quarterback earns the large money; his physical therapist keeps his bad ankle working. If I have made it sound here that all these cases were solved by virtue of my father's contacts and *savoir faire*, and, later, by my ingenuity and Richard's brains and hard work, then that does not do justice to the others in our organization. We are indebted to many people, including fine surveillance operatives and investigators like Cal and Timmy, and a lineage of secretaries including Chris, the Wellesley grad from Idaho, who was brilliant enough to have done many other things, but loyal to us for almost a dozen years.

But there was one non-family member whose unsung status meant more to us than anyone else's, and she deserves a special mention.

In 1985, as our business was expanding, we realized we needed to hire another full-time employee. What we were particularly looking for was someone who could go undercover at Gems and Luxury (Dorothy had put in almost two years, more than a full tenure for UC agents), and where — even after we had caught at least a dozen people stealing — the theft problems were continuing. I advertised the position in the *Boston Globe*, without mentioning the undercover aspect, of course, and soon had more than twenty responses.

We have always preferred to hire people with a demonstrated interest in criminal justice, but no experience. We want to train our employees ourselves. Often, we have had applicants who have done something else for five or ten years, then decided they were ready for a change. They had a real curiosity about people, they would tell us. Or, they had a passion for TV shows about private investigators. Or they just had a sense they would love the work and be good at it. Or, worst of all, they were ex-cops or State Troopers who already thought they knew how to do the kind of work we do. We always steered clear of these applicants because the last thing we wanted was to get someone set up, say, in an undercover position, and have them decide a few weeks later that the profession did not suit them after all. For the first couple of weeks, in fact, we always just let the UC agents do their regular job and refrain from asking questions. We want them to get settled in the workplace, and be accepted there.

210

In the fall of 1985 I went through the responses to the *Globe* advertisement, and saw one that caught my eye. Her name was Karen Nasson, she had just earned a degree in Spanish and Sociology from Emmanuel College, and was working part-time as a volunteer dispatcher for the Somerville Police. We arranged an interview at 45 Bowdoin Street.

During that first meeting, Karen seemed very nervous, but I could sense right away how intelligent she was, and that her interest in investigative work was not a passing fancy. As I always did at the close of an interview where the person impressed me, I suggested she go home and think about the job for a few days. I would think about it, too, talk with Richard, and then we would have a phone conversation and see what the next step might be. Karen called a couple of days later and sounded unsure — she was interested in becoming a police officer and didn't want to make a commitment to us that might interfere with that career. In the meantime, I had a chance to talk with several other candidates, and I knew she was the one we wanted. I asked her to come in again, and told her that working with us for a three-month trial period would be, at worst, good experience for a career in criminal justice, and, at best, the start of a lifelong job. It turned out to be the latter.

Karen was only about five feet tall, solidly built, with shoulder length brown hair and a preference for slacks over skirts. I think the only times I saw her in something other than a pair of pants was at Richard and Siobhan's wedding party, and at her mother's funeral. According to what Dorothy tells me, Karen did keep a skirt in her car in case she had an appointment that required dressing up, but she was, at heart, a slacks-and-blouse kind of woman. She was also extremely efficient, hardworking, loyal, and, in some ways, a walking contradiction in terms.

Around the office, for example, she was unfailingly quiet

211

and polite. But neither Richard nor I liked to be in a car when she was behind the wheel, because she would inevitably have one hand on the horn and be gesturing with the other, swearing like a truck driver at anyone who got in her way.

When she was not on the road, she was tender-hearted almost to a fault: she wasn't really satisfied with the work of her hairdresser, but couldn't bring herself to voice a word of criticism, never mind leave for another shop. At the funeral of our son, J.D., she was so stricken she couldn't speak, and walked out of the church in tears before the service ended. And yet, if some poor clerk treated her impolitely, or denied her access to records she knew she had a legal right to see, Karen would be in the clerk's face, and, more often than not end up writing a letter to his or her superior. Here's the first part of one such letter, written after a registry official would not let her see the driving history of a person we were investigating:

*Mr. Daniel Grabauskas*
*Registrar of Motor Vehicles*
*One Copley Place*
*4th Floor*
*Boston, MA 02116*

*January 26, 2000*

*Dear Mr. Grabauskas:*

*I am a private investigator who visited the Copley Square branch of the RMV to obtain a copy of a driving record (not my own) on 1/26/00. I was in the process of conducting an investigation in anticipation of litigation for Atty _ _ _. The woman I encountered in Customer Assistance, J _ _ , has to be the rudest person I have ever dealt*

*with in my life. She was completely unreasonable and com-
pletely unaware of the rules regarding the availability of
driving records.*

And the first part of the response, which she received ten
days later, went like this:

*Dear Ms. Nasson,*

*Registrar Grabauskas has asked me to respond to your
letter of January 26, 2000.*

*Please accept my apology for the incident that occurred on
January 26, 2000 when you came to the registry office at
Copley Place to obtain a driving record.*

*As you point out in your letter, the registry employee you
spoke with did not describe the correct procedure for obtaining the driving record of a third party. The registry employee has been instructed on all the correct procedures regarding
accessing agency records. Additionally, she has been counseled on the preferred technique to use when dealing with
customers.*

*. . . . . . .*

*Again, my sincere apologies for this regrettable incident.*
*Ralph Rooney*
*Director of Customer Services*

There are dozens of letters like this in Karen's files.

Though she had never spent much time around my father
(she was doing undercover work when he died), Karen shared
with him that out-of-fashion idea that people should do their
job well . . . and courteously. She was a logical, level-headed
woman who dealt in facts, and who could put together an airtight report, complete with documentation that would make

any trial lawyer want her at the table in court. She would track down people tirelessly. Even after we had gone over budget on a case, she would continue to look — I remember getting emails that she had sent at 3 a.m., titled *"I got him."*

At the same time, she would come into the office and tell me she had been to see a palm reader that weekend, or that she "just had an intuition" we were going to get busy in the coming weeks. Usually, she was right.

This was the person — with her five adopted stray cats, her love of sports (she bet the football pools, kept spread sheets with the entire season's results and once traveled all the way to Toronto to see Ray Bourque inducted into the Hockey Hall of Fame), her penchant for bringing in candy for our kids and *Boston Strangler* film memorabilia for Richard and me, and for regularly giving gifts to the people who cleaned the office — that we decided to place in an undercover position at Gems and Luxury Jewelers.

Karen was assigned to the Gold Room. Her job was to spend the day walking from one cabinet to another with a basket and an order sheet, picking out diamond rings, ruby bracelets, silver-and-opal necklaces and so on.

Well liked by her fellow workers and keenly observant, Karen took to this work immediately. She was not hesitant about fingering thieves, but she was especially pleased if one of her reports ended up leading to a promotion for some co-worker she liked or admired.

In the days before she had her own office key, I would come to work early on a Tuesday and find her pages lying on the other side of the mail slot, everything expressed clearly and in detail. After some time at Gems and Luxury, she became particularly suspicious of one co-worker, a married woman in her mid-thirties. Nothing on any of our surveillance cameras indicated that this woman was stealing, but Karen's close observation and intuitive sense both pointed to her as being a thief. Gems and Luxury told us, when we went undercover in their operation, that they had a policy of prosecuting anyone who was caught, not just firing them. They wanted the police to arrest the thief and march him or her out of the building in handcuffs. Stealing a few pairs of running shoes is one thing; walking off with a diamond bracelet is something else, and they did not want to go to all the trouble of paying for undercover agents only to have a thief caught and released like some prize trout in a Montana stream.

So, as Karen zeroed in on this woman, I started spending time at Gems and Luxury, too, sitting in a small room with a guard, studying the closed-circuit television monitors. The thief must have understood how the sophisticated cameras worked, and where their blind spots were, because, though I watched her closely I couldn't see any evidence that she was stealing. I told Karen, and we agreed that, when she was sure the woman had stolen something and had the item on her person, she would turn her Red Sox cap around backwards — the signal for us to act. On my third or fourth afternoon at G & L, I watched her turn her cap around, as casually as if she needed a better view of a drawer of sapphires. When the shift ended, I stood with the guard at the metal detector and started a conversation with the woman as she stood in line. The detector sounded its alarm. Most likely the woman was about to claim it was the wire in her bra that had set it off, but I could tell something was strange by the way she was slurring her words. After a couple of exchanges, I held out my hand, palm up, in front of her. She spit a diamond ring into it. We escorted her into the security office and waited for the police to arrive.

All of us showed up for her trial at District Court . . . all of us except the woman herself. A warrant was issued, customary practice in such cases, but, contrary to what most people believe, I knew no one would actually spend a lot of time looking for her. If the thief happened to be stopped on a traffic violation, the warrant would show up and she would be brought in; otherwise, she was moving on to other work.

I do not know what ultimately resulted from the woman's arrest and failure to appear, but some years later when I was about to board a flight at Logan Airport, I recognized her. She was working one of the security lines, the other end of the camera this time, checking the bags of passengers to make sure they weren't carrying anything they shouldn't be.

So much for thorough background checks.

Over the course of her first two years, Karen worked three important undercover operations for us — Gems and Luxury, a Route 128 company called HiTech, and a wallpaper manufacturer in South Boston. She thought it likely — I am inclined to agree — that the illness that later claimed her life came from exposure to glues in one of the later two jobs, though the process those chemicals may have started in her cells did not manifest itself for another decade and a half.

After two years of undercover work, we felt it was time to move Karen into another aspect of our business. For a short while we had her doing surveillances, but this proved to be a weak point: she would call the office in tears and tell me she had lost the trail of someone she had been following for hours.

It was at about this time — early 1987 — that Richard and I realized we would have to computerize the operation or we were going to be left behind. Karen took this idea and ran with it, teaching herself how to use a computer (we started out with two IBM PC's, one for secretarial reports and the other for research), and then seeking out the appropriate databases that would aid us in background information and character profiles. For example, one place we go to find information on an individual is the property assessment records, available at any City

Hall. Karen discovered there were databases that had entire assessment records on line, whole telephone books on CD, skip-tracing data bases. In the old days, when Social Security numbers weren't used by identity thieves to the extent they are now, we could get that number from the Registry of Motor Vehicles, plug it in, and harvest all sorts of information on a given individual. But in those days, we would also spend vast amounts of time driving around Greater Boston from one municipal office to another, looking up the information we needed, or filling out Public Records Forms so that a clerk would agree to do it for us. The advent of the Internet changed all that — though, unlike other states, in Massachusetts you still cannot get criminal records on line.

It is important here to note that we do not undertake these searches casually. Over the years, I have had plenty of requests — some serious, some not — from people who wanted me to find an old girlfriend or boyfriend, dig up a little dirt on a person who was giving them a problem, or do a background check on someone who had just started dating their daughter or son. Unlike some private eyes, who will find anyone for anybody, anytime, we do not involve ourselves in that kind of thing — first, because, in certain cases, it would be illegal; and second, because, more than some businesses, our survival depends on a reputation for honesty and diligence and we do not trifle with that. If someone did engage us to find an old friend, we took payment only with the understanding that we would notify the friend first. Once we found them, we would call or email and say, so-and-so hired us to locate you and we have done so. If you do not want anything to do with this person, say the word and we will keep your location and other information confidential. Lately, though, we have even stopped doing that. Now we work exclusively through attorneys; there is just too much risk, too many improper ways such information could be used by the wrong person.

It is also important to mention here that licensed private investigators are by law allowed access to certain kinds of records — Registry of Motor Vehicles would be one good example — that are off-limits to non law-enforcement agencies. Also it is important to note that I am not going to reveal all the ways we have of finding out things about people. Suffice it to say that, in these days of ubiquitous Internet use, very little is truly private. Volumes of information can be found on line if you know where to look and have the patience to do so. It might not be pleasant, but it is a fact, and it is easier for us than it was in the old days, when I would have to put on my coat, walk down to the Kirstein Business Library and page through shelves of Polk Directories and phone books there whenever I needed to locate someone, especially if the person lived out of state. That kind of information has always been available: now it is just easier for us to retrieve.

Experience and diligence are crucial in using these data bases, however, because the amount of information they provide can be overwhelming, and the facts themselves misleading. Karen became a master at using these Internet sites, and often "tested" them by seeking out information on herself to see how accurate they were. I used to tell people that if Karen couldn't find somebody, then, that person was dead. She had a notebook filled with the addresses of places she could go — chat rooms, newspaper web sites, registrars of deeds, Federal Court records, and so on.

The convenience of the Internet has a flip side, as we found out one January day in 2006. That morning a man called and told Chris he had put his own name into a Yahoo! search engine and was very surprised to see the engine come up with a trove of his personal information under the heading DiNatale Investigations. His name, date of birth, and Social Security number were all there for anyone to see. Business dealings, assets. Everything.

This seemed impossible to me . . . until I called the man, who was the subject of one of our investigations, and found that it was all too true.

There has not been a worse moment in my professional life. The three days that followed were not much better. To Karen's horror, we soon realized that information she had stored on a site — 170 confidential reports, plus her own personal medical and financial records — had all been made publicly available. The web manager of the site had assured her she would be the only one to have access to it, but then someone somewhere had hit the wrong key, and it had all flooded out into the public domain. It was obvious to all of us that this could mean the end of our business, so, with the help of our attorneys, we went into a frenzy of firing off letters.

It took four days and increasingly ominous threats of legal action for the companies involved — RCN, Yahoo, and Alta Vista — to agree to take all the material off the sites. To our knowledge, there were no consequences from this enormous breach — we sent out a letter to every one of our clients, explaining what had happened and the measures we had taken — but Karen was upset. From that day forward she kept all her information on thumb drives.

These days, unfortunately, I think that, even despite examples like this one and numerous news reports, we have all become partially inured to the risks posed by private information being available on line. But when use of the Internet started to be widespread, in the early '90s, there was a fresher concern about privacy rights, greater suspicion about the Internet's safety. As I sometimes do, I wrote an article for *Lawyers' Weekly* in Boston, a piece that discussed the increased use of computers by investigators. This article made its way to Larry Tye, a reporter at the *Boston Globe*, who asked if I would like to be involved in a series they were doing on the availability of information on the Internet. The series was going to be a bit different, he said. Four people — all prominent or notorious in their own way — had agreed to give the *Globe* permission to search the 'Net and see what information was available about them.

I went in to the *Globe* offices and met with Larry and his editors. We sat around a conference table and they asked me a lot of questions about my resume' and experience (I could have shown them how to do a background check on me to answer these questions, but I did not). Understandably enough, they wanted to make certain that nothing about the search would be either illegal or unethical. I assured them that everything we put into our reports would be limited to information available to anyone who knew where to look, and they gave me the four names: M.L. Carr, former star basketball player for the Boston Celtics; Arnold Hiatt, then CEO of the Stride Rite Shoe Corporation; Patricia Faley, acting director of the US Office of Consumer Affairs and head of a White House study group on privacy; and Robert Michael Layne, an individual who had served eighteen years in prison, and rebuilt his life through education there.

I gave this assignment to Karen, and within two weeks she had forty pages of information on these four individuals, including the value of the homes they lived in, the make and model of the cars they drove, their unlisted phone numbers, speeding tickets, a bit of criminal history from M.L. Carr's juvenile days (he had been arrested after a fight to defend the honor of a black girl in Wallace, North Carolina, his home town, and was sentenced to six months probation), and information about Hiatt's Russian ancestry. The subjects — Carr and Hiatt, especially — were dumbfounded, impressed, and, in Carr's case, ultimately irritated. Since the *Globe* wanted a photo to accompany the article, Karen pulled up a screen from the Secretary of State's records on Massachusetts Corporations and let the paper's photographer shoot it. It showed a company formerly owned by M.L. Carr, and included his name and home address. Since his house had been burglarized in the recent past, he was not pleased when this information showed up on the top fold of the first page of the *Boston Sunday Globe* in 1994. (In a strange twist of fate, his offices now adjoin ours.)

We did about $10,000 worth of work for this project, and asked for no pay — only the *Globe*'s agreement to let me say, in print, that we did not go around invading people's privacy for the fun of it. As a bonus, they threw in a front-page photo of me, and some flattering words about the agency — the kind of publicity you cannot pay for.

Even with the appearance of the Internet, though, certain things still needed to be done face-to-face. All through the 1990s, Karen spent her time hustling around the city from court house to Registry office, from libraries to City Halls, doing the necessary shoe-leather work that would accompany her exhaustive computer searches. Never a person who lacked energy, she belonged to a club that started off the day at 5:30 a.m. by taking brisk walks — year round. But in the summer of 2000, she started to notice she was tiring more easily on these walks, and having some trouble breathing. When her work necessitated climbing a set of stairs to interview someone or find an office, she had even more trouble. These symptoms were accompanied by persistent heartburn, and then a regular cough. She started to notice that the tips of her fingers would sometimes turn blue. She had less tolerance for the cold.

After a long series of tests that ruled out pneumonia and other possibilities, Karen went for a CT scan. It showed extensive scarring in her lungs. A lung biopsy that fall confirmed the doctors' worst suspicions: Karen had scleroderma, a disease in which the immune system attacks the body's own organs. Her lungs were slowly hardening. She was put on an immune system suppressant that made her vulnerable to all sorts of illnesses and infections, and was subsequently hospitalized twice with pneumonia. She started chemotherapy, which has been shown to slow the progress of the disease, but, as she lost weight the dose was, mistakenly, never reduced. The overdoses of chemo made it so, by December of the following year, 2001, she could not get out of bed. More painful tests. High fevers. Low red blood cell counts. She nearly died during Christmas week, but kept herself alive by walking around and around in her private hospital room (*"I figured I couldn't die if I was walking,"* she wrote in a short description of the illness), and was released on Christmas Eve. For two weeks after that she had to stay out of work and away from people, for fear she would contract an illness.

She fought on for another eight years. Long after anyone else would have gone on disability, Karen continued to work for us, slipping from 60-70 hours a week down to 25, then to 10, then to 5. She had to sleep sitting up because her esophageal sphincter had frozen in the open position. *"Every day is a struggle,"* she wrote. *"I still live with extreme fatigue, excessive heartburn, painful and stiff joints, blue fingers, tight skin that is constantly splitting open, a very persistent cough, shortness of breath, and the terrible side effects of steroids and no tolerance for the cold — but I still live."*

Until two days before she died, she was working up reports for Richard and me. It was, her father told me at the funeral, one of the things that kept her going. At that point, she was barely able to breathe. Her dad convinced her to go to the hospital. Forty-eight hours later she was dead.

Dorothy and Richard and I and our families as well as a number of her former co-workers attended Karen's funeral and cremation. At the service, I told the story of her work on the

*Globe* series, and talked about everything else she had done for us. Two days later, her cousin Alexis came to the office for a visit, and told me something Karen had kept secret: that at one point after she had been with us for a while, Karen had an opportunity to fulfill her dream and become a policewoman — she had passed the Registry Police exam — but she'd made a commitment to us on an undercover job and passed up her dream opportunity.

We have five names on our company stationery now — Phillip and Evelyn DiNatale — my mother and dad. My name. Richard's name. And Karen Nasson, 1963-2010.

# TWENTY SIX
Some Difficult Cases

*"It is possible to fail in many ways. . .while to succeed is possible only in one way."*
Aristotle

During the forty years of our family business, we have had our share of personal difficulties — the illness and death of my mother and dad, of Dorothy's mom, of our son J.D., Richard and Siobhan's boy Harry, and Karen, but there have been professional ones, as well. Every case we take on does not have a happy ending. For the most part, it has been my experience that clients understand when things don't work out. They expect you to have sufficient experience and expertise, to sincerely try to solve their problem, whether that problem is finding a thief or a missing child, helping with their defense in a criminal case, or unearthing evidence that will help in a civil lawsuit. And they expect you to charge them a fair rate for your services. I would say our success rate has been somewhere in the mid-eightieth percentile; the other fifteen percent of cases, for one reason or another, concluded in a way that left us and the client less than satisfied: the defendant was found guilty, witnesses in a civil case would not talk, we were caught in the act of surveillance or for other reasons could not get the video we needed. I thought I would mention a few of these here, to give our story some balance.

One of these less-than-successful cases came to us early in my career from an estate lawyer who was a partner at a long-established Boston firm. He was representing the sister of a man who lived by himself in Cambridge. She'd had no contact with her brother for several weeks, and she gave us photos and a description (five feet, five inches tall, fond of wearing a blue stocking cap summer and winter), his address (Putnam Street), age (early seventies), and other pertinent information, and asked us to find him. In my twenty-something naiveté, I thought, at first, that she was worried about her elderly bachelor brother, hoping he was all right. Only after I had access to his files did I learn that the man had a great deal of money and no other heirs. I didn't know it at the time, but without proof of his death, it was going to take this woman seven years to probate his estate and get her hands on the windfall.

Had I been aware of them, her motivations might have bothered me from a personal standpoint, but as a business matter they would not have come into play. Almost a year after his major heart attack, my father was still recuperating, Richard still in school. The case was mine and I intended to do a good job on it.

I checked the morgue for unidentified bodies. I had copies of the man's photo made up, went to the Cambridge police (who knew about him but did not exactly consider his disappearance an urgent matter) and made sure they passed them out at roll call. I printed up posters from the photo and stapled them to every telephone pole in a five-block radius; the posters included our phone number and a request for people to call if they had information. For weeks, I did what my dad liked to call "knuckle and heel" work: I walked the streets of the neighborhood knocking on doors, and stopping everyone I saw, asking if they had seen this man.

Many of them had. It turned out that he was a neighborhood fixture, known affectionately as Zeke the Trash-Picker, because he spent his days wandering all over that part of Cambridge, collecting objects others had thrown away. The interior of his large, wood-frame house showed the evidence of that preoccupation. Some rooms had stacks of trash higher than my shoulders — newspapers, books, magazines, pieces of metal, anything and everything Zeke had considered worth carrying home. From speaking with his sister, and from my examination of the house, I knew he did not have a drinking problem and wasn't on any kind of medication. In better years, he'd made a great deal of money in the business world, then suffered some kind of mental breakdown and spent the past decade either sitting along the Charles River — four blocks to the south — or prowling the tree-lined, close-packed streets picking trash.

This was the reverse of the usual missing persons case, in which we would show a photograph and most people would shrug, shake their head, and say they hadn't seen the man or woman. This time, everybody had seen him; almost everybody I talked to knew him, or at least knew what he looked like, though they admitted it had been several weeks since there had been a sighting.

I staked out the house, pounded the sidewalks, checked back with the cops and the morgue. No sign of Zeke. It was late November by then, ice just starting to form on the river. As I was leaving the house to go over there again on Thanksgiving morning, my father said, "Look down by the water. He might have been out there late at night. Maybe he slipped in, or maybe somebody hit him over the back of the head and knocked him in. Look for a wallet, the blue hat, anything." Back and forth I went along the shore, past the boathouses and bridges, along the asphalt lot called "Magazine Beach", where shells are launched for the Head of the Charles regatta and where Zeke had liked to hang out on sunny days, sitting there in his blue cap, surrounded by his treasures, watching sailboats and sculls on Charles.

In the end, difficult as it was for me, I had to admit defeat. We informed the lawyer and Zeke's sister that we had done everything we could but had failed to get even a single recent sighting. It did not make sense for them to keep paying us to look.

The following spring, when the ice melted on the river and the rowing teams brought out their oars and boats, Zeke's body was found pinned under the dock of the Northeastern boathouse. His wallet was still in his pants pocket, and there was no sign of injury, so, as my father suspected, he had most likely just slipped into the cold river and had not been able to get out. I read about it in the newspaper, just a few short lines.

Some years later, after the city of Boston passed a controversial residency requirement for its workers, we were hired to do surveillance on a municipal police officer. The officer was breaking the agreement he had signed, living in Quincy, fifteen miles to south, and spending a few nights a week at his mother's house in Boston to cover his trail.

By that point, we had purchased a white Toyota van, which Richard had customized for surveillances. The windows were tinted so no one could look in. For extra measure, we had blackout curtains set up around the interior. We put small beach chairs inside, a cooler, kept a plastic bottle in there for times when a toilet was not available (the sacrifices of surveillance workers!). We had an extra battery for the video system and good cameras we could mount on tripods, and there were several different signs we could attach to the sides of the van, claiming it belonged to John R. Wilson the Plumber, or A-1 Heating and Oil, or Bay State Upholstery. We sent Cal out on this job. At 5:30 one morning he parked the van a short distance up the street from the police officer's house and attempted to obtain video that showed he was living there.

Along with a guilty conscience, the subject had a cop's instincts. It did not take him long to become suspicious of the strange van parked up the street. He ran the license plate and called our office, but our secretary at the time, Virginia, had nothing to tell him. With Cal crouched down in the back behind the curtains, the officer walked up and tried to get a look in through the rear windows. Not having any luck there, he moved to the driver's door and tried the handle, pounded on the side, yelled out that he knew somebody was in there and he had better come out. He called the fire department and told them the van was on fire. When they arrived and saw that it was not, he told them it had actually been abandoned and asked them to have it towed. It was obviously a safety hazard and might contain a bomb. The fire department refused. He called the police to come and tow it, but the police had better things to do. Unfortunately for Cal, as the day went on, the temperature climbed into the nineties, which meant that the temperature inside the curtained interior of the van, with its metal roof and sides, was somewhere up in the hundreds. Another person might have just jumped behind the wheel and sped away, but Cal felt badly enough about having been discovered, and he wanted to try to preserve the bit of anonymity that was left. It is that kind of tenaciousness that makes a good surveillance operative, and a good private eye. (He is now a good State Trooper.)

As the cop pounded and threatened, and then stood outside in a stake-out of his own, Cal managed to call us on his cell phone and, in a whisper, tell us what was going on.

228

Another of our key employees at the time was Timmy O'Callaghan, a recent graduate of Northeastern, where he had played tight end on the football team. Timmy stood six foot four inches, weighed two hundred and thirty pounds, and was handsome as a model. So much so that one of our lawyer clients asked us never to send him to his office again: his visits caused too much disturbance among the mostly female staff. Timmy liked roller blading, so, while Cal sweated it out in the surveillance van, and the cop fumed, spat, and swore on the street nearby, we sent Timmy to Quincy with his roller blades and an extra key. He parked a half mile away, roller-bladed up to the van, and was in the process of unlocking the driver's door when the cop accosted him and made his accusations. The advantage of being a tight end and a man of Timmy's size is that people, even angry people, even angry people with a policeman's badge, tend not to be overly aggressive when confronting you. I was not there of course. So, I don't know exactly what transpired. Timmy said the cop gave him a hard time for a while, didn't seem to believe the roller blading story. But, Timmy held up the key, told him it was his van and that he was planning to get into it and drive away. What, exactly, was the guy going to do about it?

Nothing, as it turned out.


When it came to marital troubles, it was not always the feminine half of the relationship that required our services. And we were not always good enough, or lucky enough, to catch the cheater in the act.

At some point in the 1980s we had a call from a man I'll call Jeremy, who was sure, not only that his wife was cheating on him, but that she was operating a call-girl service in the bargain. Jeremy was about five-four and slightly built, mid-fifties, and he used hair plugs to try to cover up his baldness. His manner was so effeminate we would have taken him for a gay man except for the fact that he was married to Elaine, and they had two children. I do not know how it affected the children, but Elaine's suspected infidelities became an obsession for Jeremy, one of those cases where knowing a hard truth was preferable to being mired in limbo.

Elaine was an attractive woman in her mid-forties. For a well-off suburban mother of two, she had some strange habits, one of which was the car she drove: a bright pink Lincoln Continental. At Jeremy's insistence, Richard and I followed her for weeks, trailing her to shopping malls and lunch dates with friends, to dentist and hairdresser appointments. Nothing. Zero evidence that she was doing Jeremy wrong. Instead of being relieved when we gave him this news, Jeremy always seemed vaguely disappointed, as if, in his bones, he knew the truth of his marital situation, but needed that truth confirmed by someone else. The lack of evidence seemed only to add fuel to the fire of his jealous imaginings. At one point he became so obsessed that he had Richard come to their house and photograph Elaine's kinky lingerie, thinking the pictures might serve as evidence in a future divorce case. By pure coincidence, their house was burglarized about this time, and our friend Ernie Reid, King of Pretexting, who also did some side work as an insurance investigator, was called in to investigate the theft on behalf of the insurance carrier. He happened to see the lingerie photos, and Jeremy happened to mention that Richard DiNatale, who was involved in a separate investigation, had taken the photos. And so, naturally, Ernie called the office asking for Richard DiNatale, altered his deep voice, and said, "This is Sergeant Jake Winter of the State Police, we understand you have a penchant for photographing women's lingerie. Is there a particular color or texture you favor?"

He had Richard going for a while.

Although the case had its amusing aspect, naturally enough it wasn't funny to Jeremy. For some reason he got it into his mind that Elaine was pimping for a local sports team and one all star athlete in particular. But, we never unearthed any evidence linking that team member to Elaine. Jeremy Eltsman was someone we liked, and felt sorry for, but, try as we did we could never come up with any proof that his wife was cheating.

Cool to begin with, eventually the trail went completely cold. With some reluctance, we told Jeremy we were not going to be able to help him; he agreed, but said he would continue to try to catch her on his own. We hadn't done any following of Elaine for several months when I had a phone call late one night. It was Jeremy, excited to the point where he was almost hyperventilating. "John, John, her car is parked in front of Good Time Charlie's on LaGrange Street! Right out front! You have to come see it!"

Maybe it is a mark of my dedication to clients, or, more likely, it was a case of just feeling empathy for Jeremy, but I got out of bed and got dressed and drove down to what was then called The Combat Zone — a few square blocks of strip clubs and porno arcades just south of Boston's central shopping district. During the day, the Zone was seedy and filthy, with litter in the streets and sagging brick rooming houses above doorways where loud music played and bright lights flashed and a guy paced the sidewalk trying to get passersby in to see the peep shows and sex acts. At night, there was only one reason to go there, and plenty of reasons to stay away.

LaGrange Street formed a kind of epicenter of Boston's universe of lust (and was the place where, a few years later, a Harvard College football star would be stabbed to death during a night out with friends, a murder that marked the beginning of the end of the Combat Zone). In the past, Charlie, the owner of the eponymous bar, had hired us to do a few surveillances, to keep an eye on his bartenders to make sure they weren't putting $10.50 into the cash register when the tab was actually $15.00, to ascertain if they were working with the waitress to take cash for drink orders without ever writing them down. Richard and I and Cal and Tim had all taken turns there, but it was not a job we liked. Within a few minutes of sitting down you would be approached by one of the "hostesses", who would immediately run her hand across your back and along the back of your waist. It wasn't flirtation; but rather, their way of checking to see if you were a gun-carrying cop. (I would always put my pistol in an ankle holster before going in to Good Time Charlie's; the women never made it that far south.) You could not relax and do your job there, because it was a place guys came to get sex, and if you sat around too long just nursing a beer and not getting up to accompany one of the hostesses out to your car, there was something suspicious about you.

In other words, Good Time Charlie's wasn't the kind of place you would expect to find a faithful wife at one in the morning. And we did not find her. Yes, Elaine's attention-attracting pink Continental was parked out front. But when I went in for a quick five-dollar beer and a look around, there was no sign of her. So I sat out in Jeremy's car with him for four hours, until the sun rose, until the streets of the Combat Zone turned from lively to sleepy, and what had seemed like a boiling pot of tawdry neon excitement, showed itself for what it was — a littered stretch of city street, quiet as a passed-out drunk and not smelling much better.

"We're not going to see her, Jeremy," I had to tell him finally. And he nodded, and let me get in my car and go home. He stopped calling us after that, though I always had the feeling there had been some strange redemption for him in the sight of Elaine's Continental on LaGrange. It was almost as if he were saying, "See, John, I wasn't crazy after all." And almost as if that was enough for him.

Domestic cases were like that, personal with a capital P, as different in their details as one marriage is from the next. A certain Mrs. Fernwood had us follow her husband twice a week for years — to work, to the golf course, to get his hair cut, to the dentist. Finally, Richard sat her down and said, "Mrs. Fernwood, you're wasting your money; we can't find your husband doing a single thing wrong."

"Richard," she answered patiently, "some women like to spend their money shopping. I like to spend mine having my husband followed."

What can you say to something like that?

# TWENTY SEVEN
Pretending to be Someone You are Not

*"These troublesome disguises which we wear."*
- Milton

Not long after my father died, we had a case that, in a strange way, combined two specialties: pretexting, and trash picking. Even more strangely, perhaps, it had to do with the specialty of a German nun, Sister Maria Innocentia Hummel. She was first discovered by a porcelain specialist named Franz Goebel in the 1930s, when a German publishing company began printing her artwork as postcards. The first of the porcelain figurines based on these paintings were sold in 1935, and, though Sister Hummel died in 1946, millions of the collectibles have been sold since. Prices these days reach to as much as $1,000 for certain figurines. A Google search of Hummel brings up 385,000 pages, and there are Hummel chat groups, collectors' conventions, exchanges, and even the Nicholas E. Stephens Museum of Hummels in Rosemont, Illinois.

Our introduction to the Hummel universe came via a lawyer we had worked with when my dad had been alive, and a partner at one of the paragons of the Boston law scene. (I'll call him Jeff Green.) Jeff said he was representing a firm we will call The Cartfuhr Corporation, a local distributor of collectibles. Cartfuhr owned the exclusive right to distribute authentic

Hummel figurines in the United States, but estimated they were losing about $50 million a year to what is called trans-shipping, or the gray market — basically, people selling something they have no contractual right to sell. We had seen trans-shipping cases before: a department store selling Raleigh bikes (then two-year-old Lindsay helped me get the necessary photo documentation); an enterprising individual buying up LumberJack boots and reselling them for a higher price in Italy. But this was being done on a much larger scale.

Trans-shipping is not, technically, a crime, but a violation of civil law, and so it is the perfect territory for a private investigator. Had it been a matter of trademark infringement — as in recent cases where Gucci and Coach knockoffs were being sold on the streets of New York — the FBI would have entered the picture. But they and the local police have no interest in trans-shipping. If a business wants to stop that practice in order to protect their profits, the D.A. is not going to be prosecuting the case for them; it is a civil matter for U.S. District Court.

Jeff Green — a man I enjoyed working with — asked me to meet him at Cartfuhr's offices, about half an hour south of the city. When I arrived, I found Jeff and the owner of the company sitting in a small conference room. We made the usual introductions, and then the owner gave me a little background on his business, told me about the problem, and showed me several trade publication advertisements that had come to his attention. The ads were from an import-export firm in Manhattan that seemed to be offering Hummels at a price about twenty per cent lower than what Cartfuhr's own clients paid for them, wholesale. In addition, Cartfuhr's internal sales people had been fielding complaints from the retailers, saying they had seen Hummels for sale at the steeply discounted price at places like The Christmas Tree Shops. In order for them to compete, they would have to sell the Hummels for less than what they had paid to get them. These underpriced Hummels were even showing up on the Home Shopping Network, and a huge outlet like that had the potential to undermine all of Cartfuhr's business in the U.S. Their own people had been unable to get to the root of the problem, which is why they wanted to hire us. In outline, our job was straightforward enough: find out how these cheaper Hummels were coming into the country.

Simple as it sounded, I had the sense right away that this was going to be a complicated job — it ended up taking the better part of six months — so I asked for and received a sizeable retainer. I also had a sense that we were going to need to make use of my father's web of connections. Again, in contrast to the TV version, ours is not a go-it-alone business, especially when we're dealing with jobs outside our geographical area. If "all politics are local", as Tip O'Neill famously said, then it is probably true that all investigative work is local, too, or at least that it is impossible to do a thorough job without the kinds of contacts and territorial familiarity that only a local P.I. can have. This doesn't mean we've worked only in the Boston area — in fact, we've had cases from California to Norway to a recent (thirty-below-zero) debugging job in South Dakota. But it does mean, when we have taken on those cases, the first step has usually been enlisting the help of others in the business who know the territory well. You can see this even in major criminal cases, where the State Police and FBI often work in conjunction with local cops. Part of that comes from the fact that the locals may have jurisdiction; part of it because they know the lay of the land, the criminal culture, where to turn for information.

In any event, as had been true in other cases, I knew we were going to miss my father's ability to pick up the phone and put us in touch with investigators wherever we happened to be working. Leaving Cartfuhr's offices with the attorney's check in my pocket (in order to preserve certain attorney-client privileges, we are not paid directly by a client), I felt an odd mix of feelings, the same kind of thing that washes over me even now when we receive a new type of case. On the one hand, I had confidence we could find the people who were importing and selling the Hummels; on the other, I had no idea how we were going to do that.

Richard and I had been in that situation dozens of times, so we did what we always do: we sat in the office and concocted a strategy. Our first step was to call Tony Sterniolo, a.k.a. Tony Stern, a New York investigator my father had done some work with years before on a Gems and Luxury case. Tony and my dad had gotten along famously, Phil had paid him well and promptly, and even asked Amelia to send along a nice set of earrings for Tony's wife — the kind of gesture my dad was known for, and which explains, I think, a lot of the affection that surrounded him in the law enforcement world. Since the inquiries of Cartfuhr's sales force had led them to believe there was a New Jersey connection, we told Tony we needed a Jersey P.I. Not a problem. He sent us to Sal Cientelli, a former cop with an incredible web of contacts in that area. All we had to go on at that point was the name and address of the Manhattan import-export company, and sketchy information that showed he might be doing business with people from New Jersey. Sal said he would do some digging and let us know what he came up with.

Step two of the plan was to have Ernie Reid call up Home Shopping and Christmas Tree and pose as a dealer. This attempt gained us nothing: they would not reveal their suppliers.

Step three was to go see the Manhattan dealer in person. I decided to borrow a page from Ernie's book, use my alias (which I will not divulge here; though I will say my father taught me to use the same one whenever I could, so it would feel almost natural) and put together a made-up company called Dorothy's Collectibles. I had business cards printed, just the company name and a phone number. We put in a dedicated phone line at the office, with a sign over a brown phone saying, "Always answer this phone "Dorothy's Collectibles"". I concocted a story that, though I had made a lot of money in commercial real estate, I had always been a collector at heart, and so was my wife, and now I was trying to set her up in a collectibles business on Cape Cod.

I took the shuttle to LaGuardia in my three-piece suit, going over the story again and again in my mind and wondering if I could pull it off. I even called Jeff Green from the airport and went over it with him and his client in a conference call, trying to find any cracks and crevices where a suspicious graymarketeer might see through the tall tale.

The import-export business turned out to be a one-man operation on the second floor of a ten-story building in midtown Manhattan. I walked in, as Phil had always advised, as if I owned the place. The owner — middle-aged, curly brown hair, glasses — presided over a couple of rooms cluttered with catalogues and cardboard boxes. He seemed suspicious at first, but my story came out more smoothly than I had expected. I was from Cape Cod, I said (we have a summer house there and I used that address), and, as I had been working on starting up this business for my wife, rubbing shoulders with dealers from the small antique shops that lined Route 6A, I had heard his name mentioned as a person who could get Hummels at a reasonable price. Whenever he broke eye contact, I used a technique my father had taught me — move your eyes not your head — and tried, unsuccessfully, to see if any of the boxes had shipping labels I could read. After a talk that lasted twenty minutes or so, I left him my phony business card and returned to Boston. The man called the next day, I arranged to buy a small number of Hummels from him, but when the box arrived there was nothing we could glean from it, no information, either on the box, in the paperwork, or on the Hummels themselves, that might lead us to the people who were supplying him.

While I was pursuing the case from the Dorothy's Collectibles angle, Sal Cientelli, using one of his own innumerable contacts, had "pulled" this man's long-distance phone records and discovered that he was making regular calls to a New Jersey company I'll call Palner Brothers Imports. In addition to that, his son, Al, had staked out the Manhattan import-export office and arranged for what is affectionately referred to in our business as a "trash buy." That is, he learned the schedule of the people who cleaned the man's office, waited until they came out of the building, and offered them cash for trash. Surprised as they might have been, they were more than happy to oblige. This was, however, something we had to do with a bit of delicacy, both because we wanted to be sure the dealer did not find out about it, and to avoid breaking the law. In order to cover us on the second concern, Jeff Green and his associates went to some lengths to draft a legal brief on that subject, coming up with a concept termed "expectation of privacy." What this internal memo said, basically, was that, if you shred your papers before putting them out for trash collection, then your expectation of privacy is that no one else should lay eyes on them. But if you just toss them in a plastic bag and drop them in a dumpster, there is no such expectation and, once they are out of the building, anybody has a legal right to look at the trash. A technicality, yes. And not much purer than what Detective Calabrese had done when he pulled over the three shoe thieves.

This is the way we work sometimes, the good end justifying

— in our minds at least — the less than pure, but always ethical, means. Any honest cop will tell you the same thing: there are times when, in the service of catching a bad guy, you bend the rules . . . a bit. The potential for abuse is obvious. In the checkered history of law enforcement, there is no shortage of examples of cops and private eyes coming to believe they were above the law, and doing things, often in the name of catching a criminal, that were not much better and sometimes even worse, than what the bad guys had done. We never came close to that line. We'd buy trash, yes. We'd pretext. We'd sometimes give a hotel clerk $50 for telling us who was staying there, or a property manager a similar sum for letting us into an apartment our client owned. Looking for a young person who had disappeared, it was common for us to spread a little money around Harvard Square — to vendors and street musicians. None of that is illegal. No single case is worth risking a reputation that has taken decades to build, and none of us wants to end up on the wrong end of the law's hard arm.

There was a comical aspect to this particular episode of trash buying, which we did three times a week for a while. I would be flying home from New York in my suit and tie, having checked a duffel bag filled with coffee grounds, apple rinds, used Kleenex, and scraps of paper. Obviously this was in the years before bags were X-rayed or they would have locked me up. As soon as I arrived at Logan and claimed my treasure at the baggage carousel, I called Jeff's high-class law firm to let them know I was coming, and then lugged the duffel bag up to their offices on the twenty-second floor of a Boston skyscraper. Jeff was sitting in one of their elegant conference rooms. He had covered the mahogany table with plastic. We dumped the trash out there and went through it, piece by piece.

The fax reports we found in that trash, along with a couple of invoices, led us where the phone records were pointing, to

Palner Brothers. Their phone records, in turn — also collected by Sal Cientelli — showed that they had been in touch with a London company that was buying from the factory in Germany. It was a big break in the case, but still insufficient evidence, as far as we and Jeff Green were concerned, to enable the firm to bring the trans-shippers to court.

Ernie Reid played an important role at this point, though it had nothing to do with pretexting. He made us aware of something called Piers Database, a publicly available site, still in use, that tracks everything imported into the US — every container and tanker shipment, every new automobile and kid's toy, everything. Piers showed that the Palner Brothers were receiving large shipments of collectibles, but it did not show who the actual shipper was on the other side of the Atlantic. We tried to find a British P.I. to help us out on that end, and came up empty.

Armed with this information, I flew to New Jersey in search of something more. I met up with Sal at his offices in West Orange. He and his son Al and I went over what we had to that point, rehearsed my pretext, made a call to Palner Bros., and the next day Al and I drove to a Newark industrial park for a meeting at their offices.

The Palners were, in fact, two brothers, middle-aged Hasidic Jews wearing yarmulke, long beards, payos, and black top hats. Technically, as I mentioned, they were not breaking the law, and I think they knew that. At the same time, they surely knew that what they were doing could land them in civil court on the wrong end of a cease-and-desist order and a hefty lawsuit, and they were not exactly warm and welcoming. Al introduced me as the fictitious R. _ _ T. _ _ , gave them the Dorothy's Collectibles story, and said I was especially interested in buying Hummels, but wanted to look at other porcelain collectibles as well. When I handed over the business card, the first question one of them asked was, "Why isn't your address on this?"

I gave him the Cape Cod address, and, changing the tone of my voice slightly, asked him, in turn, why it had taken me three days to find *their* address. When they remained skeptical, I said, "Look, we're both after the same thing, here. I'm trying to make some money, get my wife set up in this business, and I know Hummels and other collectibles are big in this market right now. I'm not just talking about a little "shoppe" on Cape Cod visited by a few summer tourists. I have contacts with flea market owners all across northern New England and, either from you or someone else, I'm looking to buy something like ten thousand Hummels a month."

Later in the conversation I added the small caveat that, before I wrote them a check, I would need to see some proof that they could get me the volume I needed. But I didn't push things very hard in that first meeting. I had worked with my dad long enough to know that, in most instances, the harder you push, the farther back people lean. So all I did at that point was dangle the idea of ten thousand monthly sales in front of the Palners, shake hands, and take my leave.

I went back to Boston and waited.

Over the following couple of weeks, Al and Sal kept buying trash, and Timmy, Cal or I made more trash trips to New Jersey and Pennsylvania and brought loads of it up to Jeff Green. We were harvesting all kinds of good things: Fax records, copies of bills of sale between the Palners and the U.K. distributor, phone calls to the Manhattan import-export company. Jeff was confident we had all the evidence we needed, but we were both hoping for one last *coup de grace*. So I called the Palners and politely said I was coming to New Jersey on other business, and this was their chance. They could let me see a warehouse that demonstrated their capacity to fill my big orders, or they could pass.

They slept on the offer for one night, and then invited me down.

I made the second trip to see the Palners alone, not carrying a weapon. The brothers met me at the same industrial park office where we had been introduced, and said they were going to show me the Hummel warehouse. The warehouse was on the Jersey waterfront; we should all go together in their minivan. During that fifteen-minute trip, there was a bit of tension in the air. I am sure the Palners were wondering if they could trust me, and I was wondering if I was going to end up being carried out of the warehouse in several plastic bags, mixed together with concrete, and dumped in the Atlantic Ocean east of Red Hook.

The Palners brought me to the waterfront, pulled their van up next to a warehouse the size of a football field, and opened the door on a huge stash, pallets and pallets of cardboard boxes. Perfume, clothing, and more Hummels than Dorothy's Collectibles could have sold in a lifetime. But, as they gave me a closer look, I realized that all the box tops had been razored off so there would be no evidence of who sent them. Technically, they had been imported into the country in accordance with U.S. law: the only thing U.S. Customs cared about was that the tariffs had been paid. But that was not all Cartfuhr cared about. Satisfied that I could report to Cartfuhr that the Palners were operating on this large a scale, I gave them a check.

We arranged for a substantial shipment to be sent to the address on Cape Cod.

Once that happened, the U.K. supplier was shut down, and the Palners, the Manhattan dealer, and Attorney Green ended up settling things in a less than friendly manner in New York Federal District Court.

# TWENTY EIGHT
People Watching

*"You can observe a lot by watching."*
- Yogi Berra

S urveillance, one of the pillars of the law enforcement world, is more art than science, and some investigators — my brother comes to mind — have more aptitude for it than others. It is a tricky business. People do not like to be followed, and most people do not like to be watched — especially, as was true in almost all our surveillance cases, when they are doing something they should not be doing.

My father told me that, once, when he knew he had to follow someone up a highway in winter rush hour and was worried about losing the tail in the heavy traffic and darkness, he found the person's car, parked and empty, took off his shoe, and smashed out one of the taillights. All the way up that highway he could see one white light among all the reds.

Richard and I have never resorted to that (though, we have heard about a kinder and gentler version of the same technique: sticking some black electrical tape over the light.) But, there were plenty of times when we had to use our imagination to solve a particularly thorny surveillance problem. For one of those cases, we were hired by a New Hampshire city to follow a truckload of municipal workers who were suspected of using their own creativity to start a side business — while they were on the city clock. Because of the truck they were working from, they had access to a part of downtown shopping district ordinarily reserved for foot traffic. We tailed them just to the edge of the pedestrian district, saw where they parked the truck, and noticed that the four of them seemed to have their heads on a swivel, to be particularly concerned about who might be watching them. Years before, Richard had been an avid hunter. He knew that deer hunting blinds are often placed up in a tree because even the most wary deer — even sensing, as they seem to do, that it is hunting season — never look up. Instinct tells them that danger will come from their own level, not from above. The same is true of humans. So my brother climbed the steps to the roof of a nearby parking garage, set up his video camera there, and spent two fruitful hours recording illicit drug transactions, made from the back of a truck with City of _ _ _ printed plainly on its doors.

Another surveillance that took an unusual turn came to us from an attorney for a woman who had just been through a contentious divorce. Her ex-husband had been granted custody of their two young children for two afternoons a week, and, from things the boys said after these visits, she was concerned that the father was leaving them unattended in the yard. One problem was, she didn't know where he was living; and another: the man had a tendency to be violent. The first time she sent her brother to follow her ex's car, the ex lost him. On the second attempt, the ex arranged for the brother's car to be pulled to the side of the road by two burly friends, who beat him badly.

We knew the exact time the ex-husband would be picking

up and dropping off the children, and we knew, as well, that he would be hyper alert to the possibility of someone following him. It so happened that the woman lived in West Roxbury, so we were quite familiar with the neighborhood roads and traffic patterns. ("No way we're gonna lose this guy in this neighborhood," my brother said. The route, it turned out, would take us past the Little League field where I had made two errors on opening day, the street corner where we used to hang out with teenage friends, the pizza place where we would go for dinner on Friday nights, and the country club where Richard and I now play golf.) After thinking about it for a while, we came up with a plan to "follow" the ex in a novel way — from in front.

We worked in two cars, with walkie-talkies, over the course of two weeks. Since we knew the roads he would need to travel in order to reach his ex-wife's house, I stationed myself at an intersection a couple of blocks away along that route. Once he passed me, I radioed Richard, saying something like, "He's traveling west on Baker Street, toward the VFW Parkway." Richard would be hidden at the intersection, and would watch him cross the Parkway and head toward Newton. We now knew how he was coming into West Roxbury and we could start the surveillance at the next major intersection, Dedham and Nahanton Streets.

We waited there for him to come back with the children, and set ourselves up in front of him. Richard would linger until he saw the man coming, then pull out either directly in front of him or with one car between. The man was constantly checking his rear view mirror — exactly what we expected him to do. Meanwhile, I would cut through the back streets and hope to end up another quarter mile or so ahead of him on the route we assumed he would be taking. It took some guesswork, some luck, some watching for his turn signals. On the first few visits we eventually lost him, but every time we did, we were at a point a little closer to his destination. Sometimes Richard and I would both be in front of him in a bizarre, three-vehicle parade; at one point, anticipating his route through Newton Center, Richard made a right, I went straight, and the subject of our attention turned left. We lost him then, but next visitation day we were able to set up in Newton Center and get ahead of him again, one of us watching him come north on Parker Street, the other parked on a side street off that first left turn.

At the end of this one-of-a-kind surveillance, Richard found himself parked on the guy's own street, looking in his rear-view as the ex-husband turned into his driveway.

Sometimes, even in a serious case, surveillance can have a humorous side. We became involved in an unusual situation when a South Shore man whose wife was away invited his neighbor over for dinner. Their dinner ended with fists flying. The neighbor charged his host with assault, the matter went to court, and the host pleaded guilty to the facts and saw his case continued without a finding. During the short trial, however, the host claimed he had hit his neighbor because the neighbor had made unwanted sexual advances. The neighbor denied it, and when the criminal case had been settled, he filed suit in civil court for damages. The host's attorney, via his insurance company, called us and said it would help his case if we could find evidence contradicting the neighbor's contention that he had not made sexual advances. As a starting point, he told us he had dug up some information that the neighbor frequented a woodsy rest area off Route 95, known to be used by gay men for sexual encounters.

Cal and Timmy took the surveillance van up to the rest area, parked it, and turned on the cameras. It was the usual routine: Men would drive up, get out of their cars and stand around looking for other men. According to our cameras, and to Cal and Timmy's report, these men would signal each other by reaching a hand down and hefting their crotch. They would then pair up and disappear into the woods. At one point, a man drove up and, seeing the van and nothing else, assumed there was someone waiting inside. He positioned himself in plain view and grabbed his crotch with one hand. No response from the van. So he came a few steps closer and made the gesture again. Still nothing. He did this several times before giving up and deciding the van driver must have gone into the woods and be waiting there. It made for interesting video.

An hour or so later, the neighbor appeared and went in search of a companion.


Of all the people we have used and worked with on surveillance cases, including police officers, I rate Richard at the top of the list when it comes to surveillance of all kinds. Over the years, though, even he has had his share of difficulties. There was the time, hired by a lawyer who represented the husband in an ugly divorce case, when Richard followed the client's wife from one South Shore neighborhood to another, expecting to find her meeting with a boyfriend. Rush hour had passed. The highway was lightly traveled. It was a real challenge to keep the woman's car in view without being caught — he let her get as far ahead as he possibly could, just catching sight of her as she took an exit, just seeing which way she turned at the bottom of a ramp.

He ended up following her into a neighborhood of summer homes — most of them empty at that time of year — and then onto a dead-end dirt road there. Turning onto the road a few hundred yards behind her, my brother was surprised to find a small gang of men loitering near her house. He drove to the end of the road and parked, wondering — as impossible as it seemed — if they were somehow expecting him. Richard waited there for more than an hour, until darkness fell and he saw a car approaching with its headlights off. By then it was clear that something had gone badly wrong. But, it made no sense. He was sure the woman hadn't seen him and called ahead to alert her friends, but here came the car, four men inside. He whirled around and sped past it going the other way. The rest of the gang was still there; he raced past them, too, hurried back to the highway, and soon saw two cars tailing him.

My brother was driving a BMW, going seventy in the right-hand lane, speaking into a tape-recorder at the same time to preserve a record of the moment in case he didn't survive. One of the cars came up beside him and tried to nudge him off the road. Richard steered into it and the driver fell back. He put the tape recorder aside and moved his car up to eighty miles per hour. The second car came up close behind him and rode his tail at that speed for a mile or more. Richard stomped on the brakes; the car following him swerved and went off the road, into the grass of the low shoulder.

When he made it home, my brother called the lawyer and asked him what the hell was going on. "Oh, I forgot to tell you," the lawyer said. "A little while before you left, the guy called up his wife. They got into an argument and he told her he was going to have her followed that afternoon. Sorry about that."

Another time, Richard was asked to take photographs of the home of a man suspected of faking an injury. The man claimed he had to build a wheelchair ramp for the deck at the back of his house, but the lawyer suspected he was lying. Richard's wife was at work, and it seemed like a quick, drive-by job, so he asked a neighbor to just run him and his young son by the house. They had taken exactly two shots from the road, when the man who claimed he was disabled came out, enraged, jumped in his car and sped along behind them, leaning on the horn and flashing his lights. Richard's three-year-old son was in the back seat, so this time there was no thought of racing away or jamming on the brakes. Instead, he told the neighbor to drive to the local police station, right into the lot there. The man did not follow. There hadn't been any wheelchair ramp, but the lawyer wanted more detailed evidence. "You're going to have to go back," he told Richard.

"Not gonna happen. The guy's a maniac. The only way I'm going back to get pictures of that deck is if I'm in an airplane."

"Hire one, then," the lawyer said.

So my brother did. He and another friend flew in low and banked. Richard took the wheel, and the friend — a specialist in aerial photography — hung out of the window with his camera. There was the so-called disabled man again, out on his rampless deck with a pair of binoculars, shaking his fist at them.

But the finest job my brother ever did on a surveillance, and one of his biggest adventures, occurred on another divorce case, when he was just out of college. The married couple were very wealthy, and had a primary residence in New England and a ranch in rural Kansas where they raised show horses. Our client, the husband, had been told by the ranch foreman that, during those seasons when he was at the New England house, his wife liked to entertain a male friend. Often overnight. Since it was clear to the husband that the marriage should end, and equally clear that there would be some bitterness about the financial arrangements, he and his lawyer contacted my dad and asked him to get hard evidence of the infidelity. My father was too ill to do the work himself. I was, thankfully, on vacation. The job fell to Richard.

My brother flew to Topeka, rented a car, and met with the ranch foreman in a not very classy motel not far from the property. The foreman had brought along the retainer — $10,000 in hundred dollar bills — and Richard carefully counted out the money, putting the new bills in stacks of ten. When the foreman left, Richard wondered where he was going to keep all that cash. The situation was, for him, something like what the River Shoe case had been for me, a kind of baptism of fire, a graduation to a new level of responsibility. Or, as he put it, "I knew Phil would kill me if I screwed up." He ended up staying at the motel for a week and kept moving the money to different hiding places in the room, afraid the cleaning woman would discover it and a) decide he was a drug dealer and call the cops, or b) keep some or all of the cash for herself.

On the second day, he drove out for a scouting run. My father was always good about telling us to take our time on stakeout jobs, get a solid lay of the land, put a plan together, do not rush things if you don't have to. Following the directions the foreman had given him, my brother found the property without much trouble. The trouble came from the fact that the couple's home was miles down a dirt road with no houses on it, deep woods to either side, and that it sat so far back off this public road that it was barely visible. Richard drove the length of the road three times, looking for a way to find a stakeout spot close to the house and get the incriminating photos the client wanted. He noticed that railroad tracks ran through the trees, and he calculated that, judging from the angle of it and the hillside behind, the tracks must pass fairly close to the house.

Next morning, very early, he put on his hunting fatigues, drove down the road, parked the car in a logging lane well out of sight, and hiked a mile and a half down the railroad tracks in the dark. Richard had made a good guess: the tracks passed within a hundred feet of the house. One problem was, he needed to get closer than that in order to obtain clear proof that the boyfriend was living there; another was that a thicket of brambles and undergrowth stood between him and the house. He had no choice but to try to go through it. When he was only two steps in, something jumped in the shadowy undergrowth a few yards in front of him.

It was dark, he was alone in the woods, Richard thought he was being attacked and nearly threw the camera over his shoulder in surprise. The commotion turned out to be caused by one of the largest deer he had ever seen, a trophy if it had been in season and he had been armed. My brother pushed on, found a tree close to the house, climbed far enough up into it so that he was well hidden, and waited.

The woman came out first, got into her car and drove away. After another half hour a giant of a man emerged. He was smoking a cigarette and accompanied by two dogs, a muscular boxer and a more ragged looking mixed breed. Richard managed to get one photo of the boyfriend, but the sound of the shutter alerted the dogs, who started barking, and sniffing their way toward him. Another few seconds and they stood growling near the base of the tree.

"I was wondering," he told me, "how I was going to explain to this guy what a kid from Boston was doing up in a tree in his girlfriend's back yard with a camera around his neck and hunting fatigues on."

But, the boyfriend called the dogs back inside and left for work. Richard waited a suitable time, then he walked through the bushes again, down the railroad track, drove back to the motel and called Phil with the good news.

The news, it turned out, was not good enough. Phil called back later in the day to say that the client wanted photos of the boyfriend's clothes and other belongings *inside the house*. The client owned the house, knew the front door would be left unlocked, and gave his permission for my brother to go inside; Richard's job would be to slip through the door when the couple was away and take some photos.

So the next day he parked his rented car in the trees, walked down the railroad tracks — again in the early morning dark, and returned to his position in the tree, managing to get even more photos. When the woman and then the man left the house, and after they had been gone for the better part of an hour, my brother climbed down and made his way to the front door. It was, as the client had promised, unlocked. Richard entered and made it about twenty feet across the dining room when he heard a fierce growl: he had forgotten about the dogs.

The mixed breed seemed uninterested, but the muscular boxer slid down off the couch and, snarling, came up to within a few feet of him.

I'll let Richard take the story from there.

"I love dogs," he said, "so I got down on the floor and went into my doggie mode. I started talking to them in baby talk. 'Uncle Richie is here now, that's my boy, what a good boy you are, come over here, that's right, what a good boy!'"

Five minutes later my brother was going through the rooms and the dogs were nuzzling at his heels, keeping the good man company as he took pictures of oversized boots, jeans, and denim shirts.

# TWENTY NINE
People Watching II

*"The haft of the arrow had been feathered with one of the eagle's own plumes."*

-Aesop


S ometimes the surveillance is counter surveillance, as in work we did for a man who later became a good friend, Bob Jasse. Bob had grown up poor, his father a middle-weight boxer and, later, manager of a tough bar near Suffolk Downs race track.

An affluent and dignified man, Bob used to like to tell the story of several bookies who had a sort of office in the attic of his parents' house — also within sight of the track. The book-ies would engage in a practice known as "'past posting", that is, taking bets on a race after it had actually started, a kind of ille-gal activity to the second power. The bookmakers would be on the phone with a client and have their binoculars trained on the race track. "You want to put a hundred dollars on the number three horse, Standing Water? No problem. Race is just about to go off." And there was Standing Water, running dead last at the first turn, thirty lengths off the pace.

After a stint as a Navy corpsman in Korea, Bob went to college, then Wharton Business School. He started a company called HiTech, that made, among other things, windows for commercial airliners. The comptroller at HiTech was an old friend of ours from Gems and Luxury Jewelry, Lonnie Tarcic, and when they had some less than satisfactory experiences with another investigator, Lonnie recommended us. "Bob can be a little tough to work with at first," he warned me, "but I think you'll end up liking him."

Our first assignment was to find the biological parents of Bob's wife who had been adopted at birth. While we were certain it meant a great deal to the couple to have this information, it also felt like a test of our abilities. The previous investigators had followed a paper trail back to an area of rural Iowa, then lost it. We followed the same trail, with a small twist. Richard got on the phone with all the country clerks and town administrators he could find in that part of Iowa and did what my father had always counseled us to do in those situations: he asked for help.

There turns out to be a big difference between speaking to a stranger, on the phone or in person, and saying, "Hi, I'm a licensed private investigator from Massachusetts and I need to find out the names of the birth parents of _ _ _". And saying, "Hi, I need some help. I'm a licensed private investigator from Boston and I'm trying to find _ _ _ ." Another of my father's sayings was, "You can get more with sugar than with vinegar."

In our experience, this approach works as well in rural Iowa as in Boston's inner city: if you approach people with some consideration, most of them want to be helpful. Richard has a good way with people, and it took him two days of phone work to find the right person, a woman in a clerk's office in a small town in western Iowa. She had lived in the town for almost seventy years. So comprehensive was her knowledge of the locals that she did not even have to check the records to answer Rich's questions. Once he had earned her trust, she gave him, not only the name of the birth mother, but a whole family history.

Bob was pleased. On the heels of that success, he moved us on to a more complicated problem. He had just bought a company in Los Angeles and, although he had a non-compete clause in his contract with the former owner of the company, he suspected him of breaking that agreement. From certain things that had happened shortly after the sale, he worried that either somebody inside the company was leaking critical information, the phones were being tapped, or both.

"Phil," I said to my father, when I told him about the case "who do you know in L.A. who can help us with electronic counter-surveillance?"

In his own way, my dad was like the elderly woman in the Iowa town hall: he had the names at his fingertips. "Mike Easter," he said, without checking his Rolodex. "But don't tell him who you're working for until he's driving you to the building. The guy is the king of self-promoters. If he knows where you're going, he'll go there himself and plant half a dozen bugs just to make himself look like a hero."

I flew out to Los Angeles, and Mike and I went over to Jasse's new company. I sat there in the various offices, watching, while Mike, wearing headphones, ran what looked like a small transistor radio with a huge antenna over every square foot of the walls. Nothing. We had better luck when we went outside to a 4' x 4' metal box on a knee-high pole. Every wire in there, every phone line into and out of Bob Jasse's new company, had a sister line clipped close against it. A hole about the size of a half-dollar had been cut out of the back of the box, and these sister lines ran in a tight bunch through that hole and into a much smaller box on the ground. Mike showed me where the recording device had been in that smaller box, and how the wires had all been cut when it was removed.

That night I met with Lonnie Tarcic at his hotel and gave him my report. Lonnie called Bob Jasse, and no bugging device was necessary for me to hear Bob's voice all the way across the room.

Bob owned companies up and down the east coast, nine in all, if memory serves. The Los Angeles situation led to him commissioning us to debug all of his many buildings and offices, which paid for our own armory of sophisticated equipment — including a spectrum analyzer that swept all the frequencies from 1 MHz to 1 GHz. An old friend from my college days, Charlie Bell, has been invaluable in this kind of work. He is an electrical engineer who does counter-surveillance as a sideline, and he has helped us ascertain, on numerous occasions, if a client is inadvertently transmitting business information to a competitor through bugged phones or offices. Surprisingly perhaps, cell phones are more difficult to bug than the old-fashioned radio phones, because they are continually changing frequencies. But anything else that is wireless — portable phones, intercoms — can easily be intercepted from short distances.

Over the years that we've been in business, surveillance equipment has evolved to the point where there are all kinds of fancy devices available. This equipment used to be found only in specialty shops, used by professionals; now any of it can be purchased on the Internet with little trouble. Using one of these new inventions, you can take video or still photos of someone while standing a few yards away holding what seems to be a computer bag. One end of the bag sports a small hole with a camera set up behind it. Other than that, though, we do not get much more technical than our Cannon Pro video cameras with a 6X telescopic lens, and the various changes of clothes that we keep on hand so we can fit into whatever disguise the situation calls for. If a surveillance becomes more technical, we make use of Charlie, almost a partner and the kind of specialist who can wire an office where stealing is suspected, or dissect a phone system to see what kinds of information are available to which people in a company.

Society has evolved, too, in ways that have a bearing on surveillance work. It is no longer comfortable for our employees to do a stakeout that involves sitting in a car near a school or playground. No longer acceptable to ask directions of children on a country road (or anywhere else; I tell my operatives never to do it.) In our region, at least, religious cults are less active than they used to be, so we have many fewer cases involving parents asking us to help rescue their son or daughter in that way. The divorce laws have changed, as I mentioned earlier. When it comes to surveillance, what is left, for the most part, aside from some criminal complaints, are insurance company cases. Over the years, these cases have increased in frequency while other work has lessened. I don't know if it is a mark of a societal change or not, but there seem to be, on the one hand, many more people with dubious disability cases; and, on the other, a greater reluctance on the part of large corporations to admit wrongdoing in a case of a legitimate injury to one of their employees.

We work with litigators of all types — civil, criminal, corporate — and we do surveillance work on behalf of the defendant's insurance company, as we have always done. Unlike some investigators, we have never kept our eggs in the basket of one or two big insurance companies or law firms. These days, we are as likely to be taking videos (still photos are rarely used for this type of thing) of a so-called disabled worker as he builds a stone wall around his property, as we are of an overloaded truck owned by a firm that claims it adheres strictly to the shipping laws.

In all of these cases, we still use the guidelines our dad passed on to us so many years ago. We drive nondescript cars, dress to blend in and make sure to take along food (but not too much to drink). We also remember to fill the gas tank, empty the bladder and have: extra batteries, a good sense of the neighborhood and a big reservoir of patience. A measure of courage is involved as well. We've had our share of ugly encounters, and in those cases, what is most important is a good instinct for trouble, and the flexibility and creativity to change plans on a moment's notice.

As Richard, a master at the art of surveillance puts it, "Never assume. Never take anything for granted."

# BOOK FOUR
## Good-Bye to Bowdoin Street

# THIRTY
The End of An Era

*"Lost is our old simplicity of times,*
*The world abounds with laws, and teems with crimes."*
- Anonymous

By the late 1990's, the agency had grown to the point where the first floor of 45 Bowdoin Street was too small for us. A secondary consideration was the fact that the parking situation, troublesome enough in the early days, had become all but intolerable. There were only a handful of metered spots on Bowdoin Street. If you used the nearby public garages, you would have to be out by 6:00 p.m. or pay a hefty additional "event fee" if there was a hockey or basketball game that night at Boston Garden. The meter maids had a ze-ro-tolerance policy for five-minute double-parking, so if one of our employees or a client needed to drop something off, or one of us needed to stop into the office for a quick delivery or to check a file, we were out of luck. Dorothy told us we were pay-ing more than $2,000 a year in parking tickets, in addition to the garage fees and our $1200 monthly rental bill. It was time for a change, but change was not easy after all those years.

One option we considered was to stay where we were, make the office space larger, and deal with the parking troubles as best we could. Despite our relationship with the meter maids, this solution appealed to us, in part for sentimental reasons. 45 Bowdoin had become a kind of home away from home. In fact, by that point, both Richard and I had worked there longer than either of us had *lived* anywhere else. Maria had told us on more than one occasion that she wanted to give us first chance to purchase the building if there came a time when she could no longer manage it. ("Johnny, I always told you and Richie that you boys would always have the first shot to buy it from me if I ever sold.")

That time had come. Jimmy had passed away from lung cancer in 1997. Maria was approaching her eightieth birthday — too old to be changing the sheets and dealing with troublesome tenants — so Richard and I asked her to meet with us about a possible purchase.

We had visions of finishing the basement and putting in a spiral staircase, of completely renovating the upstairs rooms and turning them into condominiums that could be used by state legislators or students at Suffolk Law, just around the corner. We did some research to ascertain the fair-market value of the building ($304,500 was the assessment) and then had a sit-down with our landlady.

Frail and gaunt by then, walking with the help of a cane and sometimes forgetting to put in her dentures, Maria had lost some of her mental acuity but not much of her feistiness. We told her we had reached a point with the business where we would have to have more space or move out, and we offered her $450,000 for the building plus the right to live there as long as she chose to — "life estate" is the legal term.

She thought we were trying to cheat her. The fact that we had the assessments done, comparing the building to similar properties, the fact that we would have to make a major investment to renovate the small, shabby, bathroom-less upstairs rooms that hadn't been touched in fifty years — none of that mattered to Maria. We were trying to cheat her, period. It was not a negotiating position as much as a mindset that had frozen in place over the years. Maybe it came from her time earning money the hard way, dollar by dollar in the beery bars and dance halls a few hundred yards from where we sat. Whatever its source, the attitude was as deeply entrenched and firmly set as the pilings of the city's new skyscrapers. Possibly, if Jimmy had been alive, he could have helped her understand that our motives were honest, the price fair. But Jimmy's passion for Lucky Strikes had finally caught up with him, and Maria's only living kin was a son from an earlier marriage who didn't work and — to our eyes, at least — didn't seem to want to do anything more than wait around for his inheritance. That inheritance, I would guess, turned out to be 45 Bowdoin Street.

It was probably just as well. A City of Boston ordinance required anyone buying a rooming house to keep the license active until the last tenant voluntarily moved out. It was illegal to evict anyone. We were not keen on the idea of running a rooming house, doing repairs on weekends and being called into the city at 2 a.m. to settle a dispute or deal with a drunken tenant. And, ultimately, it would have been a stretch to cover the cost of the purchase and renovations with rental or condo fees. In days when we had to go from the Registry to the Secretary of State's office to the court buildings to the Kirstein Library, digging up Social Security numbers and criminal histories, the office's central location had been a huge advantage. Now, however, most of that work was done in front of a computer screen; where at one time you would have to visit a client to pick up a report or diagrams of an accident scene, now that is accomplished via fax and email.

The neighborhood had changed, too, not so much in a bad direction as in a bland one. Long gone were the days when we would arrive to a chorus of "Richie!" "Johnny!" "Whattaya doin?", and feel ourselves a part of the Beacon Hill circus with its unselfconscious characters and connection to the life of the street. There were no more Eddie Immanellis *"dragging hot dogs through the garden for ya"*, or Freddie Rainiers selling hot shirts. In my brother's words, the block had "started to lose its fabric." Odd and annoying as it could sometimes be, that fabric had made our working life much more interesting.

So, with some reluctance (for one thing, we hated to lose the 4115 phone number), we started to cast around for other locations. An office in the city would have meant high rents and more parking problems, so we thought about finding space in one of the new buildings that lined Routes 128 and 495, highways that form concentric half-circles to the city's western side. But doing that would have meant traffic issues and more commuting time, and it would have been difficult for Karen, Chris, Cal and some of the other employees, who had been with us for years. We wanted to make life as easy as possible for them. Less altruistically, we wanted something fairly close to the golf club so we would still have the option of sneaking away for nine holes at the end of a summer workday. After months of looking, we found a location that met these criteria, and in the summer of 1998 we moved the operation four and a half miles west, from Beacon Hill to the Brighton section of the city. 1500 square feet. Four large second-floor rooms with our own parking lot, easy access to the Massachusetts Turnpike, and views of the skyline — just right. On the walls we hung autographed posters of Boston sports stars, a framed *Yankee Magazine* story about Phil's funeral, *Boston Strangler* movie posters Karen had found for us, and a painting of the office at 45 Bowdoin that I had commissioned for my father when he was recuperating from the big heart attack — a copy of which adorns the cover of this book.

As if that move was a symbolic ushering in of a new stage of the agency, we started to see the work landscape changing. "It's leg work, all leg work and more leg work," my father had said in a 1970 *Boston Globe* interview. But, that was not as true as it had once been. We left our guns at home more and more frequently, spent much less time following cheating husbands and wives, and much more time investigating auto accidents, major construction incidents, and more minor events we called "slip and falls". More time behind the computer and less time doing the "knuckle and heel" work that had been the heart and soul of things at the start of the agency. Instead of the Polk Directories, we had the Internet; instead of microfiche, we had Microsoft; instead of weeks tracking down missing children who had run off with a lover, we spent a day interrogating workers at a biotech firm — where someone had left semen on the mouthpiece of a telephone — finally wringing a confession out of the culprit.

Society was changing, too, as it always does. Cell phones — nonexistent in our early days — were outlawed in court because they were being used to photograph witnesses, and the photos would then be passed around to make it easier for friends of the accused to seek revenge. With the increase of casual sex among minors, we have seen the accusation of rape used with almost equal casualness — which can work to undercut the seriousness of those cases in which a rape does occur. If the accuser is a minor, then her name cannot be used, which means that police can show up at your door and tell you your son has just been accused of rape, and when you ask "Who is accusing him?" you will not be told.

We started to notice that, more and more often, people were unwilling to involve themselves in anything outside their own small sphere. They were reluctant to help an accident victim, give testimony about something they had seen, or aid in the investigation of a missing person. This may have something to do with the enormous increase in lawsuits we have witnessed during this same period of time. As happy as I am to have work coming into the office, and as much as we like to help injured clients receive compensation when someone else is truly at fault, there are times we turn jobs away, amazed that a lawyer thinks he has a case when what occurred was obviously a simple accident and not the result of negligence; amazed at the people who know how to use the law for their own benefit, but seem to lack any sense of the moral consequence of what they do.

At this point, I should include a few words about our work with lawyers, a critical aspect of our business.

Naturally enough, for a working-class kid, when I first started in the business I was sometimes intimidated by the famous-name Boston legal firms and their high-powered attorneys. My father helped cure me of this problem. One of the more remarkable facets of his character was that he had friends and acquaintances across the whole socio-economic spectrum, from the poorest manual laborers and petty thieves he might have sent away for a short stint, to judges, Attorneys General and movie stars. Whether this trait came from his upbringing on the streets of Dorchester, the fact that his father enjoyed a similarly wide variety of friendships (from Joe Kennedy Sr. and Richard Cardinal Cushing to the toughest beat cops), or the years he had spent seeing humanity in its most unvarnished form, I do not know. But, I watched the way he talked to hard-guys, and I watched the way he interviewed frightened young women, and I watched the way he sat down with high-priced lawyers and elicited the same degree of respect he gave them, and it was all another lesson for me.

Still, at the start, when I would be sent to a fancy office with a mahogany desk, a glitzy secretary, and a three-piece-suit Harvard barrister in residence, I would feel like I had stepped into a higher plane of existence. I remember collecting a report from one of these lawyers, who had the most gorgeous secretary on earth and an office right in the heart of downtown, and having him say, in a condescending tone, "Now be very careful with these. I don't want to see these documents blowing around the Public Gardens after you leave here," and biting down hard on my tongue to keep from telling him what he could do with his documents. When I complained to my dad about it, as always, he brushed it aside, told me not to worry, reminded me that the guy put on his tailored pants one leg at a time like the rest of us. But, as usual, I learned more from his example than from any particular advice he put into words.

All those feelings reside in the past. Familiarity with the law profession has not bred contempt (except in a few cases) but it has bred comfort. It is not boasting to say that, over the years, Richard and I have come to see how valuable we are to civil and criminal lawyers, and how a job carefully done on our part greatly increases their chances of success.

We have also come to realize, first-hand, a truth one encounters in dealings with any profession: there are great lawyers and there are terrible ones. In fact, it has gotten so we can tell within about five minutes which species we're dealing with. Good lawyers will have their cases mapped out long before they ever go to court. They will have a solid idea just what is needed in terms of statements and testimony, and they will allow us sufficient time to find the witnesses and procure that information in the proper written form. They will know when to settle and when to go to trial, and that decision will have everything to do with the facts of the case and the client's situation, and nothing to do with the lawyer's need to make a tuition payment or his lack of confidence. If a large settlement is involved after a successful civil suit, they will often arrange for an estate lawyer to be brought in to help a client who has gone, overnight, from having no money to having a great deal of money. Again and again, on the heels of a large settlement, we have seen new problems arise when relatives and "friends" come out of the walls with their palms up, and what should have been lifetime security for an injured person turns into just more misery. Good lawyers will inevitably be the ones who pay us promptly.

Bad lawyers are sloppy and disorganized, and often wait to call us until the statute of limitations is about to run out, or the case is on the verge of going to trial. They expect their lack of planning to become our emergency, and sometimes it does. They will try to cut corners on the investigative end of the case, saving themselves a few hundred dollars and putting an innocent man at risk of going to jail, or a crippled client at risk of being left with no money. In one sad case, a young woman paralyzed in an auto accident was left penniless because her lawyer insisted on going to trial when he should have settled.

Bad lawyers will put their own financial exigency before the client's, and it is often these same people whom we have to chase around town for months in order to get our fee. In several instances, we have ended up suing lawyers who failed to pay us after an inexcusably long period of time. Once, after obtaining a judgment for non-payment of our fee, we even procured a warrant for the arrest of a particularly troublesome lawyer. I sent her a fax saying the warrant would be served the day before Thanksgiving if she didn't have the money to my office by five o'clock that afternoon. Shortly before five a secretary stopped by with the payment.

From observing and being part of the system over all these years, we have come to the sure understanding that, if a person finds himself or herself in trouble, he or she should never assume that the legal system will automatically operate in such a way as to clear the innocent and convict the guilty. It is a good system, all in all, but it contains as many imperfections as the individual human being and it is equally subject to the snares of laziness, corruption, and power. As in so many other aspects of life, money makes an enormous difference. Get the best lawyer you can afford, and have him hire the best PI he can afford, and your chances of success improve exponentially.

Like almost all investigators I know, we see about 75% of our business come through attorneys' offices. In Boston, as elsewhere, the legal community is tight-knit and there are not a lot of secrets. Good quality work on the part of the investigator — locating witnesses and encouraging them to talk; providing thorough, accurate, legally astute statements; putting together visual and written documentation that describes, say, an accident scene in clear terms; making certain the attorney is never surprised in court — these kinds of things echo around the community like paid advertisements playing again and again on a popular TV show. And the reverse is also true: do sloppy PI work and the word quickly spreads, and the phone stops ringing.

I have a final pair of cases to present. One of them — to me, at least — shows the proper use and value of a lawsuit, and the other shows a crass disregard for a basic sense of decency. Both of them are recent, and each in its own way typifies the type of work we see now.

In the first case, we were approached by an attorney we knew well — I'll call her Angela — who was working on behalf of a man I'll call Adrian. When Angela first contacted me, in the fall of 2007, she said that Adrian had been arrested on charges of raping a minor. It is not the kind of case anyone particularly likes to be involved in, though my father, no bleeding heart, always insisted it was important for everyone to have a defense, no matter what the crime. Again and again — sometimes when we were doing court-appointed defense work at a very low fee — he reminded me that you should never assume guilt before it is proven, and you should never shy away from working as hard as you can to help someone get a not-guilty verdict. It is the prosecutors' responsibility to work equally hard to secure a conviction, he would tell me. Without fair effort on both sides, the whole system breaks down.

Rape of a minor is one of the most straightforward charges in that system. There are no extenuating circumstances. It does not matter if the young woman (in one or two well-publicized cases the minor has been a young man, but this is rare) swore up and down that she was of legal age. It does not matter how old she appeared to be, how she was dressed, what or how much she had been drinking, what she said, how she acted, what the relationship between the two people had been prior to the charge, or what his or her past behavior looked like. Either the man did it or he did not, end of story. In addition to that relatively cut-and-dried legal aspect, there is an unsavory personal one: while occasionally the relationship is between a slightly older boyfriend and a younger girlfriend, often it is more sordid than that, a much older man taking advantage of a much younger girl.

In this instance the circumstances sounded even less appealing: the victim was seven years old, the accused was her grandfather. But I knew Angela as a hard-working, hard-hitting, no-nonsense attorney, and so I drove down to the South Shore to meet with her and find out more information.

The grandfather — we are calling him Adrian, and changing other details here — had retired after a long career at the electric company. He and his wife lived in a modest house in a suburban town, and Adrian spent much of his time worrying about his two young grandchildren. Part of the reason he worried so much was because his son and his son's live-in girlfriend had a history of drug and legal problems. The son, Mark, ostensibly a union painter, had trouble holding a job. His girlfriend — I'll call her Ginny — was unemployed and collecting welfare and food stamps, but had worked in a notorious strip club for a time. Two children from a previous relationship had been taken away from her by court order.

Mark and Ginny and the two kids lived just outside Boston. Things came to a head in the late spring of 2007, when Adrian learned that the school authorities were threatening to keep the boy from moving on to the second grade. It wasn't a question of intelligence: he had missed school or been late a staggering forty times in his first year.

So Adrian and his wife decided to put the boy in a special tutoring program. Not only would they pay for it themselves, but Adrian would make the thirty-minute drive every morning, dealing with the rush hour traffic, and take his grandson to these special classes. Sometimes when he arrived, the boy was dressed, fed, and ready to go. Just as often he was not. Sometimes the younger girl would come along, too, and she and Adrian would have a snack, work on coloring or learning letters, or hang out in the playground until the classes were finished.

This routine went on for several weeks, at which point Ginny decided she no longer wanted her son in the tutoring program. It was, Adrian suspected, just too difficult for her to get up at that hour and get the children ready to leave the house. He and Ginny and then he and Mark had another in a long series of arguments with threats and name-calling on both sides. But, in the end, there was nothing he could do: no more tutoring program. Later in the summer, thinking of other ways they might help the grandchildren, he and his wife invited the kids — and one of the boys from Ginny's earlier relationship — to spend a week with them at their home. They paid for the boys to go to a baseball camp, took them to the beach and out for meals. At one point the kids came home with a lot of sand on them, and Adrian got out the garden house and gave them an outdoor shower — the kids in bathing suits, soaping themselves, squealing in the cold water.

Over the rest of that summer there were more arguments, all of them along familiar lines. Adrian accused the couple of not being good parents; they accused him of meddling in their private life; the children were caught in the middle. Though he knew Mark and Ginny did not want him to, Adrian would sometimes drive up to their neighborhood and scout out the situation. One early September day he saw his grandchildren riding their bicycles when they should have been in school, and that was the tipping point for him. He called the Department of Social Services and filed what is called a 51A — basically a charge of parental neglect that warrants a home visit. Weeks later, in a separate incident that would bear on this case, Ginny called the police to report that Mark had been drunk and abusive, and had punched one of the children and verbally abused him. The police arrived, examined the boy (no injury was discovered), and filed a report. Mark was made to leave the house and seek treatment for "anger issues." Adrian's name was not mentioned.

Eleven days later, Ginny paid a visit to the police in the town where Adrian lived. In a deposition there, she stated that her daughter had told her that, on the summer visit, Grandpa had touched her inappropriately. To bolster this made-up story,

Ginny further stated that she had mentioned this to the police in her city when they had come to evict Mark from the house. That police department, she said, had advised her to go to the police in Adrian's city and file a complaint.

At that point, without checking on the story, the police in Adrian's home town called him into the station and formally charged him. His name went into the newspaper; a GPS bracelet went around his ankle. He was forbidden from seeing his grandchildren and from going within four hundred yards of a school (which was difficult, since he lived across the street from one) and advised to get a lawyer.

Angela related all this to me on my first visit — in early November of 2006 — and gave me a file to take home and study. "You'll see what kind of a man he is when you meet him," she said. "You'll see what kind of bullshit is going on here."

By the time I had studied the various police reports in the file, and gone to talk with Adrian and his wife, I had so little doubt of Adrian's innocence that I told him, "If I can't help you on this case, I'm going to give up my license and start selling hot dogs for a living." For one thing, it was clear from the reports that Ginny had never mentioned her daughter's alleged abuse when the police came to evict Mark. That part of the story was purely made up, and so was the assertion that police department A had told her to speak to police department B, in Adrian's home town.

The deeper I probed into the facts of the case, the worse it smelled. Ginny, it turned out, had a rich legal history. In an affidavit filed almost a decade earlier, she had admitted to lying to police in order to get back at someone "in anger." In addition to several drug charges and the loss of custody of her first two children, she had, for a time, even lost custody of her son: in 2000, when the boy was twenty-one months old, Mark had gone to court and pleaded with a judge to give him sole custody. In that affidavit, he said Ginny would get off work at 1:00 or 2:00 a.m. and not come home until 6:00 or 7:00 a.m. or later. Usually she would sleep until noon, paying no attention to her child. Once, Mark had come home from work to find the boy locked in the bedroom with his mother passed out on the couch. The affidavit ended with this line: "Please don't leave my child's life in this woman's hands."

For a while after that court appearance, the couple had split up. But then there had been a reconciliation. A second child was born, a daughter. Ginny stopped work, went on welfare and food stamps — which meant that, now, Mark was living with her illegally. In the interim, she seemed to have refined her skills in working the system and using it as a means of revenge. She filed a restraining order against a neighbor — Adrian suspected it was her drug supplier — then rescinded it a few months later. Now she was trying to turn it against her childrens' grandfather.

Adrian insisted, vehemently and repeatedly, that he was innocent.

Usually, in a case like this, we keep our feelings private and restrict ourselves to doing what the lawyer pays us to do — preparing the best defense. If he wants court records, we will get them. If she wants an employment history, we will unearth it. Witness interviews? No problem. We will then hand over the material and let the attorney do his or her work. But Adrian's predicament struck me as particularly awful. After thousands of interviews with all kinds of people, I think I have a finely tuned sense for when someone is lying, and it was clear to me that Adrian was not. Nothing I found in his background argued otherwise, and nothing I found in Ginny's background made me wonder for so much as a day if she was sober and trying to protect her little girl. To make matters worse, when I delved into the details of the case — the police work, and the so-called evidence compiled by the Assistant District Attorney — all I saw was sloppiness and inconsistency. Rape is a horrible crime, a mix of violence and humiliation, a kind of torture that leaves victims scarred for decades. We have seen that scarring on many occasions. What we were seeing in this case was something else.

Though Adrian's lawyer, citing these same observations, argued more than once for dismissal, it was an uphill battle. No judge wants to dismiss charges of child rape only to have the defendant arrested on a similar charge a month or five years down the road. It's a certain path to the front page of the *Boston Herald*: CHILD RAPIST RELEASED BY BLEEDING HEART JUDGE. Probably because of the flimsiness of the evidence, though, Adrian's lawyer did succeed in getting the D.A.'s office to reduce the charges from rape to indecent assault. Still, Adrian refused to accept a plea. He wanted to go to trial.

Before that happened I took some extra steps I almost never take in a case like this. First, I brought the folder to my father's cousin Babs, who happened to have been a police prosecutor for over twenty years (and who had been indirectly responsible for my meeting Dorothy). I wanted to know if I was missing something, if some bias I was not aware of was causing me to take Adrian's side when I should have been more neutral. Babs went through the documents one after the next and said, "This isn't right."

Next, after consulting with Angela and getting her permission, I made a trip down to see the arresting detective, a man I'll refer to as William B.

In the station, I sat across the table from detective B. and for forty-five minutes laid out the obvious flaws in the case, the absurdity of it. First, Ginny had made up the story of talking to

277

her local police about the alleged abuse, and saying they had told her to speak with the police in Adrian's town. Second, Mark had told one police department he wasn't living with Ginny, and told another — in Adrian's home town — that he was. In her medical intake report, which we found in a court docket, Ginny stated that Adrian had masturbated while putting his fingers inside his granddaughter; in the first report that had not been mentioned . . . and it seems like a detail that would be difficult to forget. The police in Adrian's town had charged him without ever having questioned the young girl about what had happened. Add in the fact that Adrian's record was unblemished, and Ginny's was spotted and scarred, and it seemed to me like an open-and-shut false accusation.

"Look," I said to Detective B., "This guy's life has been ruined. Look at all this. You've been around. You know what's going on here. This woman's playing the system, and she's using you to do it. She needs to get Adrian out of the game so she can stay on the dole. Call her in for a second interview and have her go over these inconsistencies. I bet she'll admit she's lying."

All during my presentation, Detective B. had seemed bored, or offended, or both. When I was finished, he said, "It's out of my hands. Can't help you."

I have to say here that it is an attitude I have seen before, in the worst kind of burnt-out cops. The fact that they are dealing with human lives seems to have been forgotten somewhere along the way. We all like to think that every police detective involved in these kinds of investigations, and every District Attorney involved in prosecuting them is ultimately interested in putting the truth in front of the jury. That is simply not the way it is. Working for the defense in a recent Greater Boston murder case, I was able to locate someone who told me when and where she had seen the accused man's car — testimony that supported the defendant's alibi. "Did you tell this to the police?" I asked her. Yes, she had; she reported it to two Boston detectives in fact. Confronted with this on the stand, one the detectives said, with a drop of sarcasm, "Oh, I guess we just misplaced that report."

I would be the last person to suggest that there are not a lot of great police officers on the job, and not a lot of dedicated D.A.'s working for much less than they could make in the private sector. But I have seen plenty of cops lie in my time, too, under oath, and enough prosecutors who are only trying to build a reputation for themselves — so they can run for office, or move into a lucrative private career a few years down the road. On the one hand, that kind of behavior is disappointing, sometimes disgusting; on the other, it acts as a motivator for us in the work we do for defense lawyers. Few things in our professional life are as satisfying as helping to exculpate someone who has been wrongly accused.

We worked on Adrian's case for months, tracking down medical and legal records while Angela hammered away at the judge and Adrian and his wife simmered in a stew of public shame and private agony. Eventually, one year after my first meeting with Angela, and five months after my unsuccessful visit with Detective B., the case went to trial. On the first day in court, with Adrian and his wife and Angela and Ginny and Mark and even the two children all present, I noticed the young Assistant D.A. going back and forth between the conference room and the bench. Once, twice.

Before the proceedings could get underway, she announced, with an unfortunate smile in direction of the defense team, "Your honor, the State wishes to drop all charges."

Which is what happened.

A good outcome, except that, between the lawyer's fees and our charges, Adrian was out something like $50,000. His name would always be associated with child rape. He would probably never see his grandchildren again, and have no relationship with his son. And, where would he go to get his reputation back?

That Christmas he sent me a thank-you note and a gift certificate to a restaurant I like. Part of the note said that he and his wife were taking legal action to try and get custody of their grandchildren, and part of it said, *"I'm glad you didn't have to quit and start selling hot dogs."*

The other case was a construction accident — hideous and unusual — on one of the Big Dig sites. As the largest construction project in American history, Boston's Big Dig — which, among other things, moved an ugly section of overhead highway underground and opened a pedestrian zone from downtown to the waterfront — drew laborers from all over New England. It was a boon to unions and construction companies, and to lawyers, too. When you have a construction project of that size and complexity, you are going to have a lot of accidents, and with accidents, you often have lawsuits. That work goes to the lawyer's office first, and then to us. In fact, it is not unusual for Richard and me to read about an accidental death or injury in the Boston papers one day, and get a phone call asking us to investigate it, the next.

The best-known, and most disturbing example of that happened shortly after the completion of the Ted Williams tunnel. A woman driving her family to the airport was killed when a roof tile fell on her car and crushed her. Within a day, we had been called by both sides in the lawsuit.

But the case I am describing here happened a few years earlier and a mile or so to the east.

The accident occurred in one of the hundred-foot-tall narrow structures called "vent towers", that bring stale air up from the tunnels to the surface and funnel fresh air back down. Eight-foot-long X-shaped metal rods were being used to hold the forms in place inside these towers while the concrete was hardening. Once it had set, the X braces were stripped away, a bolt at the crossroad was removed, and the brace could be folded into an "I" shape. Workers in the bottom of the tower were putting these folded-up braces into bundles of thirty or so, wrapping them in a leather binding, and attaching the bundle to a hook on the end of a long cable dangling from a crane boom. On signal, the crane operator would lift the boom a few feet, jerk the bundle twice to tighten the wrapping, then hoist the bundle out of the chimney-like tower and set it in a pile for removal.

Something went wrong, the binding on one of these bundles did not hold as it was being lifted, and eight-foot metal pieces began raining down on the workers inside the vent tower. They tried to run, but there was not much in the way of an escape route, and little time, besides. One of the pieces went through the skull of a worker I'll call Luis, piercing his head from temple to temple. Impaled in that terrible way, Luis fell down and bled profusely, but he did not die. Firemen and ambulances were called. The EMTs tried to put Luis on a stretcher and have the crane lift him out, but the piece of metal was wider than the mouth of the tower so they had to lower a band saw into the vent tower, cut the metal to either side of Luis' head, and then get him out.

Somehow he survived, though he would never speak again. His family hired an attorney, and the attorney hired us. Massachusetts law states that you cannot sue the company you work for, so the question became: was this a simple worker's compensation case, which would mean something like $700 a week for Luis for the rest of his life? Or was there a third-party involved that might have been negligent?

Union workers, even traumatized union workers, are not reluctant to testify on behalf of a brother. (Although I remember, in the course of investigating this accident, getting into a shouting match with one Italian American co-worker who lived in the North End. He refused to tell me anything about what had happened, did not care about helping anyone but himself, and I felt ashamed because of our shared heritage. Yet, after we had argued with each other for a while, his wife invited me to stay for some spaghetti.)

From our first inquiries through discovery and deposition, we learned that yes, at one point, there had been a safety engineer on the job; and, yes, he had been working for the general contractor. More depositions yielded a name. The problem was, the man's name was a common one, he was no longer with the project, and no one seemed to know where he was working now.

Let us say the safety engineer's name was Andrew Clark. Karen began a surname search via data bases and RMV records, and we called all the Andrew Clarks we could find. This was made more difficult by the fact that cell phones are often handed out to people on a construction site, then collected again after their job is finished. So there were a lot of dead ends. A lot of, "Yeah, I've heard of him, but this isn't his phone anymore."

But then, after scores of calls, I reached a voice mail message that ended with, "Have a safe day," and I had found my man.

We ended up meeting at his new workplace in a railroad yard in New Jersey. Yes, Clark said, the supervising General Contracting company had known about this procedure; they had even had meetings that showed they were involved in the direct supervision of this particular job. And yes, he had warned them it was unsafe. And yes, he would be happy to sign an affidavit to that effect.

While I was not privy to the amount, due to confidentiality agreements, I would guess that Luis and his family ended up with a settlement of several million dollars.

In the midst of the cases we get now, I sometimes wonder if the sense of personal responsibility has eroded completely in our society, or if I am just seeing things through the jaded eyes of middle age. On some days, it is painfully obvious that the hope of squeezing out more profit on the corporate side, or finagling a set-for-life windfall on the personal side, leads companies to cut corners at the risk of consumers or employees, and individuals to lie, cheat, and steal in the hope of never having to work again. There are days when the legal system looks like the only tool that will make some corporations consider the safety of their workers. And other days when it resembles a different tool, one designed to make life easier for the cheaters and manipulators of this world, the drug-addled Ginnys who will sacrifice everyone to keep their monthly check coming. (On those days I think of a case that involved a black man who tried to help a drunken white woman who had gone into a bar in Roxbury — a black neighborhood — yelling racial epithets. The man counseled her to leave, even offered to drive her to the nearest train station. She accepted . . . and later charged him — in another case that was ultimately dismissed — with rape.)

We have, I guess, entered the Age of the Lawsuit. And the age where laws designed to help one person, often seem to end up just hurting someone else. (In those moods, I think of a Cambridge, Massachusetts case in which a tractor trailer making a tight turn killed a man standing on the sidewalk. It took

Richard almost six months to track down witnesses and get their statements. The reason for this long delay was the use of an exemption to the Freedom of Information act that had been originally intended to protect witnesses whose lives might be endangered by testimony. This loophole/exemption now enables the redaction of witnesses' names from police reports, even when — as was the case in Cambridge — the witnesses are more than willing to give their statements to us.)

Although the laws and attitudes have changed, the underlying causes of our cases — accidents, sloppiness, cheating, stealing, greed, lust — have remained as constant as human nature. (I think of a recent call from a woman who had been scammed out of a significant sum of money by a man posing as someone who could help her children get into good colleges. The woman lived part of the year overseas; the con artist had spent years earning her trust, then asked for and received a large payment for future work, and disappeared.)

In order to keep our balance in this profession and a semblance of sanity in our personal lives, Richard and I have to make a continuous effort not to turn cynical. This is not a simple challenge. Often, I think of my father's experience — the kinds of crime he saw in the Back Bay, the backstabbing and pettiness he experienced in the Department, the egregious acts of a man like Albert DeSalvo, on the one hand; and, on the other, the inability of the legal system to bring him to trial and close the case. "You don't know the things I've seen," I remember him saying to my older sister when they would argue about what time she had to be home after a date. "You don't know what's out there like I do. You don't know what can happen."

I now have a better idea what he was talking about. In the face of all that — the grievous accidents and various shades of human evil; the bizarre characters like the guy who kept a five-foot-long lizard behind chicken wire on the bottom bunk, with his young son sleeping on the top — Richard and I and our colleagues wage a daily struggle to balance compassion and clear-headedness. We do what we can, on the one hand, not to be fooled. And on the other, not to turn into men like Detective B., for whom police reports are just documents, just paper, just a route to a paycheck, with no human being on the other side.

# THIRTY ONE
Caution and Gratitude

*"There was only one catch and that was Catch-22, which specified that a concern for one's own safety in the face of dangers that were real and immediate was the process of a rational mind."*
- Joseph Heller

It is not always bad behavior or careless police work or a failure to listen to safety engineers that casts a shadow over our world. Sometimes the negligence is combined with pure bad luck, the harsh hand of fate. Luis is only one recent example of the kind of tragedy and pain we see on a weekly basis. Just to cite a handful of examples from the past few years: a woman who was killed when she was driving eastbound on the Massachusetts Turnpike and a westbound tractor-trailer lost a wheel, which came bouncing across the median and onto the roof of her car; a retired man who went out for his morning walk in his very quiet neighborhood and was killed when a young driver, blinded by the sun, ran into him; a man who was paralyzed after being hit in the neck by a storm door that flew off its hinges in high wind in Boston's Chinatown section; a young girl who was killed in South Boston by a police car speeding to a fight in the housing projects; men and women on a tour bus in Norway who saw their spouse or seatmate decapitated when a passing lumber truck lost its load and the wood peeled the side off the bus as if it were a tin can; kids maimed on carelessly inspected amusement rides, paralyzed when diving into swimming pools, drowned in hot tubs; a worker killed when a metal drum he was cutting open with an acetylene torch exploded and blew him into pieces.

If these brief accounts are disturbing to read, imagine how disturbing it is to have to interview the husband or wife or brother or sister or parents or witnesses, sometimes only hours after the accident. Or, to sit in the first-class section of an airplane on a trans-Atlantic flight, taking signed statements from the survivors of that Norwegian bus crash. Though I have done this for forty years, there are still days when I wake up wrapped in a feeling of dread, knowing I have to go into an inner city apartment or drive out to some quiet suburban town that day and take a statement from a father whose daughter was killed by a drunk driver two days before, or a wife whose husband survived Vietnam and then was paralyzed in the barber's chair when a carpenter, working with a pneumatic nail gun in the next room over, accidentally missed the stud and shot a nail through the sheetrock and into her husband's neck.

A side effect of this, and something you rarely see on television shows that portray private investigators, is that it has made Richard and me particularly careful parents, *too careful*, my two grown daughters would say. For instance, I never let them go on carnival rides, because, in Massachusetts, the rides have to be inspected only once a year, not every time the show is taken down and set up again somewhere else; in addition to that, the inspector is not paid by the state, but by the company that runs the amusements! I give them fifty dollars to put in their shoe in case they find themselves in a situation they do not like, and need to get away from there in a taxi; I tell them that, if they are with a boyfriend who wants to have a few beers and show off by driving fast, they can call me at any hour and I will come get them. If my wife is driving and the pickup in front of us is carrying a load of construction supplies, I'll ask her to stay one hundred yards behind it because we had a case of someone nearly being decapitated by a flying 2 x 4, and plenty of other accident cases caused by poorly secured loads. I'll tell the girls to be careful how they dive into a swimming pool, not to take their eyes off a child they are babysitting — not for a minute, to be constantly aware of their surroundings, and to trust their intuition and leave a party or an area or a date if they start to feel things are not right. I will not go fishing with my cousin Jack if he gets too far from land because we had a case where a small fishing boat was hit and demolished by an ocean liner.

None of this adds up to paranoia. I am not a particularly fearful man. In fact, there is a way in which this work has made both Richard and me almost fearless. We have dealt with so many different kinds of people, had men bring out guns when we went to interview them, had tough guys threaten us, gone unannounced to knock on a door deep in the New Hampshire woods, stepped into a small room in a maximum security prison to speak with men we knew to be cold-blooded murderers. I fly all over the place, in planes large and small. I still go into housing projects most non-residents without a badge and a gun would stay away from — even the police almost always go in there with a partner. It is just that decades of having a front-row seat to all kinds of accidents and their ramifications is something that changes you.

The other way it has changed Richard and me — the flip side of having seen all those tragedies — is that we have come to appreciate the present moment more instead of continually trading it for some future we might or might not have. When Phil died and we inherited some money from the sale of his home, Dorothy and I decided to join the Charles River Country Club, a place where I had caddied as a boy. Rich joined four years later. While it might have been wiser to have put that money into a retirement account, I have seen too many people who never lived to spend their IRA (and besides, we love golf too much; we have made great friends there, entertained clients, and have always believed that you can learn as much about a person by playing eighteen holes with him as you can knowing him for years off the course). Without being unreasonable about it, we have tried to live by the expression "coffins don't have pockets". Some of that, like some of the caution I instill in my girls, might be just who I am. But, some of it comes from what I have seen on this job.

Growing up as the child of a street cop, I think there is a built-in understanding that your father might leave for work one day and you will never see him alive again. This was not talked about in our home, but surely my mother was aware of it every waking moment.

The following passages are from video interviews my sisters conducted with my nephew Myles, who asked them what it was like to grow up as daughters of a policeman:

EVELYN,

*I remember one time him coming home and it was very early in the morning. He must have been working nights. He came home, and he was on crutches because he was chasing a criminal in a back alley and he must have hurt himself. I remember his gun, when I think of my father, I think of his gun; it was "the gun". The gun was placed in his bureau in the top drawer to the far right underneath his underwear. And we were told as children never to go near it. It was almost like it was just this THING that was there*

289

*that was so dangerous, even walking by it you felt chills up
your spine because you knew the gun lived there . . . I used
to sometimes ask if I could see it and he would get very serious and say, "It's not a toy; it's not a toy."*

JEAN:

*I always used to wish he was a postman or a teacher or
something, and he wouldn't know so much and he wouldn't
be able to tell me what would happen to me if I did such
and such. He'd say, "I know these things, don't you think
I see these things?" Well, if he was a postman what would
he see? Letters with stamps. He wouldn't see anything, I'd
be able to do what I wanted.*

While private investigating work doesn't carry with it the
same level of daily risk as the work of a street cop, there have
been moments, for both Richard and me, when we ended up in
situations we were not sure we would walk out of alive. In the
course of one investigation of a religious cult, I found myself in
a Boston apartment sitting among a group of very agitated cult
members who wanted me to do surveillance on one of the other members. They were looking for evidence that she was using
drugs, evidence that she was having sex with other men — anything and everything to show she was unfit for custody of the
couple's child. Their requests were so unrealistic, and their
body language and tone of voice so close to deranged, that I
thought the situation could explode at any second. I asked to
use the bathroom. Behind the locked door, I took my gun out
of its holster and slipped it into my jacket pocket, where it
stayed for the remainder of the conversation.

Anyone, in any line of work, in the course of even safest-seeming daily activities, can find himself or herself at death's door. (My dad always taught me move to one side after I knock on a stranger's door; you never know who might be inside, and if he would start shooting.) It is just that some types of work make it harder to pretend that we are invulnerable, that death waits many years down the road. It is also an individual matter: working as a private eye, a cop, or an ironworker on a high-rise construction project, does not necessarily bring one to an appreciation of the fragility of human existence and the preciousness of family and friends.

But, for Richard and me, it has worked that way. Being forced to face the kinds of terrible grief we have seen, week after week, year after year, has been a continual reminder of both the unpredictability of daily life and the importance of gratitude for and appreciation of the people we love. Bearing witness to infidelity, greed, addiction, negligence and their consequences has been a series of object lessons in the wisdom of avoiding the cardinal sins. And we have learned, too, that it is absolutely essential to leaven all this with a sense of humor. You will not find us sitting down and talking about our life in private investigation without telling some funny stories, laughing at ourselves, trying to take the dark edge off the experience whenever we can — for our own sake, and for the sake of the people we live with.

I have tried to do some of that here — give a sense of the work we really do, not the TV version of it, and include some of the humorous tales, as well. In putting these stories together, I have often had occasion to remember the storefront on 45 Bowdoin, both the raucous laughter of the members of our little circus, and the way passersby would cup their hands to the glass and look in, expecting a glimpse into a hidden layer of human life.

Richard and I and our families have had more than a

glimpse, over all these years, and it has been my intention here to share a portion of those experiences. During the writing and the reflection, I have thought many times about my father's life, about the monstrous twist in the mind of Albert DeSalvo, and the way his actions continue to echo in the lives of innocent people. My father worked at the edge of that hurricane of trauma and savagery — the strangling victims, the molested women, the families sharing that suffering — but even those lesser winds changed the direction of his life, and ours, albeit in much less painful ways. I suppose it gives credence to the idea that we live, not in isolation, but in a web of life where all our actions — good and bad — create a ripple effect that touches everyone else. We have laws intended to regulate that behavior, but it is one of the mysteries of the human condition that, generation after generation, century upon century, people continue to live outside those laws — to cheat and steal and kill and hurt — and risk the consequences.

For better and worse, that is the world my father immersed himself in every day, and this is the work he handed on to us.

THE END

## Some Other Books By
## PFP / AJAR Contemporaries

*Blind Tongues* by Sterling Watson
*the Book of Dreams* by Craig Nova
*A Russian Requiem* by Roland Merullo
*Ambassador of the Dead* by Askold Melnyczuk
*Demons of the Blank Page* by Roland Merullo
*Celebrities in Disgrace* by Elizabeth Searle
(eBook version only)
"Last Call" by Roland Merullo
(eBook "single")
*Fighting Gravity* by Peggy Rambach
*Leaving Losapas* by Roland Merullo
*Girl to Girl: The Real Deal on Being A Girl Today* by Anne Driscoll
*Revere Beach Elegy* by Roland Merullo
*a four-sided bed* by Elizabeth Searle
*Revere Beach Boulevard* by Roland Merullo
*Tornado Alley* by Craig Nova
*"The Young and the Rest of Us"* by Elizabeth Searle
(eBook "single")
*Lunch with Buddha* by Roland Merullo
*Temporary Sojourner* by Tony Eprile
*Passion for Golf:In Pursuit of the Innermost Game* by Roland Merullo
*What Is Told* by Askold Melnyczuk
*Talk Show* - Jaime Clarke
"What A Father Leaves" by Roland Merullo
(eBook "single" & audio book)
*Music In and On the Air* by Lloyd Schwartz
*The Calling* by Sterling Watson

CPSIA information can be obtained at www.ICGtesting.com
Printed in the USA
BVOW02s1100090914

365803BV00001B/1/P